UNITED STATES Sloop-of-War *Portsmouth*

Alfred Sully THE CONQUEST OF CALIFORNIA

SULLY'S original watercolor, here reproduced, is untitled, but the best available evidence seems to indicate that it was intended to represent either the battle of San Gabriel or the battle of La Mesa. Although the artist did not arrive in California until the following year, his services were often in demand to illustrate the books of his fellow-officers. This picture may have been painted to accompany the account of one of the participants in Stockton's campaign.

BY JOSEPH T. DOWNEY

Ordinary Seaman, USN

THE CRUISE OF THE

PORTSMOUTH, 1845-1847

A Sailor's View of the Naval Conquest of California

Edited by HOWARD LAMAR

New Haven and London

Yale University Press

Contents

MAPS

APPENDIX

Preface

NEXT to the pleasure of acquiring a long-sought treasure as the climax of diligent search and patient angling, the greatest joy in a librarian's life is the occasional rare book or manuscript that turns up so unexpectedly as to seem a gift from the gods. Such was the case with this book. In the fall of 1955 a letter from the Chesapeake Book Company offered an anonymous journal of a naval enlisted man in the California conquest. Intrigued, we asked to have it sent for our inspection. Soon after there arrived a package containing a tall quarto volume, bound in somewhat shabby half calf, together with an unbound but sewn quire, the whole amounting to some two hundred fifty pages. The bound volume bore the not very original title: "Odds and Ends or Incidents of a Cruise in the Pacific In the U.S. Ship Portsmouth from Jan. 1845 to May 1848. By Fore Peak."

The volume once opened, it was immediately apparent that this was not the usual sea journal, containing only wind, weather, and courses steered, with occasional brief notations of events. Rather it was a full-bodied and racy portrait of life in a man-of-war, seen from the lower deck. Moreover, the account of the Navy's share in the conquest of California contained much new and significant detail. For the naval officer's viewpoint of these events we already had a respectable handful of journals and letters, both published and in manuscript. But this was something entirely new, and somehow a way had to be found to acquire it.

In this crisis we turned, as we so often had before, to one of the Yale Library's best friends, Frederick W. Beinecke. Himself an ardent and discriminating collector of western books, he immediately perceived the importance of this journal, and most generously acquired it and presented it to the library. To place us further in his debt, he also presented to us the original painting by Alfred Sully which serves as frontispiece. No words are adequate to convey our gratitude.

The treasure thus secured, we turned to the problem of identifying the author and tracing the history of the manuscript. The name Joseph T. Downey appeared on the inside cover of the manuscript, and it was apparent that the writer had been ship's yeoman. Correspondence with Colonel Fred Blackburn Rogers, whose expert knowledge of the naval side of the California conquest has so often been generously afforded us, made it apparent that only Downey could be the author. The Navy Department was able to furnish the outlines of Downey's naval career, but except for his later reappearance in California, the rest of his life is completely unknown. We were equally unsuccessful in tracing the history of his manuscript, for it had turned up at a country auction, been purchased by an antique dealer, and sold in turn to the Chesapeake Book Company. The lack of a full history for both manuscript and author matters little, however. The story speaks for itself—and him.

ARCHIBALD HANNA, JR.

Yale University Library
April, 1958

Editor's Introduction

ONE AFTERNOON in December, 1844, a young sailor named Joseph Downey stood on the deck of his ship and watched a new sloop sail slowly through the gray choppy waters of Norfolk Harbor. A light winter storm was blowing, and it had already covered the strange ship with a ghostly coat of sticky snow. The handsome vessel—for despite the storm one could see that she had a wonderfully clean sweep of line—was the new U.S.S. *Portsmouth*. She had just completed her first run at sea, and had come down from Portsmouth, N.H., to take on a full complement of men before joining the American Squadron in the Pacific.

In her brief history the *Portsmouth* had already acquired a good reputation. Designed by Josiah Barker, the master shipbuilder of the Portsmouth Navy Yards, she had handled so well in her first heavy storm that her crew, many of whom were experienced tars from the old *Constellation* and the *United States,* were full of her praises. Her captain, Commander John Berrien Montgomery, was not only a veteran of the War of 1812, but was noted for being a just, God-fearing, kindly man. It was not surprising then that young Joseph Downey, restless after a year's shore duty, should sign on board the sleek new ship. He joined her crew as an Ordinary Seaman on Christmas Day, 1844; and before the *Portsmouth* had been a month at sea, Downey had so impressed his superiors with his quickness, intelligence, and above all, with his wit and affability, that he was rated a Yeoman and put in charge of the ship's log.

The origins and early life of Yeoman Downey—who was to write the sketches presented in this volume—remain something of a mystery. Navy records indicate that he was born in Louisiana in 1820, and that he had enlisted (January 10, 1843) at the age of twenty-three. After a year's service as a Landsman on the U.S.S. brig, *Boxer,* he had been transferred to the U.S.S. *Pennsylvania* and rated as an Ordinary Seaman. No records explain what he did before entering the Navy, and although he once admitted that he was a "good scholar, an apt pennman, and well-versed in the Spanish language," he did not reveal his source of schooling. But sometime before 1843, Downey discovered that he possessed a talent for writing humorous sketches; that, indeed, he had a positive love for that pastime. He confessed once that it was "born within him to manufacture a jest." Downey's own description of himself, written under a pseudonym, is perhaps the most candid and revealing one could hope to find:

> Now among said ship's company was a wild, harum-scarum blade yclept Joe [Joseph T.] Downey, who had passed through many a grade on board said ship, from yeoman to confidential clerk to the executive officer, down to one of the after-guard and steady sweeper of the quarter-deck. His love of change and irresistable thirst for mischief prevented him from holding any one place long at a time. Joe was good enough in his way, but his was a bad one for a man of war, and this way, bad as it was, he seemed determined to have, despite of law, gospel, or that stringent argument, the *cat* [o'-nine-tails]. Joe was a favorite with the crew, and didn't give a d – – n for the officers, and his fate though a checkered one, suited him well enough and he was happy.[1]

By his own report we learn that Downey kept a journal while on his first cruise aboard the *Boxer*. He wrote not so much for himself, however, as for a small if somewhat roisterous public—his fellow-sailors—to whom he read his compositions. One can easily picture the short, fair-skinned, brown-haired sailor (for so the Navy records describe him) sitting on a keg in the ship's storeroom, his blue eyes aflash with pleasure, as he recites an outrageous version of some shipboard incident to a roaring group of listeners.

Unfortunately the whereabouts of Downey's first journal is unknown, but when he went aboard the *Portsmouth*, he determined to write a similar set of sketches—apparently with some hopes of publication, for he appended a formal preface to his manuscript and took the trouble to provide himself with the pseudonym "Fore Peak." He also cast a thin disguise over the members of the crew who came under the scrutiny of his sometimes sarcastic pen. Despite

1. Fred Blackburn Rogers, editor, *Filings from an Old Saw: Reminiscences of San Francisco and California's Conquest, by "Filings"—Joseph T. Downey* (San Francisco, 1956), pp. 52–53.

many difficulties—at one point the ship's officers attempted to confiscate Downey's writings for fear that they contained plans of a mutiny!—he kept his promise and for two years (January, 1845 to May, 1847) recorded his impressions of life aboard the *Portsmouth*.

Odds and Ends is perhaps most notable for its candid picture of the life of an enlisted man in the United States Navy during the 1840's. Downey traces his wants, his foibles, his superstitions and hatreds in a vigorous, sometimes impudent manner that is highly refreshing. His purpose was to amuse, not to preach or reform. Thus his descriptions have both a ring of authenticity and a happy lack of self-conscious moralizing for the future reader's benefit, which so many naval officers of the time wrote into their own chronicles of life at sea.[2] Quite obviously, too, Downey was an amateur writer with little sense of literary organization. His journal will never replace Richard Henry Dana's classic *Two Years Before the Mast* (1840). Yet Downey was by all definitions such a true "old salt" that he managed to capture the "below decks" atmosphere and the raucous, childlike spirit of the *Portsmouth* sailors in a firsthand way which Dana could never have done. One should remember that Downey was neither a stand-offish observer nor an unsullied hero. He was in many ways a smart-aleck, opinionated, and saucy fellow who, so the ship's log reports, was flogged with the "cat" four times in five months for the assorted misdemeanors of "lying," "disobedience," "insubordination," and "drunkenness on duty." The sketches have an unbuttoned charm which make them a lively, if less literary, supplement to Dana's book. Indeed, Downey's account is closer in spirit and manner to that found in J. Ross Browne's *Etchings of a Whaling Cruise* (New York, 1846) than to that of *Two Years Before the Mast*.

Despite the worlds of difference which lie between the amateur chronicler and the professional author, there exists a remarkable similarity between parts of *Odds and Ends* and Herman Melville's

2. See as examples: Reverend Walter Colton, USN, *Deck and Port; Incidents of a Cruise in the U.S. Frigate Congress* (N.Y., 1860); Fitch W. Taylor, *The Flagship or a Voyage Around the World in the U.S. Frigate Columbia* (N.Y., 1840); George M. Colvocoresses, USN, *Four Years in a Government Exploring Expedition* (N.Y., 1852); William Maxwell Wood, Surgeon, USN, *Wandering Sketches of People and Things in South America, Polynesia, California* (Philadelphia, 1849). And for a pompous British officer's account: Lieut. the Hon. Fred Walpole, R.N., *Four Years in the Pacific in Her Majesty's Ship "Collingwood" from 1844 to 1848* (London, 1849), 2 vols.

account of his own life aboard the U.S. frigate *United States,* which he portrayed in *White-Jacket; or The World in a Man-of-War* (New York, 1850). Melville's hero, Jack Chase, who was a captain of the foretop, strongly resembles Jack Ratlin, a foretopman aboard the *Portsmouth* whom Downey openly admired. Both authors tell the same anecdotes and in one case they both use the same punch line (see below, pp. 17 ff.). The first lieutenant in *White-Jacket* bears a startling resemblance to Lieutenant John S. Missroon on the *Portsmouth;* and curiously enough, the Purser's Steward in *White-Jacket* sounds very much like Downey himself. Both treat the ship's character types in much the same way.

One should not conclude that Melville and the fun-loving Downey ever knew or influenced one another,[3] for Downey's pastime of sketch-writing was a common one on all vessels. Melville himself reported that during his trip on the *United States* three or four enlisted men kept journals of the cruise, and one specialized in sketches of comical incidents which he hoped to have printed at the end of the voyage. The sailors "vied with each other in procuring interesting items to be incorporated into additional chapters" Melville stated; which is precisely what happened on the *Portsmouth* the day it was known that "Fore Peak" was writing a book.[4] On Downey's own ship we now know that Commander Montgomery and Ship's Surgeon Marius Duvall each kept private journals, while Lieutenant Joseph Warren Revere was collecting notes for his book, *A Tour of Naval Duty in California* (New York, 1849). Last, but not least, Lieutenant Henry B. Watson was assiduously writing up a history of the small detachment of Marines on the *Portsmouth,* over which he had command.

Downey's original purpose was not so much to chronicle a naval odyssey as it was to spin amusing yarns. With an eye for the ludicrous in the activities of human beings, Downey worked that rough and ready practical joke vein of American humor, represented in his own time by Augustus B. Longstreet and Johnson J. Hooper, and

3. Some of the same crew who served on the *United States* while Melville was on board were now on the *Portsmouth,* so that Downey may have heard some of the same anecdotes which Melville had heard the year before. Melville's first cousin, Stanwix Gansevoort, was an officer on Downey's ship, but this seems to have been a coincidence of no significance.

4. Herman Melville, *White-Jacket* (Boston, 1922), pp. 44–45.

soon to be exploited by Mark Twain. Downey had read Dickens and admitted that he admired "Boz"; nonetheless, the situations and dialogues of the humorous sketches in *Odds and Ends* are all unmistakably American. Downey pursued his role as the ship's wit, in fact, so deliberately that once when he was in the brig facing serious charges, he carried on what seems to have been a hilarious duel of written words with a fellow-writer from another vessel anchored nearby. Stories, jokes, humorous insults were rowed back and forth in the cutter and read on each vessel as the crew laughed.

While Downey was consciously recording humorous incidents and less consciously reporting on shipboard life, the accident of fate gave him a more serious and truly exciting theme for his notebooks, for the two years during which he wrote marked the high point of the patriotic and expansionist movement in American history called "Manifest Destiny." His term of service not only coincided with the Mexican War, his ship was in San Francisco Harbor when the Bear Flag Revolt began in June, 1846. Downey was in the small naval detachment which raised the Stars and Stripes over the sleepy and largely deserted town of Yerba Buena (soon to be called San Francisco). Later he served as town clerk to Lieutenant Washington A. Bartlett, the first American alcalde of that town. But most important of all, Downey was in that strange conglomeration of mountain men, volunteers, soldiers, and sailors under the joint command of Commodore Robert F. Stockton and General Stephen Watts Kearny, who marched from San Diego overland some 150 miles to recapture Los Angeles in 1847. His eyewitness accounts of this expedition and of the resulting battles of San Gabriel and La Mesa, while often amusing, are also a valuable historical document of a major event in the American conquest of California. What is more, it is an account by an enlisted man with an enlisted man's view. As one reads the pages of Downey's dog-eared notebook, one captures a glimpse of the bearded Frémont and his incredibly ragged soldiers, and one sees Kit Carson smoking a cigar while coolly firing at the enemy at San Gabriel. Downey and the reader laugh together at the exuberant, uncontrollable Stockton as he calls for a military band to play celebration music as soon as the battle is won. But one also hears the slangy conversation of the common sailor, sees him get drunk on the wine found at Mission San Luis Rey, hears him swear at the lack of food, and watches him trick his officers by clever ruses. And still more significant, Downey's pages suggest in an unconscious way, just how vital a role the American Navy played in the conquest of California.

When Downey and his fellow Portsmouths returned to their ship in San Diego, he seems to have realized that the fun and glory were now past. He closed his journal and requested to be discharged and returned to the States. But the Navy, short of men and fearful of continued troubles in California, kept him on duty at San Jose and other Pacific ports for another year. He was honorably discharged May 12, 1848, when the *Portsmouth* was decommissioned.

The rollicking and, by now, hard-drinking Downey returned to California again in 1853. Undoubtedly the gold rush drew him back. How he came and what fortunes fell his way, it is impossible to say; during the spring of 1853, however, a local newspaper, the *Golden Era,* printed a series of articles entitled "Filings from an Old Saw," which purported to be a firsthand account of the conquest of California. Here was part of Fore Peak's *Odds and Ends* in type at last. Although he had abandoned "Fore Peak" for a new pseudonym, "Filings," the stories, even to minor details, were the same as in his journal. Downey's strong opinion of some of his officers and shipmates had become more mellow by this time, so he did not hesitate to identify some of the men whom he had once so carefully disguised. On the whole, his 1853 articles are less accurate than his sketches, but they serve as a valuable supplement to his earlier version.

By 1853, Downey, still seeking fun and companionship—and perhaps audiences as well—caroused nightly in the rooms of a set of friends whom he dubbed the "jolly sort" of San Francisco. What happened to this convivial young sketcher after that year can only be surmised. "Peak," "Filings," and Downey disappear forever after this last hearty flourish of the pen.

The editor has attempted to preserve as fully as possible the flavor and character of Downey's manuscript by retaining his peculiarities of spelling and punctuation. In some sketches, though, Downey wrote passages of dialogue without quotation marks in such a way that they were rather confusing. These and other passages have been punctuated for the reader's convenience.

Complete names of the persons Downey chose to disguise have been included in brackets after the initial reference; or, if the person has more than a passing importance to the narrative, he has been identified in a footnote. Where a character appears infrequently, his name is repeated. Some of Downey's disguises proved impossible to penetrate, and where this was true, no attempt was made to footnote the negative fact.

Most of Downey's dates and accounts are correct so that only occasionally do they have to be rectified. On the other hand, Downey, in writing for his fellow-sailors, often assumed an intimate knowledge of shipboard and California events which his present day readers might not have. Consequently, a few brief editorial introductions and insertions have been made in the text. Finally, it seemed useful to append a list of the ships in the Pacific Squadron, a muster roll of the crew Downey knew so intimately, and maps of the *Portsmouth*'s voyages, as well as of those areas of California which Downey treated in his sketches.

Among those who have been of inestimable help in the editing of Downey's *Odds and Ends,* I hasten to express indebtedness to Archibald Hanna, Jr., Librarian of the William Robertson Coe Collection of Western Americana in the Yale University Library. He not only acquired Downey's journal, he identified the author, and then kindly allowed me to edit the manuscript. Without his excellent suggestions and his successful efforts to secure other relevant materials, *Odds and Ends* would have gone to press in a far less complete form. Equally valuable have been the research findings of Colonel Fred Blackburn Rogers of San Francisco, who recently published Downey's 1853 newspaper articles, "Filings from an Old Saw." Colonel Rogers' painstaking search for the proper identity of many persons mentioned by Downey has saved me hours of labor. More recently Colonel Rogers published *A Navy Surgeon in California, 1846–1847: The Journal of Marius Duvall* (San Francisco, 1957). Duvall was aboard the *Portsmouth* when the Bear Flag Rebellion began, and when San Francisco was occupied in July 1846, so that his record is yet another valuable eyewitness account with which to check Downey's version. At present he is engaged in writing a history of the U.S.S. *Portsmouth,* which work should throw even more light on the Navy's important role in the conquest of California.

Many of the confusing details to which Downey made only passing reference became clear when the officials of the Henry E. Huntington Library allowed me to use their extensive collection of Californiana. Relevant manuscript letters from the "Fort Sutter Papers," the W. A. Leidesdorff Papers, and fugitives from other manuscript collections at the Huntington proved of great value. The "Log" and "Muster Roll" of the *Portsmouth* and Downey's service record were kindly furnished by the United States National Archives and Records Service from their Navy Department files.

In the preparation of the manuscript for publication, Mrs. Ruthe Smith of the Yale Western Americana staff rendered Downey's often faded and difficult handwriting into readable typescript; Mr. William L. Owens, my assistant, peered for weeks at a microfilm copy of the *Portsmouth* Log searching out references to Downey; Mr. William T. Waller has also been of assistance. Lastly, I am indebted to James T. Babb, Librarian of Yale University, and to John H. Ottemiller, Associate Librarian, for their permission to publish this volume in the new Western Americana Series. For any mistakes in the correct rendering of Downey's words and in the explanatory footnotes, the editor alone must be responsible.

H. R. L.

New Haven, Connecticut
March 31, 1958

THE CRUISE OF THE PORTSMOUTH

1845–1847

No Offence Shipmates—I meant none
Tis true Heaven bestows gifts—and withholds them
It has been pleased to give me a fertile imagination
For the manufacture of a Jest

OLD PLAY

Preface: Joining My Ship

WHAT IS A BOOK without a preface? Tis a ship without a helm, a steamboat without a starting bar, a railroad car without a track, in fact 'tis no book. A Preface in my idea is of no earthly use, but as my humble opinion cannot alter the customs of the world, I suppose I must give one to my book. To the point then at once. When I commenced the following pages, I had not the most remote idea of ever committing them to the tender mercies of the public; it was attempted more to amuse myself and pass my leisure hours away than anything else, but as page after page was added to the volume, the praises of those of my shipmates to whom I was accustomed to read them, stimulated me to renewed exertion, and as the Cruise drew near the close, I yielded to their Entreaties and determined to trust my little Craft in the sea of public opinion, well knowing, 'twould make but small odds whether she sank or swam.

My last night ashore was spent with those, who, but the acquaintances of a day, had become very dear to me, and a pang of genuine sorrow shot through my heart when the last farewell was said. A tarry of one year had sickened me of "life in a Guardo," and a fine prospect opening to me, I determined to embrace it, and was consequently transferred Bag and Hammock on board the U.S.S. *Portsmouth*, bound on a foreign cruise.

It is a very curious feeling that comes over the recruit, when transferred from one Ship to another. New and strange faces are continually peering at him, and a sensation akin to homesickness comes over him. But a few days suffices to drive the novelty away, and that once gone, he is hale [sic] fellow well met with all hands. I never felt more real sorrow than at leaving the old *Pennsylvania*, there were some kindred spirits with whom I had long comingled [sic] and one who was dearer to me than a brother, but a rover like me seldom forms lasting affection for anyone, and every new face brings its own charm, so, though I for a little time thought the separation would unman me, yet it soon wore off, and with a hearty God bless them all, I started with a light heart.

For my own edification I determined to keep a sort of Journal of incidents that might transpire, be they ludicrous or serious, and I have done so. As my motto states, no offence is meant, and should any one in looking over these pages, and comparing the dates, recognize any passage in which their own sayings or doings are caricatured, I pray them to remember 'tis in no unkind mood that it is done, only to raise a laugh for them and their shipmates. To the balance of the world into whose hands they may perchance fall, all I have to say is, if you have had patience enough to read all this tiresome rigmarole, and yet feel inclined to travel with me the whole cruise, you must not expect to find any thing very historical, or descriptive, but merely the impression matters and things have made upon a self-tutored son of Ocean.

The Start

AFTER one or two false starts, and the usual quantity of Galley Yarns, on the morning of the 23rd January, 1845, the long expected summons of "All Hands Up Anchor" resounded through our Ship.[1] It was a welcome one for many reasons, one of which was that it was the dead of winter, and very uncomfortable for all, and we were bound at once into a warm climate; another was that a sailor never thinks his time begins to wear away until he is fairly at sea. Time

1. The United States sloop-of-war *Portsmouth* (20 guns) was built and launched in 1843 at the Portsmouth Navy Yard, but was not commissioned until November 10, 1844. John Berrien Montgomery, Commander of the *Portsmouth*, was under orders to join the U.S. Pacific Squadron. The *Portsmouth* is described in detail in Howard I. Chapelle, *The History of the American Sailing Navy* (New York, 1949), pp. 436–438.

hangs heavy on his hands while in port, whilst at sea, the days slide almost imperceptibly away, are hardly noticed in their passage. At all events, for weal or woe, we were off. The Capstan Bars were rigged, the messenger passed, the Chain unbitted and brought to, the Boatswain and his mates had a long whistle, all to themselves, the Fifer struck up "Old Dan Tucker," the Capstan flew round, and the anchor came merrily to the bows, when running out our hawsers, we were taken in tow by the Government Steamer *Engineer* and were soon under good headway, and bade a long adieu to old Norfolk. The *Jamestown* (which as well as ourselves was a bran new Ship) had dropped down the day before, and as it was the wish of the Department to test the powers of sailing of the two vessels, we were ordered to proceed as far as Madeira with her. The *Jamestown* was to all appearances a lovely craft, a double decked sloop built after the most approved model, and by one of our most experienced Constructors, and the people in the vicinity of Norfolk were wont to brag high upon her anticipated sailing qualities.[2] Our Ship was a beautiful specimen of Yankee Architecture, and when we lay in dock, was pronounced by all who saw her as a beautiful model, and some of the Carpenters in the Yard were bold enough to venture the assertion that the *Jamestown* would be pawled to beat her. Our crew was composed for the most part of true born Yankees, though of course we had a small sprinkling of all Nations, yet they one and all boasted loudly of the weatherly qualities of their Ship which they had well tried in her passage from Portsmouth round to Norfolk, when they had experienced one of those severe gales, so common on our Coast in the Winter, in which she had proved herself so staunch a craft, that they placed all Confidence in her. Nor were their praises confined to her weatherly Qualities, but they also blowed a large quantity of wind about her sailing, and it would have been deemed rank herasy [sic] for any person to have hazarded a remark that she might by any possibility be beaten. We had received at Norfolk a few recruits, of whom I was one, but by far the greater portion had joined from Boston, and were old Man-of-War's Men, who had been

2. The United States sloop-of-war *Jamestown* (20 guns) was built and commissioned at the Norfolk Navy Yard in 1844. The *Jamestown*, Robert B. Cunningham, Commander, was under orders to join the U.S. African Squadron as its flagship. Commodore Charles W. Skinner, Commander-in-Chief of the African Squadron was also on board the *Jamestown* during its maiden voyage. For a detailed description see Chapelle, *ibid.*, p. 440.

paid off from the *States* and *Constellation,* and after having their spree out, had again hunted up the Rendezvous flag, and entered into a mutual agreement with Uncle Sam for 3 years. As a matter of course being old Shipmates they worked together, and despite the many little difficulties in the way, seemed determined to be happy if such a thing was possible.

Having thus given a short sketch of our ship and Crew, we will now join her in Hampton Roads, where the *Jamestown* is lying at anchor. As the wind was dead ahead we came to also, waiting for a favorable chance to go to sea, and the little Steamer put back to Norfolk. The next day she came down again bringing the mail, an officer from her came on board with final orders for us, and I had a chance of shaking the flipper for the last time with my old Shipmates. After a short tarry she again left us for good, and I remained on deck, watching her as she receded, and as the intervening point shut her out from my sight, I felt of a reality that the tie which bound me to the Guardo was sundered and were it not for shame's sake, could have wept. This would have been foolishness, and I shook all serious thought off, and looked forward with hope for a guiding star to the future. The bustle incident to getting a Ship ready for sea, will soon drive dull care away, and plunging Head and Ears into work, the past was lost in oblivion, the future unthought of, uncared for, and the present alone occupied my mind.

Jan.ʸ 24th.

Wet, cold and disagreeable, wind blowing almost a gale from the Northward. All hands busily employed getting ready for sea.

Jany. 25th

A bright morning, a clear sky, and a fair wind from the Southward. Everybody's face seemed to look smiling and happy: what a change the weather will make in the Countenance.

At daylight hove short. At 11 A.M. Commodore [Charles W. Skinner, aboard the *Jamestown*] made signal to get underway, and proceed to sea. Every man sprang to work as if it depended solely on his exertions to get the Anchor *Up and down.* *"All Hands Loose Sails,"* up fly nimble Topmen, and down falls heavy Canvass. The Fifer plays Yankee Doodle. The Capstan literally spins round, the Anchor is at the bows, she feels the breezes, she moves, Hurrah, Hurrah, we're off at last. Farewell to the Land for a month at least.

4

The Race

AS STATED in the preceding chapter, it was the wish of the Department to test the sailing qualities of the two new vessels, the *Jamestown* and the *Portsmouth,* consequently we were ordered to sail together.[1] Previous to our departure the topic of conversation in any circle you might get into in Norfolk was the probable result of the Contest, and the several merits of each vessel were canvassed, and from the Cabin to the Fore Peak they were overhauled and judgment passed on their build. As a matter of course the good people of Norfolk were prejudiced in favor of the Ship built at their own Navy Yard, and it was sacrilege almost, to dare assert that any thing could beat her, yet there was not wanting among the Knowing Ones a few who were willing to hazard not only their opinions but also to stake a few dollars on "Old Poverty Hollow," as our Ship was familiarly called. The Jamestownians, however, were all kind, and dared not post the money.

The excitement ran so high that I have even seen the arguing parties come to blows, and I have no doubt very many were glad when we sailed, as it would put an end to the contest of words. The Constructor of the *Jamestown* would not for a moment even harbor the idea that a Down Easter could build a ship that would compete with his; so positive was he that we could not do so, that when we sailed he went down in the *Jamestown,* to enjoy his triumph and return in the Pilot Boat.[2] As before stated, when the Commodore made signal to weigh, our boys sprang to work with a will, and before the *J* had got her anchor we were under way, and as we passed our Captain hailed, and informed the Commodore that he would heave her to when outside the Fort, salute his Pennant as she passed us. Accordingly, as soon as we cleared the Roads and got into the Bay, we hove our Main Topsail to the Mast and waited for her. We had not long to lay before she came gallantly along, under Topsails, Top Gallant

1. The race between the *Jamestown* and the *Portsmouth* symbolized the passing of an era in American naval history for they were the last large sailing vessels ever to be built by the United States Navy. Hereafter the Navy constructed either partially or wholly steam-propelled ships.

2. The builder of the *Jamestown* was Foster Rhodes.

5

Sails and Courses, and as she glided by, so swiftly and smoothly did she move through the water, that I heard one of our Lieuts. on the forecastle say "We may, we must beat her, but if we do, we have got to do our best," and so thought everyone. As she passed we saluted with 13 guns, which she returned with 9, and we squared away and followed in her wake. By the time we were fairly off again, and had got our Top Gallant Sails set, she was nearly or quite a mile ahead.

Now came the tug of war. Cape Henry Light was only ten miles distant, and if we could pass her before she arrived abreast that it would be more than the majority even dared to think of. But some of the harum scarum fellows, that so often blunder into the right, were loud in their declaration that we should do that. The wind blew quite fresh, and as our beauty gathered way, the anxious faces on the forecastle, poop, and peeping out at the port holes, showed plainly how intense was the excitement. Though the weather was quite cool, and standing in the open air anything but agreeable, yet I am sure there was not an individual on the Lower Deck, save the sick. All, Stewards, Cooks, Loblolly Boys, and even the Sable Sons of Africa who do congregate around the Galley, dropping pots and pans, leaving cookery to look out for itself, forgetful of the sundry lashes of the Cats neglect might bring upon them, might be seen popping their wooley heads above the Combings of the Hatch, and grinning from ear to ear, hazarding remarks on the contest. Bets, and long odds were freely offered on our ship, but no takers could be found, though the tallest kind of credit would have been given.

After a lapse of perhaps 10 minutes, which seemed an age to the gazers, it could plainly be seen that we were gaining on her. As soon as the Commodore saw this he prepared to send aloft Royal Yards. Our Quartermasters were up to snuff and twigged the move, and we got all Ready too. As soon as the Signal was made "Sway Aloft," up went ours, as clear as day, but some how or other his got foul. After a while they got them up, and then made Signal "Sway Across," here again we were ahead; their Main went all Ship-Shape but their Fore and Mizen [sic] were *all ahoo*. Our youngsters chuckled loudly at it, and the Old Salts shook their heads, and said 'twas surely an omen; if we could beat them in small things, we would certainly do so in large ones; and ended by prophecying that a goodly number of poor fellows would drink their Grog with the Ducks tomorrow morning.

While matters were in this position, dinner was piped and Grog rolled, but incredible as it may seem, yet no soul budged. Eating and drinking were all forgotten, everything was made subservient to the Great cause now pending. Slowly but surely we were gaining on our far-famed antagonist; every breath seemed hushed, perfect silence reigned fore and aft. She did not fail us in this pinch, but nobly did she perform her part. We each had as much sail as was necessary, and a fairer race could never have been contested. Creeping up by degrees, we reversed the old Proverb which says a "Stern chase is a long one." We were now alongside, still we shoot ahead, and ere we had come up with the Light, "Old Poverty" shot ahead in gallant style, thus beating her, and badly too, before the wind.

As our quarter shot clear from her bows, a long heavy breath from all announced the close of the Contest, and a strong tendency manifested itself on the part of our fellows to cheer their good ship, but good discipline prevailed, and this crow over a fallen adversary was omitted. A General Dive was now made for the Berth Deck and Grubbing was the order of the Day, between mouthfuls of which the different merits of the two vessels were discussed in all their bearings, and had the Hon. Secretary been on our Berth Deck that day, I have no doubt but that he would have been fully convinced that the *Portsmouth* was the Bully Ship.[3]

When we again returned on deck we found ourselves some 3 or 4 miles ahead and outside the Light. The *J* now hove to [to] discharge her Pilot. We followed suit, but as the Pilot Boat was much nearer to her than to us, she ran first along side of her. By the time the Boat had run up to us and taken ours, she was up and off some distance ahead. As the Boat shot under our stern I caught a look at the beaten Constructor, and a more woe-begone looking countenance I never saw. He was pointed out to me and another and, Poor Old Man, we all pitied him, but then we could not help it; if our ship would sail the fastest it was no fault of ours. By the time we were ready to square away she was some 3 or 4 miles ahead, but nothing daunted we cracked on, and long ere the sun had set we had again passed and took up our station on her weather bow. This double beat settled one of the disputed points, *i.e.* as to which was the best before the wind.

The Breeze freshed up as the sun fell and before dark we had stowed our Royals and sent down the Yards, stowed the Top Gallant

3. Downey is referring to the Secretary of the Navy, John Y. Mason.

Sails and made every thing snug. We kept our proper distance, without any extra trouble, save that of hauling up the courses, when we would shoot too far ahead and setting them when she had caught up again. At 8 o'clock, Hammocks being piped down, the Watch was called and thus commenced our first night outside.

Jany. 26

Nothing very interesting occurred these 24 hours. It still blew a fresh gale from the N.W. At 12 M. 250 miles from Norfolk, *Jamestown* reefed topsails, and of course we had to follow suit, though if our Old Man could have had his way, he would have given her Steering Sails. Oh, the misery of sailing with the Commodore, and he in a slow ship! Towards night the Gale increased, but our beauty was all right and tight and from all appearances made much better weather than the *Jamestown*. At 8 P.M. sent down Top Gallt. Yards. The last we saw of the *Jamestown* she was still astern.

Jany. 27th

At day break *J* discovered far, far astern. Shortened sail amid a shower of curses from all hands, who are anxious to get into warm weather. At meridian she came up, and considerable bunting, as Jack says, was talked between them.

Jany. 29th

This morning broke and to our great joy the *Jamestown* was nowhere to be seen; however our joy was short lived, for soon after sunrise she was discovered, and again we hove to for her. As soon as she came up it was evident that she was in some way crippled. As soon as [she was] within signalizing distance we found she had sprung some main spars, but which we could not find out. At all events it was something out of Kilter. When she came up she signalized us to lay by her as she was repairing her main rigging. If ever any ship was made unlucky by having a quantity of anathemas put upon her, she certainly would be, for I never heard so many heartfelt curses breathed against any one thing as there were against that Ship.

This sort of humbug lasted 2 days, by which time the wind had moderated and the weather became much warmer. This was just her play, and while the wind was light she would shoot ahead of us during the day, as her canvas was much heavier than ours, but when night came, and the dew thickened our sails, we were off again, and morning would find us again ahead. All this time we had fair winds,

8

and though it was very agreeable, it was getting rather too uninteresting. We had conclusively beaten her before it, and so confident were we of serving her the same on a bowline, that all hands were praying for 24 hours of a fresh head wind; at last on the

30th Jany. it came and a cracking one it was too, and with it also rose the excitement. The Commodore [Skinner] said he was ready, and so were we, and after a close contested match of 12 hours it was at last conceded by all that we could out carry, fore reach, eat to windward and make better weather than she could. They tried all sorts of ways such as trimming &c. but 'twas of no use, they were bound to be beat. We ran on, keeping about the same position until the

12th Febry., when having a fine Top Gallant breeze the Commodore determined to make one more struggle for the palm, and honor of Virginia, but 'twas of no use, we beat her worse and worse, and to prevent us from crossing dead to windward of his fore foot, he ordered us to take position on his lee quarter and remain there. We shortened sail to do so; this was just at dark. Soon after 6 o'clock we missed her light and hove to, burned blue Lights and False Fires, got no answers, could see no *Jamestown;* at daylight she was not in Sight, and to the great joy of all the Old Man [John B. Montgomery] determined to crack on for Rio, where we arrived on the 27th, making the passage in 32 days.[4] How we lost her, unless she hauled down her light and tacked ship, is a mystery, but such was the result of the long talked of Race. For 2000 miles we had run her, and beat her so bad that in sheer despair she bolted.

4. Downey was so completely oriented toward the life and activities of the crew, that he rarely discussed the officers aboard the *Portsmouth* except to complain about some injustice they had perpetrated. The editor has included information on the officers, therefore, wherever it may be helpful to the reader. Since Downey does not mention the *Portsmouth*'s captain, John Berrien Montgomery, other than as the "Old Man" or "Our Captain" until late in his narrative, a few biographical facts concerning Montgomery's career and nature seem in order here. Born in Allentown, New Jersey, in 1794, Montgomery first entered the Navy in 1812. He "fought creditably" on the *Niagara* at the Battle of Lake Erie in 1813. After the war he served first as a lieutenant in the African Squadron, then as executive aboard the *Peacock* and the *Constitution,* and for a time as the recruiting officer in Philadelphia. He became a commander in 1839 and five years later was assigned to the *Portsmouth.* His biographer writes of him: "He was of modest nature, an eminently just man who made the Scripture his daily study. No quarrels or serious mishaps marred his service career." "John Berrien Montgomery," *Dictionary of American Biography,* XIII, pp. 97–98 (hereafter cited as *DAB*); see also the *Army and Navy Journal* (April 26, 1873).

General Quarters

HAVING finished my account of the Race, and got my ship fairly at sea, and matters and things well settled, it is now time to look about me and pick up incidents to found yarns upon, for the amusement of my friends, and the public. This is not a hard matter, for any man who is disposed to write sketches can always find lots of timber to work upon on board Ship. There are always some characters on board, the every day actions of whom will afford plenty of themes. Life at sea is not, as a Landsman naturally enough supposes, an unceasing round of sameness; no, far from it—the grand routine it is true is always the same, but the variety, the spice, the little by-play, which savors as it were of life everywhere, is never quiet for a moment, but changes so often and quick as almost to defy the pen, be it ever so smart to note each ludicrous or serious incident that may present itself.

A person who intends to keep a record of the doings "before the mast" must in the first place select his characters (of whom there are always plenty) on whom he may play. Sailors generally have an unconquerable antipathy to having their name appear in a book, but assume a feigned one and you may portray incidents that happened in such a manner that none who were present at the time could help identifying the individual, yet it is all right enough. Like all other men they have no objection to enjoying a laugh at the expense of another, but let any little foible of their own be brought up, and they forthwith get offended, and a fellow has to be very careful how he steers his trick if we would get along well, after it is once discovered that he is writing a book. I had learned all these things last Cruise and was somewhat prepared for the task before me.

Among others whom I selected for peculiar subjects to aid me in getting through my work was Brush, our Painter, a cool calculating long headed Yankee, smart as a Steel Trap in his way, but rather backward in showing it.[1] He had by some "Hocus Pocus" been inveigled away from his shop in Boston where he was doing well, had got on a spree, and was, under the influence of Liquor, induced to

1. Downey usually gives the reader many clues to the identity of the person about whom he is writing. Since no painter is listed on the muster roll of the *Portsmouth,* "Brush" is one of the few unidentifiable characters in Downey's sketches.

sign that dreadful paper, and before he rightly knew where he was, he was sent "holus bolus" on board the Guardo. He said it was all one to him where he was, he never could lay up anything ashore, and if he didn't have anything due him when the ship was paid off, it would be all the same to him, and beside all else, he should have seen some of the world.

I asked him one day what was the cause of his leaving home and coming to sea. "Why," said he, "you see when the old *States* come home, I was on a spree and used to cruise with the Sailors; wal, I seen them have 2 or 300 dollars, and nothing else to do but try and spend it as soon as possible, so I concluded it must come mighty easy, and that all I had to do was to ship, and I should have my pocket full too, but I rather guess I got sucked in this time." Brush was installed Captain of the Paint Room as soon as he joined, and though he growled at it, he could not get clear. Being rather green he was often imposed upon, but his ready tongue often turned the laugh intended for him onto his opponent.

An incident occurred to him soon after we had got to sea and left the *Jamestown,* which was not only very laughable but is also an excellent one to commence my series with, and so here goes. As before stated we were running along with fair winds and clear weather, and of course a portion of the Ship's Company were exercised each day at the large Guns. There is no part of the duty more irksome to the sailor as this, yet at the same time while growling about it he will acknowledge the necessity of it.

Among others who were inveterate against it was Brush, and when roused from a nap in the Store Room to go to quarters, he would swear a batch of notes enough to sink the Ship. He however congratulated himself that he had only two days in the week in which this sort of play was to be enacted, when horror of horrors, the word was passed that until further orders Thursday of each week would be devoted to *General Quarters.* This cut poor Brush to the very soul; he could, he said, have stood the exercise of his Gun pretty well, but "Come to board," and all that, he couldn't come that.

"What on earth is the use on't," said he, "don't they suppose we git enough on't at Exercise, but now we must have the Devil's own time, goin' through the moves the whole blessed afternoon? I wonder if they are foolish enough to believe a feller's a going to wait, in a fight, till the Captain of the Gun says 'turn sponge, cock lock, blow match,' and all that sort of thing; no, by Golly if I do, I'll be darned if ever we do git into action, and one of the enemy comes in range of my gun, I shall blaze away as fast as ever I can, stuff the powder in her, and if she hits anywhere about where they are, they'll think old parson Miller has come sure enough with the day of judgment under his arm!"[2]

It was of no use to argue with him, or to bring forward the usefulness of the maneuver in order to get the men at home about the Gun, and able to fill one another's place in case of accident, to proceed with some sort of order when boarders were called away, and know how to act in case of fire. "It's all very nice," said he, "to talk about, but you jest give me the natral impulse, and I'll beat your tactics all holler."

If by chance any person would hazard the remark that practice would make perfect, he would laugh at them and say, "I know better than that. I used to train in Boston among the Militia; well I turned out for five years, twice a year to muster, and we used to have Sham Fights and all them sort of things, but do you suppose I know any more 'bout fiting than I did afore? No indeed. When a feller gits hold of that 'ere tackle he can only pull as hard as he can, and all the Exercising in the world won't make him pull any harder. I go in dead agin all such extras, and if I had my way I wouldn't have 'em cast adrift again this whole cruise. Anyhow, I hope it will rain tomorrow like all possessed, and then I guess they won't have any on it, but if they do I won't stand it long, for I'll git the cholic, or run the Gun over my toe, and if I git on the List, I shall be all right."

But despite his prayers, the eventful Thursday came, and a bright, beautiful day it was, rather warm, but still not too much so. As the day wore away, Brush found another new cause for dissatisfaction, for it was his dog watch below from 4 to 6, and this was the identical two hours picked for the onslaught. This was the unkindest cut of all, for it deprived him of his sleep, and if possible he growled and grumbled more than ever. However, at 7 bells evident preparations were being made for the long talked of operation; Brush, who when

2. "Brush" referred to William Miller (1782–1849), a self-taught minister who, by tract and sermon, preached that the world would first be revisited by Christ sometime in 1843–1844, and then be destroyed by fire. The movement attracted many followers and great national attention until Miller's final predicted day of judgment (October 22, 1844) passed without incident. "William Miller" in *DAB*, xii, pp. 641–43.

he knew there was no chance of a get off worked as cheerfully as any one, was all about and full of life.

At 8 Bells the Drum beat, and all hands repaired to their stations. I caught a glimpse of Brush as he ascended the Ladder, and could not help fancying that his face wore rather an air of discontent, and to tell the truth there was nothing very enticing in the prospect of an hour's hot work in the broiling sun. The men were mustered, and the 1st Luff, ascending the poop, gave the order to cast loose. After exercising from the Quarter Deck for a few moments, the order was passed "Officers of Divisions, go on," and they in their turn gave "Captains of Guns, go on," so that before you had hardly time to think, every Gun fore and aft was at work, each striving who should load and fire quickest, and even the powder Boys, catching the enthusiasm, flew about like mad, and one little fellow who hailed from Buffalo, actually got so awfully excited that he split his trowsers in a most melancholy manner.

Whilst these things were transpiring forward, Brush at one of the after Guns was making himself as miserable as possible. His station was 1st Loader and Pikeman—as the first, it was his duty to insert the cartridge into the muzzle of the Gun. To do this he was obliged to lean forward some half way out of the port. Upon his first attempt, just as he had got himself balanced, some mischievous wag gave him a sly shove in the stern, and away he went, nearly out of the port.

"Hello," then sang out Brush, "who ever you are, if you do that again I'll make my fist and your Countenance acquainted in a manner that won't reflect much credit on you."

"Silence!" said the Officer of the Division.

"Oh yes," muttered Brush, "it's very easy to say silence, but he most tumbled me overboard just now, and I am violently opposed to all such unlawful measures."

"Silence, I say!" said the officer again.

"Yes, I'm all silence now, but you see if there's a goin to be any victims in this Engagement, I don't want to be the first, and so I thought I'd put in my protest."

This sally occasioned a great Laugh all round, and by the time that had subsided, all the Pikemen were called to repel boarders. Brush seized his Pike, and away with the Crowd he sallied, seeming however to have no fixed purpose, as he would move when they did, and when they stopped he came to a dead halt also.

13

"Repel Boarders!" was the order. Brush looked round as if in utter amazement, but never stirred hand or foot.

"Why don't you repel boarders?" sung out a reefer close in his ear.

"Because," said Brush, very composedly, "I don't see anybody round here to repel; them 'ere fellers are all my shipmates, and I don't like the idea of ramming this thing into them."

"Well, 'repel the Enemy' then."

"Now," said Brush, "you talk. If you'd a said that afore, I should have been about. Jest you show me where the enemy is, and by gosh I'll walk into him right away."

"Go through the motions."

"Now," says Brush, "I don't see the use of that, 'cause like enough if there was any enemy coming over the bulwarks, I should drop my pike and run away, and as the 1st Lieut. said we must go through the motions just as if we were in battle, I don't think I should like to have the folks laugh at me, so if you please, I'll stand right here."

"Well," said the reefer, "either you are a fool or else you wish to be thought one."

"No Sir, I am no fool, nor I don't want nobody to think so, but I goes in for strict obedience to orders, and —" something else he would have said, but alas for him, some lawless rascal in passing him (unintentionally, of course) pricked him with the point of his cutlass. This was too much, even for his good humor, and so dropping his pike he sung out lustily—"Murder, murder, murder."

"What is the matter?" said the Officer in charge.

"Why there's Brush the Painter, has been asleep all the afternoon, and has just fell down and stuck a pin in his leg, and it has awakened him, and he's crying about it," said our old Gray headed Mast man, with his nose all askew.

"Taint no such a thing," said Brush, "I'm severely wounded in a vital part. I feel I shan't survive. Oh, please have me sent down to the Doctor. I knew 'twould be so. Oh, I'm a victim, a victim of misfortune, and if you have any regard for me, have me carried below before I faint."

"Nonsense," said the officer, "come here!"

"I can't, not for a thousand worlds I couldn't, my leg is all to pieces, I know it is!" So without any more ado he planked himself down on a spar, and there he stuck in defiance of threats or entreaties.

14

Meanwhile, as if in a regular action, the alarm of "Fire" was given, the Pumps manned, and the Carpenter's Mate who had the pipe directed it as he was ordered. After playing aloft for some moments, he espied Brush sitting disconsolate and alone upon the spar, and the spirit of mischief entering strong into him, he directed the whole force of the water full upon the poor fellow. No sooner did he feel the water than a new idea seemed to have taken possession of him, for dropping off the spar he fell sprawling his full length on deck, and struck out as if swimming, bellowing at the same time at the top of his voice for the Life Buoy. This was too ludicrous to be easily borne. All hands from the Commander down were convulsed with laughter, and when order was in a sufficient measure restored, the order was given to "Secure." As soon as the water drained off from Brush, he gathered himself up and dove below, and swore roundly that the next time they had General Quarters he would either go on the List or join the 4th Division.

Last Cruise

"Most unkind Daniel, to speak such biting things of me"—OLD PLAY.

FOR WHAT PARTICULAR REASON I could never discover, there is a natural tendency among all Sailors to use the phrase which heads this chapter. Our crew was mostly composed of old man-of-wars men and by far the greater majority of them had been Shipmates before, either in the *States* or *Constellation,* and the humane character and seamanlike propensities of their old Commanders was the subject of many pleasant reminisences to them, and many a dull hour was passed away spinning yarns about matters and things "last cruise." Now Jack is a professed growler, and if anything goes either wrong or particularly well with him, 'tis all the same, he must have a growl. If they are ordered to clean in blue they will growl, and if in white, 'tis the same, and if allowed to do as they please and not clean at all, then they curse the bloody dirty Ship and say, "Twant so last cruise." If you say they were a long time performing any piece of Ship's Duty, they will growl, "If we were twice as long Last Cruise nobody would care," and if done very quick, they could have done it twice as quick Last Cruise. Now our ship, though strict, was very easy to get along in, but 'twas no use, they must have their spells of cursing the bloody ship and all that belonged to her.

Nothing will ever check growling but making a joke and having a surfeit of it. A surfeit we had, and one that put a stop to Growling for a whole month. It occurred in this wise. Among other outfits to a Man of War is a Carpenter, who is generally a very useful and necessary man. But unhappily for us, in drawing lots for our share we drew a complete blank, or in other words, got a thing that minded almost anything else but his own business and seemed anxious to have a finger in everybody's mess and stand nobody's watch. He was withal very inquisitive and rather ignorant, and soon became a but[t] for all hands to crack their jokes at.

He was a stout, squat, ill-made clump of a man, who had been but a few years in the service, and who, 'twas said, had grinned himself into the situation he now occupied, from the fact that he was servile in the lowest degree to an Officer, and never addressed one, but with a grin on his face. Now a smile or a grin is quite agreeable when a handsome set of teeth are to be displayed, but when, as in this case, they were an ill-made, deformed, and withal a very dirty row of masticators brought into view, combined with a horrible breath and a villainous manner of squinting through one eye, when addressing you, a conversation with our Chips was any thing but agreeable.[1]

The subject now on the tapis seemed to have imbibed the idea that nothing short of toadyism to our first Lieut. could secure his good graces, and consequently when before him or in his hearing he was all servility, yet when his back was turned he allowed his vile mouth to utter phrases he would not have had him hear for his ears. He could be heard if not seen from the grey of the morning until twilight, flying about shouting at the top of his voice for Dennis or some other of his Crew, meddling with this or that job, displacing

---

1. Downey's "Chips," whom he also calls "Mr. W." on occasion, was undoubtedly George Wisner, carpenter aboard the *Portsmouth*. Although born on Prince Edward Island, Wisner had settled in Massachusetts, and as a citizen of that state had entered naval service, December 30, 1841. See *Register of the Commissioned and Warrant Officers of the Navy of the United States* (Washington, 1846), p. 64. Hereafter cited as *U.S. Naval Register*.

tools and creating confusion wherever he went.[2] When all else failed, he would run forward, stick his head down the Forecastle Hatch and bellow out, "Where's that Ship's Painter?"

Poor Brush, green though he was, was gifted with a small share of common sense, and evinced the Annoyance Chips was to him by heaping all sorts of imprecations upon his head. One day, after an unusual hard run from Chips, Brush sat down and seemed ruminating for some time, at length he raised his head and said, "I'll tell you what it is now, that old feller haint got hard sound sense enough to enjoy good health, and if I was in his place I'd get in some Ship and go right straight home and tell my mother I wouldn't dew. He'll keep his mouth open till some of these days there'll come a squall when he's looking to windward and he won't have sense enough to turn round but will get full of wind and bust, and that will be the end of him."

Among other foolish and unnecessary things he proposed to the 1st Luff was to have all the combings of the hatches and the waterways scraped and kept bright. It looked so neat, he said, and when he was asked what was his object in making so much additional work for the men his only answer was "That's the way we used to do in the *Vincennes*." 'Twas the same with any job he proposed, when inquired of as to the utility of it, all he could answer was "Well, that's the way we used to do in the *Vincennes*."[3]

Our combings and waterways were nicely blacked and to all appearances were well enough, but by dint of hard persuasion and incessant grinning he prevailed on the 1st Luff to have them scraped, and one bright morning just before going into Rio all hands were called to Quarters and the Job was commenced. Loud and deep were the curses that were uttered by the crew upon his head, some of which he must have heard, but he paid no attention to them, but kept sculling about decks rubbing his hands and grinning from ear to ear.

At last he approached one who was digging into the wood with all his might, making as rough a track as a plough over a field. "Look

2. Henry Dennis was carpenter's mate aboard the *Portsmouth*. See Fred B. Rogers, "Personnel of the *Portsmouth*" in *The Society of California Pioneers, Publication for 1954* (San Francisco, 1955), pp. 22–24, for a conveniently available muster roll of the *Portsmouth*'s crew as of 1846.

3. Wisner had served on the United States sloop-of-war *Vincennes* (20 guns) in 1843 and 1844. See *U.S. Naval Register*, 1843, 1844.

here, my lad," said he, "you are spoiling that 'ere waterway, where on Earth did you learn the art of scraping?"

The man he addressed was a wit in a quiet way, and the idea of annoying Chips was stronger than the fear of the Cats, so he merely answered without altering a whit his rough manner of working, "Why this is the way we used to do in the *Vincennes.*" Chips started as if an adder had bitten him and turned away. The effect was soon noised about, and fore and aft, aloft and on deck the same thing assailed his ears.

The right chord was touched and the crew eagerly seized the opportunity now offered of venting their spite upon him. Did he go forward, some fellow would immediately stop his work and begin, glowingly, to describe to an admiring crowd the beauty of something on board the *Vincennes,* and when he would turn to go aft a loud fit of laughter would burst upon his ear. He dove down upon the Berth Deck to get clear of the annoyance, where he found a Marine descanting upon the beauty of a Cutlass Rack on board the *Vincennes.* Forward he ran to the Fore Passage, where the Yeoman [Downey] was busily engaged ornamenting his Store Room, and as Chips descended, the first word that greeted his ears was, "Don't this look as well as the Store Room on board the *Vincennes?*"

He could stand it no longer, but cramming his fingers into his ears, he rushed on the Quarter Deck and up to the 1st Luff [John S. Missroon], exclaiming, "Sir! Sir! I claim protection from you!"[4]

"What is the matter Mr. W.?" said the 1st Lieut.

"Matter Sir? Why mutiny, insolence, insubordination is the matter!"

"Explain yourself, Sir!"

4. Missroon, a native of South Carolina, entered the Navy in 1824 as a midshipman. He was appointed passed midshipman in 1830 and three years later received his lieutenancy. In his earlier sketches Downey spoke well of Missroon, who appears to have been an able officer and a trusted favorite of Montgomery. As yeoman, Downey was in constant contact with the vigorous, strongly positive Missroon, and the former's cocksure manner and impertinent wit soon brought about a clash of personalities between the two men. Downey's remarks about Missroon grow increasingly hostile until in the latter half of the journal he dubs Missroon "The Autocrat."

Missroon became a commander in 1855, and during the Civil War, he was promoted to the rank of commodore. He died in October, 1865. See Thomas H. S. Hamersly, ed., *General Register of the United States Navy and Marine Corps* (Washington, 1882), p. 500 (hereafter cited as *Gen. Nav. Reg.*); see also Seymour Dunbar's introduction to Volume IX of "The Fort Sutter Papers," MS in the Henry E. Huntington Library.

"Why just listen one moment, there, do you hear that?" said Chips, as some fellow bellowed out "This is the way we used to do, last cruise in the *Vincennes*."

"Yes Sir," said Mr. M, "but there is nothing alarming in that, 'tis an expression I hear from the men every day in regard to their former cruises."

"Well but Sir, it aint that they mean, they are only blackguarding me—that is a phrase of my own—they were none of them Last Cruise in the *Vincennes*."

"A phrase of your own," exclaimed Mr. M. smiling, "really Mr W., when you can by any manner of reasoning or argument prove to me that any word in the English Language belongs solely to you, I will severely punish the first man I find using it, or anything else of yours, always provided," added he with a broader smile and a meaning look, "the reason or argument is not such as you used to have 'Last Cruise in the *Vincennes*,'" thus saying he turned upon his heel and left poor Chips standing in the middle of the Deck, aghast with Eyes and mouth staring wide open, nor was he roused from his stupor until he heard a wise remark of Brush who was working near, "Look at the Carpenter," said he, "with his mouth wide open. I wonder if that's the way they used [to] catch flies 'Last Cruise aboard the *Vincennes*?'" This roused Chips and he darted down to his room, declaring loudly that the Service was going to the devil. Hearty bursts of Laughter greeted his ear as his head disappeared below the combings of the After Hatch, and this little affair was talked over many a day after it transpired, and never failed to excite a laugh at the expense of Poor Chips.[5]

5. In *White-Jacket, or the World in a Man-of-War* (1850), Herman Melville tells a remarkably similar story about an old salt who keeps recalling the time "when I was on board the *Audacious*." See p. 17 in the 1922 edition.

"Murder Will Out"

GOOD NATURED READER do not start or let your blood run cold at the sight of our motto, as nothing very alarming is about to be related, for 'tis but an incident which occurred one day on board our Ship, which goes far to prove the old proverb of "Tis a long lane that has no turn" to be a true one. Our Ship was in a certain manner a temperance Ship, not exactly a *Teetotaller* but a Temperance Ship.

Our Captain [Montgomery] was very religious and looked not with the eye of scorn but with that of pity on a drunken man; he had prohibited the Carriage of liquor as sea stores to all but our Ward Room Officers, and the quantum of grog served out at the tub was duly watered after the most approved style. Our Officers were all of them temperate men, but still indulged in a glass by the way of a stimulant to their memory of sprees ashore. Various were the excuses invented among them to gratify their tastes, and when all else failed, they were sure to have a certain dryness of the stomach seize them, which nothing but a "Cockroach" (the cant name for a Gin Toddy) could be found to allay.

During our stay in Rio, the stock of Roaches had been replenished, and for the first few days after we left every thing was to all appearance going on famously.[1] But some way or other, an idea seized upon the brain of one of the holders of *stock* that his Capital was decreasing faster than the drafts he made upon it accounted for, or in other words the Expenditure exceeded by far the Consumption. He pondered on the matter some time and finally came to the conclusion that some one of the Boys employed in the Ward Room must have been attacked with the prevailing Mania, and following the example of his Superior Officers, have administered a Roach or two to himself.

Now this was but a suspicion, but one which required an analysis,

1. The *Portsmouth* arrived at Rio de Janeiro, February 28, 1845, and while being reprovisioned was inspected by Commander Daniel Turner (1794–1850), then in charge of the U.S. Brazil Squadron, and by the American Consul at Rio. See "Log of the USS *Portsmouth,* November 19, 1844 ff.," in Records of the Bureau of Naval Personnel (RG 24), Department of the Navy, The National Archives (Washington, D.C.), entries for February 28 to March 8, 1845 inclusive. (Hereafter cited as "Log of the *Portsmouth.*") See also Daniel Turner in *DAB*, XIX, pp. 59–60.

so a meeting of the Stockholders was called, and various were the means proposed to detect the offender. To sit in the Ward Room the whole day and watch was by no means pleasant in the prospective and moreover if it was as they suspected the thief would never commence his operations while a guard was kept; this therefore was out of the Question. At last however our young medico proposed that a large dose of Tartar Emetic should be put into the bottle, the height of the liquor marked and placed in the usual position, and frequent visits made to it, so that when they should find that any of it had been purloined, they might be on their guard to detect the delinquent, from the Effects of the Dose.[2]

Accordingly this was done, and all the officers left the Ward Room, to give a clear field for the Operation. It was agreed that the Chief of the Stockholders should make the inspection of the Bottle and report proceedings every half hour. The day wore slowly away and no signs of a successful solution of the mystery developed themselves until at his periodical visit at $\frac{1}{2}$ past 3 he discovered that the Magical Jug had experienced the effect of an Ebb Tide to the tune of some 3 or 4 inches. With a heart bursting with Joy he hurried on deck and disclosed the intelligence to the Conspirators, who forthwith repaired to the forecastle, to watch what unfortunate individual should suddenly be taken sick and compelled to visit the head.

They stationed themselves upon the forecastle chest and patiently awaited the elucidation of a mystery which promised them so much amusement.

They had not yet tired their patience when slowly creeping up the ladder there appeared a face—Ye Gods—such a face—Pallid as a corpse—Elongated one moment to the utmost degree of tension then again compressed into the smallest possible space, his Eyes starting from their sockets, and hair standing short on end with fear that he had been poisoned.

Reader did you ever see a poor fellow afflicted with sea sickness? If not, you have one sight to witness that will cause you to smile, no matter how humane or sympathizing your nature may be. If you have, you may be able to judge of the sight which now presented itself to the watching trio. The poor fellow between fear and deadly

2. The "young medico" was undoubtedly Charles H. Oakley, assistant surgeon aboard the *Portsmouth*, who had entered the Navy, October 2, 1844, and was on his first cruise. *U.S. Naval Register, 1845.*

sickness was able hardly to walk, and sat down upon the rail, apparently striving yet fearing to open his mouth for fear of defiling the Deck. He had evidently made up his mind that he was poisoned, and had crawled up the forecastle like "Great Caesar to die with decency."

But the man, for man it was, who of all others should it be but Jimmy Legs, one who is required by law to be the most inveterate enemy to Liquor in a Ship.[3] Now our Jimmy was a perfect Liquor hater, *and evinced his hatred of it by destroying it wherever it could be found.* He went entirely upon the Christian principle of loving our Enemies; he knew liquor was no friend of his, but he loved all his enemies and this one in particular.

But now the question arose of how could he have gotten the Liquor. He could not have gone into the Ward Room and procured it— Oh no—some one must have aided and abetted him in that—No matter how he got it—It had certainly got him—and there he sat, a perfect picture of the Knight with the Rueful Countenance. Not one of the Conspirators even dared to look towards him for fear of bursting into Laughter and spoiling the Sport, a chuckle drawn from the deepest recesses of their stomachs like that emitted of yore from old Joe Willett might have been heard, but any stronger evidence of mirth was strangled at its birth.

As a Solution of the mystery of how he obtained the dose was highly necessary, an adjournment to the Ward Room was moved, and a muster of the various servants there employed had. One by one they appeared, clean, sober, and in no wise afflicted with any disease under the heavens. The plot now thickened, until upon calling upon the body servant of the Chief Conspirator he was no where to be found. Messengers were soon dispatched for him and his name resounded along the Decks. No answer was returned, nor could the messengers who were sent find him. At length news was recd. from the Sick Bay that he was there, but too sick to obey the Summons. Here then the mystery was unravelled.

The Ship's Corporal was sent forthwith with orders to bring him into the Ward Room dead or alive.[4] The Trio of Conspirators sat in mute Array, the Ward Room Boys circled round them grinning

3. "Jimmy Legs" was John Morgan, Master at Arms. Rogers, "Personnel of the *Portsmouth*."
4. The ship's corporal was Henry Osborne. *Ibid.*

from ear [to ear]. Expectation was at its heighth when in stalked the legs and body of the Delinquent but not his face! oh no! not his face, it is the counterpart of the face we left on the forecastle. The Conspirators tried to look grave, but the fellow servants of the culprit giggled, and one of them, a little monkey looking fellow, fairly laughed aloud at the sight, but a severe look from the Steward checked him and he was at once seized with a most excruciating cough.[5]

"Come here, Andrew," said the Chief.[6] Andrew obeyed. "Poor fellow," said [the Chief] "you do look sick—What ails you?"

"Oh, I don't know sir," said he, retching violently at every attempt he made to open his mouth.

"What have you been eating?"

"Eaugh—Nothing, Sir."

"What drinking?"

"Not Eaughthing—Sir."

"Have you touched the contents of this bottle?" said he, producing the Magic Jug. At the sight of this Andrew grew if possible more pale than ever—and solemnly protested he had not touched it. "If you have," said Mr. L., "you had better acknowledge it, as it contains a certain poison and if an antidote is not administered to any person imbibing it in one half hour, he will be a corpse."

This announcement seemed to petrify the poor fellow, and falling upon his Knees, he confessed the whole affair, and in the most piteous tone called upon the Doctor to save his life, and quickly too as it was nearly half an hour since he first took the dose.[7] What was his Astonishment when instead of Commiseration he was greeted with a roar of Laughter from all in the Ward Room which fairly shook the deck and an exclamation of, "I've caught you at last!" from the Chief.

"Oh save me—save me, Doctor," cried he, almost shrieking with fear. The Doctor with tears running down his cheeks from sheer exhaustion of laughing could barely utter "'Tis no poison, 'tis only

5. It is not clear which was the steward holding the inquiry. James M. Ball and George W. Neal are listed as stewards aboard the *Portsmouth*. *Ibid.*

6. "Andrew" was probably Andrew Robinson, who was cook for the wardroom officers. *Ibid.*

7. The "Doctor" was Charles Chase, Ship's Surgeon, who had been in the Navy since 1814. He became fleet surgeon for the Pacific Squadron when the *Portsmouth* arrived at Mazatlan, Mexico, Commodore Sloat's base of operations. *U.S. Naval Register, 1845.*

an Emetic" and again rolled off into a fit of hysterical laughter. Poor Andrew saw through the trick in a moment, and starting to his feet, rushed from the Ward Room, cursing his foolishness for allowing himself to be caught, and swears roundly he will never drink any liquor in the Ward Room again.

The Black List

ON BOARD a vessel where so many human beings are crowded together as in a Man-of-War, cleanliness in clothing and person is one of the most important duties devolving upon every member of the family. A good man-of-war's man is as proud of his dress as the veriest dandy that struts up the Paved streets of any city was, and no pains or expense is spared to outvie each other in neatness of dress, but in collecting 200 men together there must of course be some who are of the Sloven order and whose sole desire seems to be just to be able to sheer clear of the law and are very much like the Whited Sepulchure of old. The laws of the Navy prescribe a regular length for hair and whiskers, for officers as well as men. Our Capt. had strictly conformed to the order himself, and was determined all under him should do the same.

Although the Regulations also prescribe the Uniform to be worn, yet every Executive Officer is allowed the privilege of suiting his own fancy in decorating the same with Tape, Stars, &c. Our 1st Luff [Missroon] had a pattern of a frock made to suit his taste and displayed it fore and aft, with the name of the owner in Black Letters ½ inch in length to be placed 1 inch below the Blue Bosom of the frock. Orders had been passed and sufficient time allowed for their execution, when one Sunday he determined that all who were dirty or out of uniform should be summarily punished—but of the whole Ship's Company who were inspected at quarters, but three individuals were found wanting.

Foremost among these was our old friend Brush, who seemed endowed with the faculty of getting into a scrape whenever there was a possibility of so doing. Next appeared an odd sort of Fish nicknamed Spouter, from the fact that he was always boasting about his Cruises in a Whaler. He would (if he had possessed sufficient sense) have been the Joe Miller of the Ship, but the small stock of jokes he had purloined from others were soon worn out, and of course by repetition became stale. Last upon the List came a little dumpy fellow yclept *Dale,* whose brains, if ever he had any, were so deeply set in his head as almost to preclude the possibility of their ever appearing.[1]

He was in common with the other two hostile to anything that savored of Exertion, and an inveterate [enemy] to Soap and Water. He was, or pretended to be, a Simpleton, in proof of which, he once boldly asked of the Officer of the Deck permission to be excused from standing a night watch, as his Pea Jacket, he said, had a great hole in it and was wet at that. This was the trio now arraigned at the mast, that great tribunal of justice on board Ship, charged with being generally filthy.

Spouter was first called upon for his defence. He urged that he had as clean a bag of clothes below as any man in the Ship, but that being that particular morning a Cook on the Berth Deck, he had very accidentally dirtied the bosom of his frock and did not have time to change it before quarters. That excuse was of no avail, "Besides," says the 1st Lieut., "look at your trowsers, they too are dirty, and even your shoes; blacking and they are total strangers, and see, one [of] them is only tied with a rope yarn, while the other does not even boast that appendage." Spouter plead hard but 'twas no use, but he had been tried and found wanting.

The next case on the docket was Brush; his was a more heinous offence—he was not only charged with filth but on this particular occasion he had been caught in an attempt at prevarication, in the following manner. He had no clean white clothes and had flattered himself with the Idea that we should muster in Blue, until it was too late to wash, so he had borrowed from some good natured shipmate a clean frock and persuaded the Purser's Steward to issue him a new pair of trowsers. When he incased his nether limbs in the last mentioned articles they were perfectly clean, and he was heard to boast when dressed that he *thought* he would pass muster this time.

1. "Spouter" is difficult to identify, but "Dale" was apparently Theodore Dale, Landsman. Rogers, "Personnel of the *Portsmouth.*"

But before the drum beat to quarters he had managed by some means known only to himself to bedaub the lower extremities quite plentifully with paint and dirt.

Being mustered at quarters he could by remaining in the background completely hide the dirt-spots and so placed himself with a self-complacent smile to await the ordeal. As the Officer of the Division passed along the line, the whiteness of Brush's frock attracted his attention. 'Twas a perfect *Lusus Natura*. How could it be possible? White as the driven snow was the frock and all that could be seen of the trowsers. He thought he must be mistaken in his man—rubbed his eyes, and looked again. Brush seeing he had attracted so much attention put on one of his most seducing smiles, and thought no doubt, he should receive some high Compliment upon his unusual Cleanliness.

Mr. B. [Washington A. Bartlett] again took a cautious survey of him—from the crown of his head he let his eye rove downward, his hair was short enough to satisfy even Mr. Sect. Badger himself—his face shone resplendant with Splendor (or Soap), his neck was not exactly alabaster, but it was clean—his collar was duly ornamented with the necessary rows of Tape and number of Stars according to the pattern—no fault could be found with the bosom.[2] Glancing still further, his eye catches the fatal mark, ah-ha, mentally ejaculated he, I thought so—this accounts for all.

"Come here, Sir—Take your station at the mast—you thought you would weather me, did you?"

Brush good humoredly strutted forth, and without a sign of surprise upon his countenance muttered forth, "I knew 'twould be so, I'd have to go to the Mast anyhow. If it hadn't been that, he'd have seen the trowsers," marched forward and planted himself upright against the mast, ready for trial.

2. Bartlett was Acting Master of the *Portsmouth*. A native of Maine, he had been appointed midshipman in 1833, but had received the rank of lieutenant only when the *Portsmouth* was commissioned. Bartlett had a serious, religious nature and was inclined to be pompous. From the very first Downey appears to have disliked him, calling Bartlett the "Tract Man." In 1846 Montgomery appointed Bartlett "Alcalde" of Yerba Buena (San Francisco) and detailed Downey as the latter's clerk. Bartlett was dropped from the Navy in 1855. *Gen. Nav. Reg.* (1882), p. 55.

Downey's phrase "even Mr. Sect. Badger himself" referred to President John Tyler's Secretary of the Navy, George E. Badger, who was noted for his strict enforcement of discipline. Leonard D. White, *The Jacksonians: A Study in Administrative History*, 1829–1861 (New York, 1954), p. 316.

"Well, Brush," said the 1st Lieut., who was at once Judge and Jury, "You are here again I see."

"Yes Sir," promptly replied Brush.

"I am sorry to see you here," said Mr. M. [Missroon].

"So am I, sir," chimed in Brush.

"You are reported to me, Brush, for being generally filthy, and on this particular occasion for an attempt at deception."

"False indictment, Sir," said Brush, "I never tried to deceive any body."

"Oh yes you did, you came to your quarters with another man's frock on, thereby endeavoring to impress your Officers with the Idea that you had reformed, and become a tidy individual. What have you to say to the charge?"

"Why, I plead not Guilty, for the following reasons: You see Sir, I'd forgot my stock of clean Linen had run so low, till I overhauled my bag last night, and when I found I had no clean frock, I went to wash one, but couldn't find a bucket before 8 o'clock and then 'twas my watch below."

"Why not wash then when you came on Deck?"

"Wall, I meant to, but when a feller first comes up, he feels kinder dull, and so I sot down to collect my thoughts a little, and the first thing I knew 'twas 8 bells and I had to go below again."

"Then you are not only guilty of Dirtiness, but you sleep in your watch on Deck, do you?" said Mr. M.

"Oh, no sir, not at all—I wasn't asleep, only fancy kinder carried me back home, and I was a thinking—"

"No matter what about," said the Lieut. laughing, "that was a bad fancy that carried you off that way. You had better not travel with her any more, you see what a scrape she has got you into now. 'Twas that same fancy I expect that led you to suppose you had a clean frock of your own on—"

"But," said Brush, "it's all the same, I'm a-going to wash this one you know and—"

"Never mind what else," said Mr. M. and turned away. Dale's turn for trial now came on, but he had seen enough of the Arguments of his fellow prisoners, and therefore when asked what he had to say very wisely answered nothing.

The Judge now summed up—the Jury rendered a verdict of guilty against the trio—and they were sentenced to be *Black Listed* and to muster every morning at 7 Bells, to be inspected by the Master at Arms and Officer of the Deck. The sentence seemed to have but little effect upon any one but Dale, who shuffled forward, blustering loudly upon the hy-poc-ri-sy of the world in general, and of Navy Officers in particular. Brush and Spouter laughed heartily at the idea. But, poor fellows, on the morrow they were sadly disappointed, for it happening to be their morning watch below, the 1st Luff deeming that nothing would rouse their energies so well as exertion, decreed that, one should be allowed the privilege of White-Washing the Berth Deck, while the others should amuse themselves by polishing the Iron Stanchions around the Galley. Spouter was accordingly introduced to a Brush and White Wash Tubs while Brush and Dale operated in the Art of finishing.

Brush said that was no punishment at all for he had worked 4 months for a man filing up screws, but never got any pay for it— while Spouter exulted in the Idea of being able to learn the first rudiments of Landscape Painting, i.e. laying on Color smooth, without any expense. Poor Dale however did not fancy the Job at all, and was loud and fervent in his denunciation of the High-poc-ri-sy of the thing.

The Jobs were at last finished, but not until they were heartily tired of them, and each one had resolved, that rather than be "Black Listed" again they will wash forever.

All Aback

THERE IS NO SITUATION in which a Ship can be placed more perilous than this, and none in which even to an uninitiated mind the Danger is more apparent. An incident of this Kind occurred to us on the night of the 18th of March, 1845, when nearly up with the Pitch of Cape Horn.[1] We had been running along for some days with a Light but fair wind and had Steerings Sails below and Aloft both sides set.

1. The vessel was off the Falkland Islands on March 18. "Log of the *Portsmouth*."

The night was rather warm, and I had lingered on deck long after my usual hour, amusing myself by following my fancy back to the States and again enjoying cheerful intercourse with a select few, in whose company I had passed the most pleasant hours of my existence. The watch on deck, save the Look-outs, were stretched on the deck enjoying a pleasant snooze, when I roused myself out of Fairy Land and betook myself to my bed in the Bay.

I had fallen into a doze when I was again roused by hearing the watch called at 12 midnight, and had just composed myself to sleep again, when I heard an unusual bustle upon deck, and presently saw the figure of a man, disdaining the common entrance to the Bay, come darting through the Grating window that separated it from the Berth Deck, pitching headlong into the hammock of *Wax End* who was dozing there, and finally panting and blowing like a porpoise settle down in one corner, and cover up his head.

My first impression was, that the man was seized with some sort of a fit, and might fall foul of me, but perceiving he had settled down very quietly, and the noise still continuing on deck, I proceeded to dress myself, and inquired of him what was the matter.

"Oh Lord, Oh Dear," said he, "I was on deck just now and Oh Dear, Oh Lord—"

"Well, what is it Matic," said another of the occupants of the Cots

"Why, the Ship was took aback!"

"Oh Hell, is that all," growled an old Sheet Anchor man, "I thought she was overboard."

"Is that what scared you so," said I?

"No, I wan't scared a mite, only a little *started*."

"Yes, and you seemed to be *started* pretty quick too from the way you pitched into my hammock," exclaimed Wax End. "I believe you've stove in some of my ribs." I now recognized the voice to belong to an Old Holder, who was not noted for possessing too much sense at any time.

"But what did you leave the door open for?" said I.

"Oh Lord, I didn't come in at the door."

"No," sang out a Dago who lay near, "he got such a devil of a start, he no stop for open de door, he come fly in de window all de same as one dama Albatross, what for you no stay on de deck if de ship is aback and pull rope, hey?"

"Because," said Old Hold, "I am very sick."

"Eh-ha-begar, den because you sick, now den if de Ship go to de bottom, you run down in de sick-a bay for de medicine to save you, hey. Begar, I hope she go down for your sake."

By this time I had succeeded in getting on my clothes and hurried on deck. Here all was Confusion, every one was hallooing and bellowing at the top of their voice, and order seemed to have been blown away by the Squall. The most contradictory orders were given, and in the mean time the ship was rapidly gathering stern way. This was however of short duration. Mr. S [Schenck], our 3rd Lieut. sprang from his berth and was seemingly with one bound on the Forecastle, while at the same moment our 1st had gained the Quarterdeck and taken the trumpet.[2] "Silence, Fore and Aft!" shouted they, and such is the habit of obedience inculcated in a good ship that in a moment, order again ruled supreme.

The necessary orders for paying her off being now given, our little beauty wore round on her heel, and bounded off seemingly as much relieved as I am sure the minds of all on board her were. When the Melee was at its height, Brush who was barely awake, seemed all at once to comprehend the danger, and he stood stock still gazing fore and aft, and shouting at the top of his voice, "Oh my patience, we'll all be drowned, she's going down, what shall we do?"

"Wal I reckon," said our Sailmaker's mate, a dumpy little Virginian (who was dubbed Man Eater), "I reckon if you are going to do anything you had better pull on this rope," at the same time putting one into his hands. Poor Brush however was paralyzed by fear, and dropping the rope, still continued to bawl out, "There she goes—There she goes, right now stern foremost—"

"Yes, and there you go stern foremost too," said Sails, and suiting the action to the word, he planted his fist between the eyes of Brush and sent him rolling into the Lee Scuppers. She gave a heavy lurch at the same time and tripping up the heels of Sails sent him flying to leeward also. He was up however in a moment, and looked eagerly round for his antagonist, but Brush had come to the sage conclusion that "discretion is the better part of valor" and had accordingly taken himself off.

When the hurry and confusion on deck were over, and the watch again sent below, the natural thoughtlessness of the Sailor reigned

2. Woodhull S. Schenck, Third Lieutenant aboard the *Portsmouth*. *Gen. Nav. Reg.* (1882), p. 632.

triumphant and Jokes were bandied about as merrily as if danger had never been near them. Pill Box, our doctor's Steward [Oakley], came in for a full share of them. He was a little spare built fellow, and not only his profession but his figure continually reminded one of the Apothecary of Romeo. Moreover he was gifted with a constitution enabled to undergo a large quantity of rest, and when once he resigned himself into the arms of the drowsy god, 'twas a most difficult job to awaken him. More than one of the Poor fellows intrusted to his care has, while suffering with pain during the long watches of the night, endeavored in vain to rouse him, and many a bitter curse have his sleepy tendencies caused to be uttered.

Now Pill Box was not much of a Sailor, and as he was in the habit of making a field bed on deck, he was as apt to get his head to leeward as to windward, if not told to the contrary. This night however when he retired he had managed to get his noddle to windward, but as during the Melee on deck the Ship had gone about, and careened over, he now lay with his heels elevated to near an angle of 45 degrees above his head. The Ship was rolling and pitching heavily, and bottles, pots and pans were jumping about and kicking up a merry tune, yet still Pills slept on as quiet and undisturbed as if nothing was the matter.

At last the Ship's Corporal [Henry Osborne] in his hourly round happening in at the Sick Bay, one of the inmates requested him to wake Pills up or slew him round, else, as he expressed it, his brains would all turn over, and he'd be a bigger fool in the morning than he was the night before. "Ah begar," chimed in my friend the Dago, "It makes but a very leetle diffrance to him, how he lay, for I bleive he got so mush brain in one end as the other."

Pills still slumbered until at last an Arm Chair having fallen over struck him in the face and awoke him, when he roused up and on being questioned, swore roundly that he had been awake before, and even on deck, though 'twas evident to all he was but dreaming. However, he slued his head to windward, and the poor devil who had so unceremoniously *started* having got quiet, and receiving an admonition from Wax End to the end that when he tried any more "ground and lofty tumbling he should dodge lower," we all settled to sleep from which we were not awakened until all hands were called, and on repairing on deck found as bright a morning as if the events before related had never happened.

Cape Horn

THE PASSAGE round this promontory is a source of dread and anxiety to the Sailor at any time, but more especially at the season of the Year in which we were to make it. It was the beginning of the Winter months in those latitudes, and long before we reached it, though the weather was mild and beautiful, bags might have been seen all over the decks, and all sorts of Old Garments, Pea Jackets and Flannels were going through a thorough overhaul, and carefully laid by against a time of need. Our Ship had been signally favored with fine weather since our departure from the States, and there were many on board who were so enamoured of it that they would hardly believe we could ever have any other, and persuaded themselves into the idea that if no Ship ever made the passage without a gale, we should be the one to lead the van in that achievement.

There were plenty of Old Salts however who stoutly maintained that such a thing could not be, and if by any chance they overheard any of the opposite party venture a remark or offer anything in shape of proof, such as "Look how fine the weather is now, and we almost down to the Cape," would shake their weather beaten noddles and sing out, "Just you wait a bit and you'll find out what Cape Horn is." No matter how fair the wind blew or the prospect looked, they were sure to prognosticate evil from it.

On the morning of the 19th Mar. being then 10 days out from Rio we made Staten Land, and our old man determined to run through the Straits of Le Maire, thus cutting off some 150 or 200 miles of the distance to be run. The wind was fresh and fair, and by 12 o'clock

(M) we were through the Straits, and our noble Ship was running per log at the rate of 13–6 bound for the Cape.[1]

It was apparent enough, even to the most sanguine of the foul weather breeders, that if the wind held in the quarter it was now for 12 hours we should be round the Cape and as times looked now at least it promised very fair. I was much amused at a sort of Conundrum I heard from one of our Boatswain's mates, a tall raw boned fellow who had spent nearly his whole life at sea, who completely silenced a youngster who was trying to convince him that because the wind was fair and the sky was clear 'twould hold so.

"Look here, my youngster," said he, "you should be like a Marine over the Scuttle Butt, 'seen but not heard.' Now boys," said he, to a large crowd that had gathered round him, "did you ever hear of anything that would take a Yankee 20 years hard work to guess?"

"No," said all.

"Well I have," said he. "When I first come round this way some 20 years ago, I was like some of you, young and foolish, and one night, I was bragging the same as that youngster that because the weather looked fair, 'twould be so, when an Old Sheet Anchor Man my chicken asked me if I knew why Cape Horn [was] like a woman? I told him no. He then said, 'Guess!' Well, I kept on guessing and cruising for twenty years, when at last I found it out."

"Well what is the reason, Sam," sung out a dozen at once.

"Because," said he, quickly casting his eye to windward, "she's d – – – d deceitful."

He had hardly got the words out of his mouth when "All hands reef topsails" was the cry, and slap, a squall from off the Pitch of the Cape took us right in end, and all yarns, fine weather and bright hopes flew down to the Leeward. In less than 1/4 of an hour we were under close reefed topsails, and dodging about much like a dumpling in a boiling pot. By sundown it blew a perfect gale, and the prospect seemed fair for us to battle the watch some 2 or 3 weeks off there.

As soon as everything was snug, the Old Salts might have been

1. Here Downey and the Log differ, for the latter indicates that they made the Falkland Islands at 2:00 P.M. By the following morning, however, the *Portsmouth* had gone through the Straits of Le Maire and was in sight of Cape Good Success. "Log of the *Portsmouth*," March 19 and 20, 1845.

running fore and aft chuckling, and rubbing their hands, seemingly in great glee at the fulfillment of their words. "There now," said an old Capt. of the Forecastle, who with the Gunner's Mate were unanimously voted Ship's Growls, "what did I tell you bout Cape Horn when you was talking this afternoon, hey? You wouldn't believe me, but now you've got it."

"But," said I, "this will blow over in a day or two."

"Oh, that be d – – – d," said he, "we'll have to lay off here a fortnight at least." This is but a specimen of the manner in which these old fellows ran on, not because the prospect of bad weather or cold fingers was agreeable to them, but because they could not now be called false prophets.

The weather was intensely cold, and frequent squalls of rain and hail burst upon us. The next morning when the Doctor went his rounds, from the Crowd assembled round the Door of the Bay, it really seemed as if Pandora's Box had been thrown on board wide open, and all the Ills that it contained had been showered upon the heads of our devoted crew. There is no man living who more sincerely pities a sick Shipmate than your true Sailor. So also there are none who more heartily despise a Skulk. Now when a man is found to be full of lip in fine weather, and at the first approach of bad, hauls on the List, he is at once denominated a skulk. Our doctor was a kind hearted old soul, who would take any man's word as to his feelings, and consequently was often imposed upon.

Among others who applied for the assistance of our Medico on this eventful occasion was a Son of Crispin named Wax End, a short stout built fellow, who in fair weather had lip and appetite enough for any two men, but who had a mortal aversion to cold, rainy watches, and all sorts of work generally, but to work off Cape Horn in an especial manner. When we first left Norfolk he had made two or three ineffectual efforts to get on the List, but as he failed, and fine weather came on, he shone out as bright as any one. But after we left Rio and drew near the Cape, he was most violently attacked with the Horn fever, and succeeded in hauling on the List.

His soul's ambition was now achieved, and all he had to do was to keep himself there while there were any cold feet or wet jackets in the prospective. To do this he was ready to become a martyr, and would no doubt have swallowed the whole Dispensary and made a gulph at Pills himself to effect this end. For the first 24 hours after he was admitted his symptoms were alarming, but they gradually wore off, and he would smile and chat as cheerful, and argue as strong as any one until near the time for the Doctor's visit, when his face would elongate, and he would be dreadful bad, till the Medico's back was turned. His was a very convenient disease, for when it had lingered a sufficient time in one part of his system it would suddenly fly off to another, to the no small annoyance of our worthy Doctor, who had no sooner pinned it up in one place and made preparations to dislodge it, than presto—it was off, and all the work was to do over again.

His ration had been stopped for the benefit of the Hospital Fund, but living on Rice, Sago, &c. did not at all agree with the cravings of his stomach, so he was in the constant habit of making frequent visits to his mess, where the enormous quantities of Bread and Meat he would back off soon became a subject of note, and at a Council of War held by his messmates, at which the Cook presided, it was unanimously voted that in their humble opinion the poor fellow was afflicted with a *tape worm*. I may as well add here that soon after we were round the Cape and fine weather came on, he got off the list, and one day very gravely assured me that he considered his recovery solely attributable to the change of Climate, in which opinion I entirely coincided, though not in the sense perhaps he intended to convey.

Thus we stood on the morning of the 22d Mar. 1845. Imagine us, kind reader, off the Pitch of Cape Horn, with a head wind, a heavy beat sea, continual squalls of rain and hail, and cold enough to satisfy even the most dainty of all the Old Salts. Our Captain however was not to be scared out of a quick passage if it was possible to make one, and during the lulls, would crack on to her in a manner that plainly showed he meant to try what she was made of. Try her he did, and she was not found wanting, for she acquitted herself to the Satisfaction of every one and many blessings were silently heaped upon the head of her builder.

A Gale of Wind has so often been described by abler pens than mine that I shall not attempt [it] and merely say that nothing out of the usual Course of such things occurred until the morning of the 23d at near 11 o'clock, when she was boarded by a tremendous Sea that shook her fore and aft, stove in two of her upper half ports, and deluged the spar Deck with water. The watch below were in their hammocks (which were kept down all the time for the comfort of the Crew) but such was the shock that every man was on his feet in a moment.

Little Jim, one of the Carpenter's Gang, a lively Joker, was sent below for some nails to repair the ports. He obtained them and was returning to the Spar Deck when she shipped another sea, which seemed to stave her whole bow in: in a moment she was waist deep in water on the Deck and poor Jim who had just cleared the Hatchway was taken full and bye, in the rear, and away he flew, Tool Box, Nails and all down to Leeward, jumbled up with pigs, geese and niggers. To save himself he let go his hold upon the nails, and had no sooner regained his feet than off again he started for more nails. On being asked if the former supply had been used, "Used be d – – – d," said he, "they've gone to the Devil, Tool Box and all, and what is more than all the rest, they've took my cap along with them." Chips, who was standing by the main mast, not having "savvy" enough to dodge, caught the whole of it on his head, and was completely drenched. When the most of it had passed, I caught a sight of his face, and a more woe begone looking countenance I never saw, but happening to look behind him he perceived an Officer looking at him and instantly assumed his accustomed grin.

This was the sum total of our disaster, and an End of the bad weather, as we were now in the Pacific Ocean, having as I heard one of the youngsters logically explaining it, just jumped into it, "For," said he in support of his doctrine, "you know the Pacific is 14 feet higher than the Atlantic, so that when that sea struck us it was the Beginning of the Pacific." Whether this was true or not I will not pretend to say, but in the course of 24 hours we got a fair wind and were soon balling it off at the rate of 12 Knots on our course for Valparaiso, where we arrived after a passage of 29 days.

As after an action a general overhaul of damage received in spars [and] rigging as well as men is had, so after a gale has abated the usual quantity of bruised fingers and toes are bandied down to the Doctor. Among others was one of so ludicrous a nature that I deem it worthy of preservation. We had among others of the Crew a Dane who bore rather a bad name among the men as a "White Mouse," or tale bearer.[2] Now during the gale Hans had managed to knock the skin from off his nose, and ran down to the doctor's Steward. Pills,

2. "Hans" is probably Hans Carl, Seaman. Rogers, "Personnel of the *Portsmouth*."

who was in a hurry, and withal something of a Wag, cut off a piece of Sticking Plaster near an inch square, that had some printing on the outside of it, and slapped it on the proboscis of poor Hans, who then strutted off on deck, having very much the Appearance of a perambulating newspaper. His nose continuing to pain him, the next day he put on a long face and with his lower lip sticking out some inch or two marched down to the Doctor.

"Well Hans," says the Dr., "and how did you get hurt?" Hans screwed his face into the most melancholy shape possible, and whined out, "You she, Doctar, der vash so big a Sea as never vash, come over ze sheep, and lift him up de Blacksmith Shop. I hold on so long as I could, to him, and let go and run foul my noshe of him, and broke him."

"Which?" said the Doctor, striving to repress a smile, "broke which? Your nose or the Blacksmith Forge?"

"Yesh," drawled out Hans, "my nose him broke de Blacksmit Shop."

"In that case," said the Dr. smiling and turning to Pills, "it seems you have made a small mistake here, you should have put the Plaster on the Forge, not on the Nose."

"No, No," said Hans, "not my noshe, ze Blacksmit Shop proke, but ze Blacksmit Shop my noshe proke."

"Ah, very well explained, but have you any pain?"

"Oh yesh, very mush great pain all down my pack."

"You must be cupped then."

Now Hans had no objection to have a pain, but he had a very strong objection to being cupped and begged so hard that at last the Dr. excused him and ordered him to remain quiet. This just suited him, so he settled himself in the Bay to mourn over his "noshe" and sew Hats.

General Liberty

[In the following sketch Downey gives the impression that the *Portsmouth,* after rounding Cape Horn, continued an unbroken voyage to Callao, Peru. Actually the *Portsmouth* dropped anchor at Valparaiso, Chile, on April 7, 1845, to deliver the French, British, and United States government mails which she had on board. While in port the Intendant of the city visited the *Portsmouth* and a messenger from the American Consulate in Valparaiso took passage to Callao. Downey's ship reached Callao on April 20, where they found Commodore John D. Sloat, Commander of the Pacific Squadron, aboard his flagship, the United States frigate *Savannah* (44 guns). With the appearance of the sloop *Warren* (18 guns) on April 22, the commanding officers of the three vessels constituted themselves into a court of enquiry which sat for a week. Not until the Court had completed its investigations (April 28) did Montgomery permit the *Portsmouth's* crew to go on the general liberty which Downey describes. In a later sketch, "The Ship's Wag," however, Downey does mention incidents of the voyage between Valparaiso and Callao.]

IT IS ALMOST IMPOSSIBLE to describe the various feelings that animate a Ship's Company when the report is started that the Commander is about to give General Liberty. A run ashore to Jack is something similar to giving a man a respite of 24 hours, who is condemned to death. He seems to think that he must live a whole life in that time, that when he places his foot upon the beach, he is his own master, and that no one has any right to interfere with him or his actions, that for that space of time he can set all law at defiance, and act just as his fancy dictates. The plan of operations is often discussed for a week beforehand, but they most generally end in one way, that they will see the Curiosities of the place, enjoy all the Come-at-able Amusements, have a horse ride, get drunk and then come on board in time. But poor fellows, many of them are sadly disappointed, and instead of following the plan laid out, are much apt to reverse the matter, i.e. they get drunk first and never think of returning to the Ship until sent for.

This is the general result of Liberty, though in our Ship, the Case was a little different. Upon our arrival in Callao there was but little work to do save water ship, yet before that could be done even, there were some discontented spirits continually on the go, urging the Petty officers to go aft and ask the Capt. for Liberty. It was of no use to represent to them the folly of such a proceeding until the work was finished; so, they could not brook a moment's tarry, and some of them worked themselves into quite a fit of desperation, because their wishes were not at once complied with.

Twas not a Killing matter however to wait, and wait they were obliged to until Monday the 28th of April, when a draft consisting of some 25 men and boys were called on deck at 10 A.M. and after receiving a lecture from the 1st Lieut upon the necessity of coming on board in due time, and of course as sober as possible, were sent on shore.[1] After they were fairly off there could be no doubt in the minds even of the most fearful, but that we were to have Liberty and those who were to go the next day, were (to use a homely phrase) in a perfect fidget, until the following morning dawned, for fear that their predecessors would not come off in time, or would kick up some row ashore that would put a stop to the Liberty.

As soon as the breakfast is piped the following day they are seen cleaning themselves, from which time until the hour of 10 they are restless, dissatisfied and eternally shifting from place to place. Ask one of them to lend you a hand and you will be sure to get a surly, "No—Ain't I going on Liberty?" Continual visits are made to the gangway and upon the arrival of a boat along side, a general rush is made, to find how many have come off, and their countenances, like barometers, will tell the news as plainly as their tongues.

We will now suppose the first 24 hours expired, and repair to the Spar Deck, and watch the first draft, as they come over the Gangway. Some few years since, it was a rare thing for a "Man-of-War's Man" to be able to ascend the side unaided, and to come from Liberty clean, and sober, was in the eyes of his shipmates disgraceful and a sure sign of a Curry-favor, or a White-Mouse for Officers. But in common with the rest of the world, the march of Temperance has affected Poor Jack also, and though to come on board drunk is not in his eyes a disgrace, yet he who comes sober and neat, is by all hands considered the most sensible of the two, and is much more heartily received, and highly praised even by the Old Soakers themselves.

Our Captain was a professed Christian, and unlike many who leave their professions at home, was a Christian if ever one existed both in practice and precept, and the crew were accustomed to look up to him in time of need as to a father. His sole delight seemed to

1. "31 men given 24 hour liberty," "Log of the *Portsmouth*," April 28, 1845.

consist in seeing his Crew contented and happy, and as this draft—with a few exceptions, came on board, clean, decent, orderly and Sober, his face glowed with smiles, and he appeared willing to overlook the faults of the few, for the good conduct of the many.[2]

I say with but a few exceptions, they were all sober, and even of this few there were but two or three very far gone, and none were noisy. One little fellow who was hardly able to keep his eyes open, when he saw the Officer of the Deck, muttered out, "I'm drunk and I'm ashamed of it." Having thus made his report, he immediately resigned himself into the Arms of Morpheus from which he was not aroused, until, as he assured me himself, "his hair pulled so hard that it awakened him."

Another, a youngster and a general favorite, with all the Cunning peculiar to a drunken man or boy, amused himself by shouting some well known air, until, his vociferations had collected a crowd round him, when all at once, he ceased his song and very gravely assured them he could whip the best man in the fleet, and having by dint of three or four repetitions of this assertion convinced himself that he was understood and no person having contradicted him, he proceeded forthwith to give illustrations of the manner in which said whipping was to be performed, in the midst of which he was arrested by the heavy hand of the drowsy God, and soon repaired to the Land of dreams.

The second draft, most of them, made their appearance in good time, but differed from the first in that, the majority of them were drunk and half naked; there were none however who were in any manner hurt, save a black eye or so, and their clothes were found subsequently and brought off by their Shipmates.[3] Wax End, who was of this draft, seemed determined to make amends for the suffering he had undergone in rounding the Cape, by remaining on Shore for some time after his Liberty had expired.[4] He staid some 3 days, when finding his services on board were not considered valuable enough to require even a Marine to be sent for him, and the beach combers, having aided him in getting rid of what ready money he

2. "2 not back from liberty." *Ibid.*, April 29, 1845.

3. The second draft to go ashore consisted of 24 men and 4 marines. *Ibid.*, April 29, 1845.

4. Most likely "Wax End" was William Brown, Seaman, who is listed as an attempted deserter in the Log. *Ibid.*, May 1, 1845.

had, and also of the proceeds of his Jacket, now beginning to look coldly upon him, and Starvation staring him in the face, he took the wise plan of returning on board again.

Among the dissipated ones, an overhaul next morning presented a sorrowful prospect; their money was gone, their clothes half ruined, and in return they had nothing to show except an aching head and sore bones. It was in vain to ask them any questions as to what sort of treatment they met with, or what kind of country it was, until breakfast was piped and grog served out, when their spirits would revive and they would become Communicative, but even then their Knowledge of the City was limited to the number of grog shops, and quality of the liquors they contained. Their stories differed as much as it was possible for any two yarns to do, but they all agreed in one thing, namely in d – – – g all Mother Gibson's horses.

One old fellow in describing his cruise to Lima said if he had carried the horse, he should have had an easier job than to make the horse carry him. He said he had to beat him all the way up. As a matter of course he was much fatigued when he arrived there, "But then," he said, "I was well treated, saw all the curiosities but one, and that was the big Church by Candlelight."

"Why did you not see that?" I asked of him.

"Because," answered he, "You see when I got down there they hadn't lit up, and so I went into a shop close bye to wait for 'em and then—"

"Well, what then?"

"Why I got so corned that I couldn't see any thing, and when I made daylight again I was half way down to Callao in the coach, so I missed the Chance." The great majority however of the Crew, could give fair statements of the place and its inhabitants, and all seemed well satisfied with their liberty.

There is always adrift in Callao as in all the South American Ports, a gang of fellows termed Beach Combers, comprised of runaway Sailors of all nations, who have a mortal antipathy to do anything but drink rum, and whose means of living, to judge from appearances, are anything but honest. They have at their head some one who acts as Master of Ceremonies or Bully, who is supposed to do or order done all the fighting. When Liberty from a Man-of-War commences, they are at once made acquainted with the fact, and a committee is appointed to meet them on the Mole, and welcome them ashore with all the honors, escort them to the first groggery, where of course as being the last comer, Jack is expected to stand treat. This ceremony being over, and Jack being inclined for a ramble, a guard of honor is detailed to accompany him, show him the beauties and keep him out of all Scrapes, i.e. from falling into the hands of any others who might fleece him. During this ramble he is plentifully plied with Liquor, at his own expense, and when he has enough on board to stupefy him, he is laid upon the roadside, and very considerately relieved of his money, hat, Jacket, and shoes, and left to the tender mercies of the weather.

The man who officiated as President at this time was named Sweeney. He had been discharged from the Frigate [*Savannah?*] as a worthless fellow, and from all accounts well deserved the situation he filled, for he was the greatest scoundrel among the gang. Among the first draft that went ashore were some who suffered severely in pocket from him.

The sober lot thought him too much beneath them to meddle with. Now notwithstanding the warning given, each succeeding draft was sure to fall into the same snare, and when under the influence of Liquor brag what they had done to Sweeney. No matter who it was, man or boy, if he ran foul of him, and was pretty drunk, of course, our man came off best, and from all accounts Sweeney must have suffered most awfully. This game ran through the whole of the crew, and towards the last degenerated into a bye word. If any one was seen roaring drunk coming alongside, he was reported as having whipped Sweeney. Among the last who went on Shore, was our old friend Spouter, who in consequence of some misdeameaner had forfeited his claim to go on his regular turn. Spouter was in Sailor parlance, a very gassy cove, and often amused himself and others by blowing a great deal of wind, or in other words bragged loudly of what he would do. He would not touch any liquor until he had licked Sweeney too—but poor fellow the temptation was too strong and when he made his appearance on board he had his face awfully cut and bruised, and was minus hat, jacket or shoes. He was quite drunk and when some one asked if he had licked Sweeney, he said no, but Sweeney and Rum had licked him. This ended our General Liberty and the bill of health as to the Conduct of the men was, I venture to say, as clean in the average as ever was presented to the Commander of any Naval vessel.

Jack Ratlin's Yarn

CREDULITY and superstition have for years been attributed to the Sailor, more from a peculiar love he has of passing away the long watches of the night in listening to a well spun yarn from a Shipmate, than from any other cause. A great portion of some seamen are uneducated, some (and not a few) can neither read or write, hence their Love of the marvelous and belief in the supernatural. To such minds as these, the fairy stories that were wont to cheer the years of childhood are peculiarly attractive, and I have often seen a group of men whose ages would vary from 28 to 50 listening with greedy avidity and breathless attention, to a story at which a schoolboy of the present day would turn up his nose and declare too foolish to waste time upon. They will often congregate under the forecastle and relate incidents of their own lives which savor strongly of the miraculous, but these yarns no matter how highly Colored were always a source of interest to me. In the performance of my promise to portray minutely the manners of seamen, this trait came in good play, and with the hope it will interest my readers as much as it did me, I will lay it before them.

We had among our crew a jovial young fellow, a Fore-Topman, who from his ability to provoke mirth whenever he chose to display it, was a universal favorite with all hands. Were there any droll sayings adrift about decks they might easily be traced back to Jack Ratlin.[1] Did a roar of Laughter greet your ear from the Larboard Gangway, you might set it down as a sure case that Ratlin was there. When the Congo Band were performing in all their glory, a close survey would have shown Ratlin, seated in their midst, thruming away on his Go-below, (as he termed his instrument) with all the gravity of the Leader of the Part-Orchestra and when all around would be convulsed with laughter, no smile would be seen upon his face, but he would look round with an expression, which seemed to say "what are

1. Jack Ratlin is in some ways remarkably like Melville's "Jack Chase" in *White-Jacket,* and Melville admired the latter in much the same way Downey admired Jack Ratlin. Of the six "Captains of the Foretop" on the *Portsmouth* it is impossible to tell which Downey chose as the subject for his sketch. Their names were: William Dunley, Henry Harris, John Hudson, John Seaman, Thomas Smith, and Charles M. Spooner. Rogers, "Personnel of the *Portsmouth.*"

you grinning at?" and yet he knew all the while, oh yes, the sly rascal was well aware it was some of his witticisms that was the cause of all.

I could never hear him discanting upon his past life, until one fine night during the mid watch I pounced upon a lot of his Topmates seated under the Forecastle trying to persuade Jack to give them an account of his Shipwreck. I joined my entreaties to theirs, and at last persuaded him to commence. It was a tale of hard times, and though I despair of giving it with any degree of the humor with which he interspersed his misfortunes, yet I shall put my best foot foremost, and try to make it interesting.

You see boys, said he, it was in the fall of the year 1839, that I having got tired of cruising ashore shipped along with a Capt. Sherman in the Whale Ship *Parker* of New Bedford with 20 men before the mast and the usual quantity of Mates, boatsteerers, etc., and Sailed from Talcahuana, bound on a cruise; well we were quite lucky, and nothing out of the usual run of Whalers occurred, until on the morning of the 14th of Dec., 1841 we discovered a school of whales. Of course all boats were lowered. Our Captain in his boat struck the first whale, and as he ran up to enter the second iron, the flukes struck him and seemed to throw him some 20 feet into the air. We all saw him when he struck the water and were standing ready to catch him when he rose. But that he never did, after some moments his hat floated to the surface, and that was the last of our old man.

This accident put a damper on all our spirits, but we soon roused and took our revenge out of the Whales, two of which we captured and towed alongside. The 1st mate now took charge, and shortly afterward we went off to the Northwest Coast, where we took 1100 Bbls of Right Whale Oil, and in August of /42 we sailed for Wahoo, via the Coast of Japan. About this time a Spaniard whom we had shipped got sick, he was so for a long time, and at last became insane, and we were obliged to put a Strait jacket on him,—he recovered from his Sickness, but became a perfect idiot. Our crew all told now consisted of 28 souls, among whom were two Kanackers, or natives of the South Sea Islands.

We were now nearly full and were thinking of returning home; our heads were full of Conjectures as to what would be the price of oil in the States, and all our old arithmetic was called into play, to calculate what the amount due each man would be, and all sorts of plans were formed as to the manner in which said sums should be spent. As for me, nothing short of a small farm would suit me, I was tired of the sea and actually persuaded myself into the belief that I should be content ashore.

Well matters were in this state when on the 14th Sept, 1842 at 12M, our Skipper got the sun, and by his calcalation we were 700 miles from the Coast, and there was no danger anywhere near us. It was blowing a gale of wind, but we had plenty of sea room and cared not much for it. It was my first watch on deck, and at 4 Bells I was relieved from the look out, and stowing myself away underneath the windlass, and was soon calking it off quite merrily, and dreaming about my farm, my wife and no matter what else, well at 8 Bells I roused out from that, and dove down into the forecastle and had just got off my jacket and trowsers preparatory to turning in when all at once I felt a most tremendous shock that threw me across the forecastle with great violence against the opposite berth.

My first impression was that a heavy sea had struck her, and as it was my watch below, of course it was none of my business, so I crawled up to windward and was in the act of getting into my bunk, when another shock more severe than the first threw me flat on my face. I now became alarmed and hurrying on my trowsers made the best of my way on deck. As I poked my nose out of the forecastle hatch, something hit me alongside the head and made me see stars for a minute—I tell you—It was pitchy darkness around me and as the lightning flashed, I saw a sight at which in spite of the dangers I could not help laughing. Every moveable article about decks had got under way and was cruising about to its own liking. There were casks, buckets, blocks, running hither and thither. The pigs, having given up in despair the attempt to sit, stand or lay still, were running races with the Cooper's Horse, and it actually seemed as if every thing was for the moment endowed with the power of locomotion and was determined to use the rare gift to the best advantage.

On making my way aft, which was a dangerous attempt, I soon found out what was the matter. The ship had drifted stern on to a Coral reef, which was nearly perpendicular and every sea was heaving her upon it with such force that she quivered and groaned through every beam of her. The Officer who had the charge of the Deck at the time was a Portuguese, and when the Capt. (Smith) who was much alarmed ran out of the Cabin, and asked what was the matter very coolly answered, "Matter be d – – d! Ship strike rock."

"Oh no," said the Capt., "that can't be—there is no rock on the chart."

"Well," said the Portuguese, "suppose he no on chart, he here under water."

"Back the maintopsail," said the Capt.

"No use," sung out the Portuguese, "she strike stern foremost."

We jumped to the braces, but after a few useless attempts gave up and sought some other means of saving ourselves. The 1st mate suggested the idea of lowering the boats. The lee boats were already stove or filled with water and could be of no use and there was such a tremenduous sea running that to attempt to lower the weather ones seemed almost madness, yet twas our only Chance and we determined to try it. My self and 3 others, jumped into one of the Quarter boats to clear her away. I kept a bright eye to windward, and seeing a heavy sea combing over, threw myself on deck, and twas well I did for in one second more she filled with water and the weight carrying the bow full away, she swung round under the rudder and was soon ground to pieces against the rock, carrying the 3 poor fellows with her.

The two Kanackers were standing on the rail, the Spanker boom broke adrift and away it flew to leeward carrying one of them named Pete with it. A young Englishman named John had endeavored to clear away a waist boat, a heavy sea crushed her, and carried the poor fellow to leeward, against the rocks; for some minutes we heard his cries, but could render him no assistance, and they became weaker and weaker, and at last ceased altogether.

All this had occupied but a few moments—our boats were all gone, and to save ourselves seemed impossible. The Capt. now recommended us to make our peace with God, as he said it was impossible for the Ship to stand it much longer. Almost as he spoke a heavy sea lifted her and she broke amidship, her decks flew up with a loud explosion and in another second she seemed to divide into 4 parts, and every soul was thrown into the water. I had long before this given up all hope but the instinct of self preservation is strong and I clung to a spar. I felt myself driven along with great velocity and supposing myself on the top of a breaker, shut my eyes and with a hasty prayer to God, awaited the moment when I should be dashed to pieces against the rocks. For some seconds I almost flew through the water, when all at once to my surprise, the sea became calm. I now sung out and to my joy was answered by 2 or 3 voices, in a few moments others replied and I knew I was not alone. I was never much of a hand for praying, but now I did pray, and earnestly too, for daylight—I could feel that I was moving through the water and yet from the shouts of my fellow sufferers was convinced I was not going away from one spot. In fact It seemed to me that I afterward found to be the Case that I was drifting round in a circle. This was caused by a strong eddy we had all got into and there remained.

The hours which elapsed before daylight seemed as years to me, and when at last it appeared but the first dawning, I perceived some large object floating near me. I paddled myself toward it and found it was the bow of one of our whale boats, containing a few fathoms of small whale line, and stowed away, seemingly well contented was our poor idiotic Spaniard. I hailed him and bid him be of good Cheer and all the answer I rec^d from him was a loud laugh. I secured the Line and left him and for hours after that shrill unearthly laugh rang in my ears.

As day dawned, I discovered my Shipmates drifting round and round in this Eddy and looking for all the world as if they were chasing one another. We all now swam together and held a council, the upshot of which was that by joining all our pieces together we made a sort of raft, which would bear the whole of us but in so doing was sunk some foot or so under water. We now strained our eyes in all directions to catch a sight of land, but in vain. In gazing round I caught sight of a man sitting on a rock at no great distance, he soon slid off from it and swam to us, and proved to be the Kanacker Pete, who was knocked overboard by the Spanker Boom, but had swam to this small rock, where he had managed to climb up, and remained all night. We now discovered how we were situated and each man I am sure, offered up thanks to God for his mercy in preserving us. We were inside the reef, having been through the mercy of God, drifted through a small space, the only one we could see. Outside the sea was raging in all its fury but here all was calm, the Current was running very strong, right through this pass and out to sea, forming an Eddy where we were. Our case was very dangerous, even now, as were we to drift out of the Eddy we were lost certain. We had no means of propelling the Craft nor Knew in what direction to proceed, we had picked up a few pounds of Salt Beef, which we now shared out, giving a few ounces a piece was all the sustenance we had and not a drop to drink.

As the Sun set, I took an eager survey all around for land, and almost shrieked for joy as I saw it. I pointed out the spot to Pete who confirmed my assertions, and soon all hands could plainly see it was a low sandy Island and one which our Capt. said was not down on any Chart. The current was setting strongly from the Island, and how could we get there. Even if we did get there it might not be inhabited, and if it was, the Savages might kill and eat us. Well what of that said I, it will be more agreeable to be eaten ashore and by human beings than to stay here and be eat by the Sharks.

One of the Kanackers proposed that if we would swim ahead and carry the line, they would dive and secure it to the bottom and thus we could Kedge her along. Twas too late to begin operations that night, so we waited for daylight and then went to work with a will. At the first peep of Dawn we swam ahead and one of the Kanackers would dive at a time. After a few attempts, he succeeded in making the line fast; we now hauled her ahead. Our progress was but slow, yet still twas sure. This day a squall of rain came on and such as had Clothes endeavored to catch some in order to wring it out and drink it but our clothes were so saturated with salt water that our efforts proved useless. Pete had a tarpaulin hat on, which caught some rain, and we all stood round and took our turns sucking it from off the rim. This was all the sustenance we had.

We now continued to warp ahead slowly. On the 5th day it rained again and thus we obtained a few more drops, thus we continued advancing but a mile a day with nothing to eat, nothing to drink, and not an hour's sleep. On the evening of the 8th day the divers made several useless attempts to find a rock, and at last found a small one, as this was our only chance we made fast to it, but were in agony all night for fear it would break away or chafe our line off in which case, we were inevitably lost.

Four of the men resolved not to abide the chance but to swim ashore, they accordingly made the attempt and started off—they had not been gone over 5 minutes when 5 large Sharks darted out, from under the raft and swam in the direction of the poor fellows. 'Twas of no use to sing out to them, as 'twould only serve to alarm them. Eagerly we watched them, expecting every moment to see them drawn under, and devoured but no, slowly they swam along and just as the Sun set we saw them rise from the water and run up to the Shore. These men having left the raft, she raised so far out of the water as to be dry. Those who were left lay down and in spite of the danger slept soundly until morning when we all jumped overboard, and by dint of hard swimming towed our raft ashore.

Well, we were now ashore, but yet our case was a pitiable one. There were 23 of us, and among the whole lot there were not clothes enough hardly to cover one. In roaming along the beach we saw a seal and soon dispatched him with Clubs—with a Knife we then cut his throat, and each in his turn took a sip of his blood, and tore away strips of blubber to satisfy our hunger. Our old Cook said he had made up his mind to die and die he would, so he strolled off and laid himself down but had scarcely done so, when we saw him again start up and run a few paces, stoop down and on his again raising up, sung out loudly, that he had found water. We all ran as fast as we were able to the spot, and found twas true but 'twas so brackish, that it ran through us as fast as we drank it. But no matter, 'twas water. We had on board the Ship a dog, a pet with all hands, the poor fellow had been saved, and landed with us; during the time we were on the raft almost famished many an eye was turned on him, but to the honor of all be it said, that when the Capt asked if we should kill and eat him, the unanimous reply was "No—Keep him for old Ship-mates sake."

We now found there were two Islands, on the smaller of which we had landed, the other was about 4 miles off and we could see there was grass and Bushes on it, so after remaining 3 days here, we started again to tow our raft to the large Island, to which we could wade easily. We arrived after an hour's hard work—found another seal, cut him up and laid the meat on the sand in the hot sun to dry; it soon became hard and quite palatable. The bushes we had seen were of a bitter kind and fit for nothing. Here by digging we found plenty of fresh water. We also found a dog here, he was quite wild, but it convinced us that some human beings had been here before us. We afterwards learned he had belonged to a British Whale Ship that had been wrecked here, and when the crew were taken off he was for some reason left behind.

We now went to work and built small huts of our raft, every man for himself and with the grass and bushes, thatched them and made them quite comfortable. We kept a regular almanack by notching a stick, and regularly as the Sabbath came, we had divine service, our Capt., who was religious, acting as preacher. During our whole tarry on the Island we lost but one day.

It was on these Sabbath day assemblages that I shone out, in the dress line. I was the only one who saved a pair of trowsers, my shirt I divided out to make clouts for those who had none. On week days I wore my trowsers as a covering for my head, and on Sunday encased my legs in them, and look as big a stiff as a young Lieut. when he first mounts his Swabs.

Thus things run on for a month, sometimes a feast of seal, and then again nothing to eat. I had found on shore a large cask, this I rolled up and made a house of it. I was now not only the best clad, but best lodged man in our Republic, for my house would shed rain. In fact I felt myself a sort of President.

In October the Typhoons set in and with them came lots of Goni's, a kind of sea bird, and great fools in some ways. They are very easily caught when they alight as it is difficult for them to raise again, this we did not know, and when one day our old cook brought one that he had caught in his hand, he was by all hands considered as something extra. Next morning I was up and off, determined to have a goose; it was not long before I saw two. I now worked all sorts of roots [sic] to get near them. At last when I judged myself within good distance I threw myself upon them catching one in each hand. I seized one by the neck and the other by the wing—Neckee was safe enough, but Wingee thinking, no doubt, that turn about was fair play, sunk his sharp bill deeply into my arm, but Lord bless you I couldn't let go, oh no, said I, my fair fellow, you bite now but see if I dont bite you bye and bye. I managed however to shift my hold and get him by the neck and off I started for my house. Now it was a week day and I had my cap but no nether garments on, and in the struggle to get free my captives placed their tallies on me pretty deeply, as they had long claws which tattooed my poor body in the most scientific manner but 'twas of no use, I could not let go, and when I got them home with the assistance of my chummy I killed them, and after I had cooked them (for we had obtained fire by rubbing two pieces of wood together) I took my satisfaction out of them. Now as I had brought in two birds, I was an extra above the Old Cook and was considered King of the Bird Catchers.

We now had plenty for a short time but the Birds seemed to know that something was wrong and would not light any more. We now bethought of a plan to catch one and tye him down for a decoy close bye. We would dig a hole in the sand and getting a long pole creep into the hole; the Goni's flying about would see this one flutter and would alight, and then we could knock 'em over. They got too old for even that at last, and then all we could do was to throw Clubs at them and knock them down. This was poor work and I was getting mighty lean upon it, so much so that one day after a hard run I had secured two, and had them slung over my shoulder, when a sudden puff of wind catching their wings lifted me off my feet, and away I went. I managed to get down again however, though much frightened, and whenever the wind blew after that, took the best of care to have their wings secured.

About Christmas time provision grew very scarce, and we cast lots to see who should go over to the Smaller Island and try for seal. I was one of the lot; we went over and killed 2 seal. While we were towing them round we found a large turtle, captured him, and got the whole safe into port in the Republic. We had a great blow out now and you had better believe we lived fat till about the middle of January. Now and then when provisions were plenty we would catch a Goni, put a tally on him of the name of the Ship and the condition of the Crew and let him go. I heard there was one of them caught on the N.W. Coast, but dont hardly believe it.

There was now nothing unusual occurred until in April a Ship hove in sight. We made all the signals we could; she saw them and hove to and sent a boat. She proved to be the *Jno. Stewart* of New Bedford. He took our Capt and 3 others on board, but refused to take any more upon the plea that he had no room. He gave us a Barrel of Bread, one of Beef, one of Pork, & some old Windsails &c and sailed after promising to come back for us when he had finished his cruise on the N.W. Coast. We now lived a little better, and had some hopes. At last on the 2 May 1843 saw another sail, which proved to be the Ship *Nassau*. She took us all on board, gave us clothes and treated us very kindly. Their Captain (Weeks) gave us a passage to Wahoo where I joined the old *Constellation*. I went home in her, was paid off with 60 dollars, and—but there goes the bell, 8, thank God it is my watch below—

The Ship's Wag

THERE IS ON BOARD any and every Ship, containing as many souls as a Man-of-War, all sorts of Characters huddled together. From the scientific old Growl of 45 or 50, to the joyous ever-laughing Apprentice boy, from the grave Methodistical looking prig to the mischief-making wag, who not only amused himself, but all around him, by the exercise of his wit. Our ship had her full quantity of Growls and Psalm Singers, nor was she at all deficient in the Wag Line, but bright among all the rest shone out an Irishman by the name of (now guess what his name was)—well any how we'll call him Troop, a true son of the sod and as clean a Marine as ever handled a musket.[1]

He was, like most of his country men, when on post, strict almost to a fault, and would no doubt from that circumstance have gained many enemies were it not for a knack he had when off duty of gathering around him a gaping crowd, who with mouths stretched from ear to ear, and delight beaming from their eyes, would sit for hours listening to Troop, who with all the gravity of a divine in the pulpit, would retail out to them stories of his Father Land, which savored so strong of the marvellous that even famed Munchausen, would sink into insignificance beside him. Whilst relating these yarns, no matter how ludicrous they were, no smile would ever cross his feature, and should any one of his hearers dare by chance to hazard a remark as to the truth of the tale, he would with his ready tongue give the offender an answer, which would effectually stop his mouth, among shouts of Laughter from the whole crowd.

Once when in the midst of a yarn from which nothing short of the cry of Fire could have drawn the attention of his auditors, he came to a sudden pause and with disappointment strongly pictured on his face, informed them that his memory had failed him on a very important point, and offered to go on, if any one would go to a certain person whom he named and procure *that* Book. When asked *what* book, his reply was, "Sure, just now ask him for *that* book, divil a

1. Downey's clues to the identity of "Troop" are so ambiguous, it is difficult to identify him, but he was probably Philip McGowan, a Marine private attached to the *Portsmouth* whom Downey made the subject of later humorous sketches. Rogers, "Personnel of the *Portsmouth*."

one of me knows its name, but ax for *that* book and he'll be sure to give you the right one."

Off starts the messenger and after a fruitless search, returned with the answer that the person named, knew nothing about *his* book. "And who the divil," said Troop, "towld you to ax for *my* book? I said *that* book, and—may the Saints preserve us, I remember now, it wasn't him I sent it to, it was old Quoin, the Quarter Gunner." Off started the messenger [in] hot chase for Old Quoin, who was an inveterate Growl, and withal could not read a word. Having found him upon asking him for *that* book, he was greeted with a shower of curses, heavy enough to annihilate any common man, and back he trotted to Troop, who having in this manner gained time, to draw upon his imagination, for a denouement to his yarn, would very gravely answer, "well if 'twasnt him, I lent it to, 'twas somebody else, and sure 'tis no matter, for now I remember what I had forgot," and forthwith proceeded with his yarn.

A whim seized upon our Marine officer [Henry B. Watson] to have a sort of memoir of the lives of all our Guard—for his own edification.[2] Here was a chance for Troop to display his powers of mystification, who forthwith, calling an amanuensis, sat down and soon covered a number of pages, in tracing out his ancestors, who he roundly swore were in a direct line of descent from the great Brian Borihome himself; his family he said was one of the best in Ireland; and owned so much land, that they were never able to raise money enough to pay the taxes. This and other pressing misfortunes, coupled with a great family pride, he said, had compelled him to leave his Country for a short time. "But wait," said he, "till Dan gets the Repale and thin you'll see boys how our family will shine again. Now just whisper, now you might see with half an eye, that my noble ancestry is recognized by the United States, for haven't they given me my clothes, my eating and dhrinking and a free passage all over the world, to make my future posterity acquainted with furrin parts, and all they ask in return is that I should devote a little of my spare time in promoting their interests. Yes and be dad, its a wife they

2. Watson, a native of North Carolina, had been a second lieutenant in the Marine Corps since 1836. His role in the conquest of California merited him a first lieutenancy in March, 1847, and the following November he was breveted captain. He resigned from the Corps in 1855. *Gen. Nav. Reg.* (1882), p. 896.

found me too, the dear darling that I left drownin herself in her own tears, when I lift home to journey on the salt seas, for the benefit of my health and," he added in a sotto voice, "of my pocket too! Sure it's me was the boy for luck when I left the sod, for swate America."

Blow high or blow low, 'twas all the same to Troop, nothing would ever disconcert him except the Cry of "Sentry Go" when in the midst of a yarn. He would declaim loudly upon the injustice of being deprived of any portion of his sleep while in port. "Be jabers," said he to me one day, "I would like the service well enough if there was a little more Equality in it. Sure and dont I do as much barring getting up on them Cross Sticks as any of the Sailor men, and pull and haul, almost the life out me, on the ropes, and be up in all sorts of weather at sea, and then by the powers, when we get in port they lay the whole long night in their hammocks enjoying Swate Sleep and I am perched up on a board out there, with no sort of amusement to kape me awake, but to watch for the bell to strike and then halloo 'all's well!' Ave I could only learn the lingo, by this and by that, I'd join the French, for they all stand watch alike there."

When the news arrived that we were to have a war with Mexico, the ideas of Troop swelled large with the thoughts of the nice things he would be able to pick up there. "By the Martial," he said, "but that Mexico is the place where all the dollars do come from. If there's any war there, it's me is the child that will make a *lob* for Mrs. Troop and the children. Sure the little Troops shall have no other but the pure stuff to play wid and Mr. and Mrs. Troop, will ride all around town in a horse and Shay. Not that I care for the dirty goold and silver, but the honor of carrying 'em home as prisoners of War you know. Och, wont there be lashings of Whiskey at my house, and the door wide open and nothing short of a quart pot to drink out of! Phillaloo—whoop—but I'm the boy for luck!"

The crowning event however of Troop's life occurred at sea, on our passage from Valparaiso to Callao. When we left Valparaiso, among the poultry laid in then, was a laying hen; The Caterer of the Wardroom Mess, who was bye the bye our Marine officer [Watson], being the first to find out the fact, claimed as his perquisite the first fruits, and chuckled loudly at the idea of having a fresh Egg for his breakfast every day. In order to secure his prize from any unlawful hands, he gave particular orders to the sentry on post, at the scuttle

54

butt, to watch when the Egg was laid, and report the same, in order that it might at once go through the proper process to fit it for the tooth of the Caterer.

Things went smooth enough for some days, 'till at length one unlucky morning, it was Troop's post at the scuttle butt; and as the usual hour for the appearance of the Egg approached, Troop grew suddenly very attentive to Madame, following every move she made, as eagerly as a cat follows the motions of a mouse on whom she is about to pounce. At this moment the Capt. of the Top [W. J. Morris] warned him to move as he wished to dash a bucket of water where he stood.

"Whist, Whist, wait a minnit," said he, "the ould hen is laying and by jabers I'm full of business, for if any harm comes to the Egg, by the Piper that played before Moses, but I am the boy that will suffer for it." Thus he continued alternately scolding and cursing the noisy crowd around, keeping all the time a wary eye upon the Coop. Seeing him thus earnest about the matter, some roguish Boys determined to have a lark with him. One of them accordingly dashed a bucket of water on his feet and legs, and as he turned to detect the offender another whipped up the Egg which the hen at that moment dropped and sailed aft with his prize.

Poor Troop, quite ignorant of the felony, not having succeeded in detecting the one who wet him now returned to his watch, and waited patiently for the Egg. For a full hour, he never let his eye even for a moment rove from the Coop, and when the Corporal came to relieve him, in giving up his orders to his Relief, he was very particular about the Egg. The Corporal, who knew it was long past the accustomed hour of accouchment, examined the Coop, and finding the Egg gone, forthwith announced his determination of reporting Troop for neglect of duty in allowing the Egg to be abstracted.

Poor Troop begged eloquently to be let off—but 'twas no go, and when he found the case surely going against him, he burst out in a shower of invectives upon the unknown offenders. "Oh, Wirra—Wirra—Murther, what will I do now? The Thieves of the World. By Jabers, but I do think they will stale me off my post entirely some day, I do. What did I ever do to them now that they should trate me that way? By the hill of Howth, ave I catch one of them, but I'll make an Egg of him. Oh by the Martial, Capt., but did any body stale it now,—may be the ould Rooster eat it—sure I've read in ould ancient books, as how the male cratur often eats the progeny—Och, ye sly looking divil, said he, looking at the Cock, ave I could only prove it on ye now, wouldn't I soon have ye at the mast for a Thief." But grieving or supposing did no good, and up to the mast went Troop, under the serious Charge of Neglect.

When the matter was investigated and Troop asked what he had to say in his defence, he strongly maintained the possibility of the ould Cock's having eaten it—"Such was the only chance, for I never had my eye off the hen for an hour barrin when they tould me to git out of the water."

"It seems however," said the officer, "that it is gone, and though neglect of duty is a great crime, yet in consequence of your former good conduct I shall let you off this time, but for the future you must be more careful of the property in your charge."

"Och good Luck go wid ye Sir. It's just myself will be that same, and if ever I'm on post when the Egg comes again, by the body of me, but I'll carry the ould hen in my arms, till the child is born, that I will."

A Week in Port

[Downey in this chapter does not trouble to mention that the *Portsmouth*, after some weeks in Callao, returned to Valparaiso, and after a short stay there, returned to Callao on June 19, 1845. It is the second stay in Callao that Downey has chosen for this following sketch.]

STRANGE AS IT MAY appear to a Landsman, there is no sphere of life in which a man can move, where the scenes are so continually shifting, or where amusement is more varied than on Ship board. True it is that at sea, or in harbor, the duties follow mechanically in the same routine, the plot marked out for our governance never varies, but the bye play is always new, and affords sufficient exercise to the mind to drive away ennui. As most of the incidents detailed in the foregoing pages have happened solely at sea, I deem that the history of a week in port will prove amusing to my readers, and shall consequently select one out of the many that offer themselves, to prove the truth of the above assertion.

On the 17th June we first saw the high peaks of San Lorenzo, after a short passage of 6 days from Valparaiso.[1] The wind was light but fair and all hands were sanguine in their expectations of getting into Callao early next day. The usual Ship's duty was not altered, but at daylight next morning an extra holystoning, and scrubbing took place, and as soon as it was sufficiently light, the forecastle was filled with the Idlers (or those who had no night watch) to ascertain by ocular demonstration what our progress was.

Various were the motives which actuated the breast of the different gazers. Some wishing to get in to hear from home, as a mail was thought to have arrived during our absence, some to get liberty, but by far the larger majority, that they might have fresh grub and all night in. When breakfast was piped, the order to "clean yourselves" proved that the old Man at least expected to get in in the Course of the day. At first he had intended to go through the Buckroom passage, which would shorten the distance some ten miles, which was a great saving, as we should have to beat up the harbor, but as the wind heading us off, we were obliged to go the old passage round the Island.[2]

As the day advanced, the wind gradually failed, and before 10 o'clock AM, it was nearly calm. There then was a large field of speculation. Would we get a breeze from off the Land or not? Opinions were divided on the subject, and conjectures were flying round at a great rate, when lo inshore of us, at a distance of a mile or so, some one descried the puff of a whale, and soon another and another until at last we could plainly see four or five of the huge monsters, seemingly rolling about in play. Getting in or its prospects were soon forgotten in the new topic. Where are they? What sort? and all such questions were uttered in a breath by the Crowd—the news was spread from mouth to mouth, and soon the forecastle was filled with eager gazers, all running, pushing and hustling each other, endeavoring to get a peep.

1. A small mountainous island opposite the port of Callao. It served as a convenient landmark to guide ships into the harbor.

2. Downey was speaking of a narrow channel between the east side of San Lorenzo Island and the Peruvian coast, called "El Boqueron" which had been anglicized to "Buckroom Passage."

Among the rest up came Brush, almost breathless with haste, and running from one point to the other, half crazy, was singing out at the Top of his voice, "Where arc they? do show me where they are;" nobody paid any attention to him and at last in despair he mittened on to Old Growl the Capt. of the Forecastle [William Griffiths?], who was never noted for good humor, and was on this particular morning as crabbed as a bear.

"What the hell are you singing out for now?" said he, "haven't you had your breakfast?"

"Why, of course I have," said Brush.

"Well what are you crying about then?"

"I aint cryin, I only want somebody to show me a whale."

"Well look over the Starboard bow there, don't you see it?"

"What, that great black thing there, that looks like a stick of wood, is that a whale?"

"Yes, do you see it?"

"Wal, I calculate no man with a pair of eyes in his head could miss it."

"Then," said Growl, who thought to raise a laugh out of him, "keep your eye on it till the sea falls."

"If I undertake that," said Brush good-humoredly, "I calculate, I should be a little tired of the job, but I'd rather do that, than try to get a civil answer out of you."

The whales soon disappeared and with them the momentary excitment, consequently we were now thrown back upon our old resources for amusement. There was no work going forward to litter the decks, and groups were collected at all points, discussing various subjects with all the vehemence of *Corner politicians* during an election. All day long we lay, seemingly not nearing the land at all, and as the sun fell, our chance of getting into port that night seemed but small. A sail now hove in sight and guessing became the order of the day, who was she? what Countryman? A Barque loaded with Stores had left Valparaiso four days ahead of us, and bets were offered that the stranger was her; no takers could however be found.

At sunset we were some ten miles off the Land, but to our great joy a breeze now sprang up, and setting Steering Sails below and aloft, our beauty appeared to pity our anxious state of mind, so slowly rousing herself from the lethargy she had been in all day she began perceptibly to near the Land. The breeze continued to freshen

58

and all doubt as to our fetching in faded away. A Barque and a Brig now came out and as they ran to leeward of us, the rays of the moon falling full on their white sails lit them up in a beautiful manner.

Preparations were now made for Communicating with the Commodore by night signals. Accordingly, as soon as we had cleared the point and shot into the mouth of the bay, our forecastle pet bellowed out his warning note, and a moment after, whiz—away flew a rocket, then another, then a line of three lights ranged on our bow, completed the Conversation. All hands were on the "qui vive" to watch for the answer, every eye was eagerly peering through the darkness in the direction where the Commodore [Sloat] was supposed to lay, but in vain. The hope of seeing the Flag Ship [*Savannah*] was almost given up, the crowd had begun to disperse, when old *Chinney* who with his glass had hung on till the last, espied a blue light, a moment after a single rocket, "All right" said he, "she is there."

In a few moments the lookout on the Forecastle reported a boat on the lee bow, and rounding to she was soon alongside; the gangway was crowded to hear the news, and see the Mail. The Officer came over the side and then the—no, not the Mail Bag but the Coxswain. He was beset on all sides by a gaping crowd, all questioning him at once. "What's the news?" assailed his ears from all sides. "Nothing—" "Any Mail?" "No—" "What ships in Port—" "Only the Frigate, the *Warren's* gone home, and the *Shark* down to Panama for the mail—"[3] "Oh Hell, then we shant get it these six months." So it seems we have brought all the news ourselves.

All this time we were nearing the anchorage, the night was clear, and a bright moon lit up the harbor. We ran close under the stern of the Commodore, then putting down our helm, shot into our berth. Splash goes the Anchor—Tweet-Tweet goes the pipes of the Boatswain and his mates, aloft fly the Topmen, the Sails are rolled up, and in a few seconds, an observer could not have told by looking at us, but that we had lain in that position for a month.

The Hammocks were now piped down, and with the exception of a few old Gossips all hands had retired. Our Gig had gone on board the Frigate, and the newsmongers remained on the Forecastle awaiting her return in order to gather up the latest "on dits" and have

3. The coxswain gave the crew incorrect information, for the U.S. sloop-of-war *Warren* (20 guns) had not returned to the United States. *Gen. Nav. Reg.* (1882), pp. 907–08.

them in readiness for retail in the morning. "There she comes," says we, "now we Shall have it." As soon as she was hoisted up, and her crew came forward, a circle was formed round them, and question followed question in great style. "What's the news? when are we going to sail? when is the mail coming—"

"Oh by the Lord," said the Coxswain who acted as spokesman, "there's no mail this three months, we shant go till it does come and as for news, there's been the devils own time since we've been gone. The English and Peruvians have had a muss, and the Old Admiral give 'em twenty four hours to settle the hash, or else he was going to open his fire on the Castle. He drew his Squadron up in a Line of Battle, and sent the Old Coal Hulk over to blockade Buckroom passage."[4]

"Well," said Pay Roll, "that's some news at any rate. By the Lord, if old Bull does get at them, he'll knock their old Castle about their ears and the cholos will have to give leg bail."

"But," says Tiller, the Coxswain, "that's not all, Mexico has declared war, and Texas is annexed."[5]

"Hurrah for that," shouted the crowd.

"By the Man of the Mast," says Requisition, "that will carry us down to California and then maybe we won't kick up hell among the Mexicans—'Twont be no Monteray War this time—I rather expect we fellows will make a spec, this cruise, of prize money after all."[6]

Having now gleaned all the particulars, discussed the several points, and fully digested the whole, in order that all their yarns might agree, the party separated and each one retired to their hammocks, and soon the decks were entirely deserted, save by the Officer and Quarter-Master of the Watch, and the Marines on post.

At the first peep of dawn on the morning of the 19th the shrill pipe

4. Upon arrival at Callao on May 7, 1845, Admiral Sir George Seymour found that a local prefect had insulted the British vice-consul. Seymour not only demanded an apology and the removal of the prefect from office, but prepared all British vessels in the harbor for action. The new Peruvian president, Don Ramon Castilla, yielded to these demands and cordial relations were restored. See Sir Albert H. Markham, *The Life of Sir Clements R. Markham* (London, 1917), pp. 44–45.

5. Again the coxswain was wrong, for when Congress voted to annex Texas on March 1, 1845, Mexico broke off diplomatic relations but did not declare war.

6. In 1841 Commodore Ap Catesby Jones, acting upon a rumor that the United States and Mexico were at war, sailed into the harbor at Monterey, California and seized the fort there. When it became evident that no war existed, the Commodore, with many apologies, retired. He was officially reprimanded for his hasty act.

of the Boatswain summoned "all hands." Man is naturally a gruff animal when first aroused, and nothing is now heard but grunting and growling at one another. After a moments delay, "Jimmy-Legs" [John Morgan] appears, dodging under the hammocks, singing out in his peculiarly musical voice, "Come, come, rouse out here, lash and carry, fore and aft." The deck is now cleared of dream bags, and Holy-Stones and Sand comes next in order. Jimmy having reported Hammocks up, now returns squealing "Trice up your chests, Cooks" —Cooks and Loafers growl and the poor Soldiers who have to clean their accoutrement, and be in full uniform at 8 o'clock, look blank enough at the prospect.

Cheerless enough it is to be sure. The Berth Deck is all afloat, Holy-Stones, Sand, Squilgees, Scrubbers and Swabs are flying about in all directions, and it is as much as they can do to keep out of the wet, without attempting to sand. If they go on to the Spar Deck 'tis all the same there, and all they can do is to wait patiently until the muss is over. By 5 or 6 Bells, things begin to assume their former quietness, the chests lowered and squared, and Jimmy, trotting fore and aft, mechanically applies to his Snuff Box and ejaculates more from the force of habit than any thing else, between each pinch, "Clear this deck all but the Cooks." No one pretends to mind the order, as they are all aware that it has no meaning, and that he only says that because he is used to it.

At 7 Bells out come the Bags and the Ship's Cook bellows out "Draw your Tea Water," the Spar Deck is clean and dried up, and precisely at 8 Bells breakfast is piped, and the word passed to "Clean yourselves!" Now for a full hour, the Berth Deck is a scene of complete uproar, but faithful to the stroke of 2 Bells comes the old yarn, "Clear this Deck all but the Cooks," followed close by "Stow your Bags." At 9 o'clock the Drum beats to quarters, all hands now repair to their respective stations, and frocks, trowsers and bright work undergoes a thorough overhaul, after which the several Jobs of the Day are commenced.

The General Duty of the Spar Deck varies each day, but that of the Berth [Deck] the routine is all the same. As soon as the messes are cleared up, Mess Chests are squared, opened, and the bright tin ware displayed. The deck undergoes innumerable sweepings, Jimmy runs fore and aft, athwartships and amidships, peeps into every hole and corner, bawls first for the Ship's Corporal, and then for some one of the Cooks, treating himself ever and anon to a huge pinch of snuff, and having worked himself up to the requisite pitch of desperation, steps aft, and with the eye of a Connoiseur scans the whole arrangement, squares this or that spit box or mess chest, and having satisfied himself that all is right, forthwith trots aft to report the same.

The First Luff now appears, preceded by Jimmy, who sings out, "Stand to your Messes," and having seen this manoever correctly performed, now falls in the rear, and cap in hand follows the functionary as he perambulates. Joy beams in his eyes, every thing is correct, all approved and as he bows him off the deck, it again resumes its wonted appearance. Noise and bustle carry the day. Loud above the whole is heard, however, at irregular intervals, the old Song of "Clear this deck, all but the Cooks."

Formalities are gone through at dinner and supper time, after which quietness reigns until hammocks are piped down, when on the Spar Deck, "De man whot playsh ze dam fine feedle" gets up his instrument, and a dance is got under way forthwith, while on the Berth [deck] conversation, songs and Laughter predominate until 8 Bells when "Out Light" sends every one to bed.

A record of one day's proceedings is a key to that of every day in Port. On the morning of the 29th, slung clean hammocks, rigged with tye-tyes, accompanied with an order to turn in all the old lashings; this kicked up a decent growl all around. At 8 all the English Squadron dressed ship in honor of the coronation.[7] The American and French hoisted English colors at the Fore and Mizen; and at 12M a Royal Salute was fired from all the vessels in Port and also from the Fort. A Ship which appeared off the mouth of the harbor at near 11 o'clock, hearing the firing and seeing that the whole squadron, Fort, and all were blazing away, no doubt imagining war was declared, up stick and stuck her off, nor did she return for 4 days.

7. Downey's dates and facts are in error here for he had confused two separate events: a celebration of the birthday of Louis Philippe of France and the anniversary of the coronation of Queen Victoria of England. The former took place, not on April 29, but on May 1, 1845. The Log for that day reads as follows: "At 8 the Squadron hoisted the French flag at the fore in compliment to the French Nation, it being the anniversary of the birthday of Louis Philipe (sic) King of the French. At meridian the Squadron fired, each 21 guns in company with the French corvette."

It is likely that Downey, writing his entries sometime after the actual event, confused this celebration with a later one in that same port on the anniversary of Queen Victoria's coronation (June 20, 1845). "Log of the *Portsmouth*," May 1, June 20, 1845.

This evening at near 8 o'clock, a loud outcry was heard from an American merchant vessel laying inside of us and as "Murder" was the only part that could be distinctly distinguished, a mutiny was as a matter of course conjectured, and our 2nd Cutter at once called away the crew armed, and in charge of one of our Lieuts. and 2 Reefers, pulled for her. The Lieut who was at all times inordinately fond of using what Jack calls "Dick" or hard words, addressed his Crew something after this wise, "Men, when we arrive alongside the Ship that constitutes the point of action, I wish you to allow your cutlasses to remain in their respective stations, until I shall ascend to her decks and take a cursory view of the same, when, if my judgment decides that such a proceeding is necessary, I shall order you to board —upon receipt of such order, you will please draw promptly, mount with alacrity and charge upon the mutineers with decision."

"Well I'm damned," said an Old Salt who pulled the stroke oar, "if I know what that means. If that sort of lingo is 'cordin to the new book of 'llowances, why the hell dont the purser sarve out a dictionary apiece, so that a feller could find out what they do want?"

The order however was not given, it turning out that the whole row was occasioned by the Cook, who had become intoxicated and refused duty, he was accordingly sent on board the Flag Ship, and when sober, again sent to his Ship.

Next day nothing out of the usual order of things occurred but on Sunday, the 22nd, after the usual cleanings of decks and crew, and a thorough inspection of the Ship by the Capt., all hands were called to muster and our Capt. proceeded according to his regular Custom, to read the Beautiful Service of the Church of England, and ended with a short but well-written sermon. No one who has only seen the sailor on shore, where he is wild and reckless, can have any idea of the interest he takes in such matters; the Crew are all collected on the 2nd Deck, the Capstan covered with a flag serves for a pulpit, and when the Capt. mounts the Shot Box and uncovers his head he is followed by all hands and from the moment that he pronounces "The Lord is in his holy Temple" reverence and attention predominate, and old Salts, who would be thought by a casual observer past all feeling, are here seen listening with breathless anxiety, seeming to devour every word, while their earnest manner, and devout faces prove that the precepts inculcated enter not the ear alone, but are treasured up in the mind. In the Course of my life, I have seen congregations of all sorts listening to the most eloquent of the divines in our happy land, as they descanted upon the beauties of Religion, but never have I seen one, where solemnity and an earnest desire of profiting by the lessons inculcated, was more strongly depicted, than on our Quarter Deck.

When Service was over, preparations were made on board the Frigate *Savannah* and the English and French vessels, to man yards and fire a salute in honor of something. Conjecture was busy to find out the cause. The Ward-Room and cabin boys were eagerly questioned, but all that they knew, was, that somebody was coming on board. Nothing however can long remain a mystery on board a Man of War and it was soon noised about that the President of Peru, and suite, were to visit the Several Squadrons.[8]

Shortly after dinner, a discharge of 21 Guns from the Castle announced the embarkation. They soon hove in sight round the Mole, the first Barge flying the National Standard with the President and Staff, the second with an Admiral's Pennant, containing his Suite. As they advanced from out of the cluster of merchant vessels, the rigging of all the Men-of-War in Port, (ourselves excepted, as we had our Top Gallant Masts on deck) were alive with men. A few moment's pause ensued, when seemingly like so much mechanism, the Life Lines were triced up and each yard was filled with men, neatly dressed in white frocks and blue trowsers. It was indeed a beautiful sight. The *Savannah*'s band struck up the Peruvian National Air, and the Petite Frenchman, determined not to be behind hand kept ting-tinging away on a small drum.

The Cortege went first on board the *Savannah* where they at once beat to Quarters, and after a short tarry they again shoved off, the Frigate again manned yards and fired a salute of 21 Guns, which was promptly returned from the Fort. They then proceeded to the English 74, [H.M.S. *Collingwood*] and immediately on their arrival, Bang! Bang! away flew more powder in the Shape of 21 Guns from each of the three English vessels in port. This salute was again returned from the Castle. Yards were again manned and another shoot-

8. After gaining her independence from Spain, Peru had undergone a fifteen-year period of anarchy (1829–44) which ended only when General Don Ramon Castilla, emerging as a strong man, instituted a six-year reign of peace. On April 19, 1845, he was proclaimed Constitutional President. The vessels were doing more than honoring a foreign chief of state; they were celebrating his inauguration.

ing match took place, when they left her. It seemed as if he or they disdained the small fry altogether, as he visited the Flag Ships only, and as the "Grande Nation" [France] was represented by only a Sloop of War (and a small one at that) they paid no attention to her, notwithstanding which Crapeau, manned yards whenever the barges came in sight.[9] Another salute from the Castle announced the debarcation, and the pageant now being over, nothing was left, but to talk over the events of the day.

Various were the topics discussed, but prominent among all the rest, with true Yankee characteristic was the probable amount it had cost. I noticed a group squatted together on our Forecastle, in the midst of which, was Old Growl, who with a board and piece of chalk, was deep in the mysteries of the Arithmatic, ever and anon scratching his head with an air of abstraction, as if he was endeavoring to pull an idea out by main force. After having filled and rubbed out the board 2 or 3 times, he found himself non-plussed, but unwilling to let the laugh go against him, he said with a very knowing air, "You see there's a figure, way in the middle there, that's wrong, but it's a hell of a Job to find it, and as it's most 8 Bells, I haint got time, but judging from appearances, it must have cost upwards of a damn sight if not more and if any of you fellows can come nearer than that, let him try it that's all." So saying, he got up and rolling his huge quid from the Starboard to the Portside of his mouth, looked round upon the crowd, but finding no one disposed to Growl with him, he straightened his legs and muttering something about substraction and ignoramuses, he descended to the Berth Deck.

Next morning bright and early we scrubbed hammocks. During the performance of this duty an accident occurred to our friend Troop which though near proving fatal was highly ludicrous. He had scrubbed his hammock and on going down the accomodation ladder to rinse it off by some mismanagement his foot slipped and overboard he went. With one hand he clung to the ladder and with the other hung to his hammock. There was a slight swell and as the ship rolled, it would duck his head under; he was so scared he could hardly sing out for help. Three of his brother Troops happening to see him ran to his assistance, but the standing place was so small they could not raise him, but yet they kept his head out of the water.

9. This was undoubtedly the *Triumphante* which had arrived in Callao on June 19, 1845. "Log of the *Portsmouth*."

Finding himself thus far safe, he instead of making an effort to extricate himself, began to bellow at the top of his lungs, "Murther—Fire—Help—Mutiny—Oh Lord Jasus—I'll drown—I know I will—Oh Walker, Walker, take my bag for Troop's no more."

His outcries so convulsed all around with laughter that it was with difficulty that they retained their hold upon him, and when at last he was landed on deck, he could not be convinced that he was safe, but continued bawling and kicking out, to the no small amusement of the bye-standers. When by dint of argument, he became certain that he was on board Ship, "By Dad," exclaimed he, " 'twas well I retained my native Courage, and held on so well, or the Sharks would have ate me sure." When afterward made the subject of a joke, "Now listen," said he, "By the Lord, it's a dale of trouble I am to all the people on board this Ship, for if I had lost my hammock the Boatswain's mate would have had the trouble of whipping me, whereas if I had lost myself the whole ship's Company would have had the trouble of fishing for me, and any way, ye have the laugh on me. Oh, if Mrs. Troop only saw me thin, but wouldn't she have been ravin distracted sure. It's me that pities her even now."

Nothing occurred of any importance during the rest of the week until Wednesday, when a ship of War was seen off the Harbor, which was soon made out to be the *Levant*.[10] All were now on the "qui vive" for a mail but disappointment availed us, she had not been to Panama. If the adventures of this week shall have interested you, Kind reader, my end is attained.

10. The United States sloop-of-war *Levant* (18 guns) arrived in Callao harbor June 26, 1845. When Commodore Sloat surrendered his command of the Pacific Squadron to Commodore Robert F. Stockton in July, 1846, he sailed home in the *Levant*.

A Little of Everything

[The *Portsmouth* left the coast of South America for a routine cruise to the Hawaiian Islands on July 23, 1845, and arrived at Byron's Bay, Oahu, on August 20. Although the vessel remained in the islands for nearly three weeks they seem to have given Downey little inspiration for his sketches. He complained that his themes "waxed scarcer" and he wrote that this part of the ocean was "the most barren in the world," for dull monotony "hangs like an incubus o'er us here." As a result the following sketches were not as well executed or as colorful as most of the others. The exhilarating excitement of a voyage aboard a new ship had worn off, and from this point until the beginning of the Mexican War both the Log and Downey's writings indicate that the morale of the crew was very low.]

A SECRET is hard to preserve on board Ship, and I had hardly begun to make any progress in my Chronicle of Events before the news flew from one to another, and soon twas known all over the Ship that "Peak" was writing yarns, to be published. The "Widow's Retreat" for so my "sanctum studio" was nicknamed, for what reason I leave you to guess, was thronged daily by expectant crowds, all eager to hear each tale as it was brought to light, and if one might judge by their criticisms there never was any thing composed under the sun that could in any way compare with them.

As a matter of Course, our author was never in want of themes, as every little laughable incident that took place in any part of the ship was treasured up and forthwith transmitted down to "Peak" to be dressed up and put into the Book. Not a man or Boy throughout the whole ship but considered himself a party interested in it and bound to supply the raw material upon every occasion, and no matter whether their contributions had foundation enough for a yarn or not, they would have been mortally offended if it had not appeared.

One eventful day while running along the line bound from Callao to Wahoo, I was most ceremoniously aroused from my meditations by a loud outcry of my name, and at once seizing my Sombrero (how Spanish I am getting) I followed the Messenger and on arriving at the Mess, appropriated to the Larb^rd Mizen Topmen, had a something of very suspicious appearance thrust under my nose and was bid to say what that was. I peered into it, smelt of it, and endeavored to masticate some of it and at last in utter despair gave it up. When I had fairly acknowledged myself non-plussed I was informed it was a cake and made under the following circumstances. The whole mess with but three exceptions was composed of Apprentice Boys, who with all the love for sweet things natural to them, had in solemn council assembled, denounced Duff as a bore, and sighed in vain for some other mess concocted from its ingredients.[1] Accordingly the Caterer, who was a shrewd calculating Yankee, but fond of Plums, had proposed to them that if they would give him the Flour, slush and Raisins he would bake them something that would do even in a pinch for a Wedding Cake. They at once consented and the cunning rascal, in the first instance devouring all the Raisins had then proceeded to mix the remaining ingredients into a heterogeneous mess and clapping it into the oven straightway reported the same to the Messmates, who refraining to eat any dinner, had reserved their appetites for supper. When the appointed hour arrived they one and all had grouped around the Cloth and awaited with glistening eyes the appearance of the long expected dish. At length the cook, opening the Chest, gently placed it on the Cloth and in one instant every knife was immersed in it. But oh horror of horrors—they could not withdraw them, and the mess stuck like Glue, and in utter despair they had sent for me to note the Cake. I had never tried my hand at blank verse but thinking this a good chance perpetrated the following. It is not all original for I have drawn largely upon an unpublished fragment of a Brother Tar—

THAT CAKE

When first with throbbing heart and anxious breast
We seized the quill and donned the Author's Crest
And sent our Efforts forth, both far, and near,
'Twas but our humble brother Tars to cheer—
To strive as best we might, to drive away
The dull monotony, that day by day
Hangs, like an incubus o'er us here,
And makes a shipboard life appear so drear.
And as these fav'ring critics, at first sight,
Hailed our uncouth products, with delight,
Cheered when we blundered, praised our very faults

1. "Duff" was the name given to a flour pudding boiled in a bag. To vary the monotony of this fare, raisins were mixed into the duff. It was as much a part of the sailor's diet as hardtack was a part of the soldier's fare.

With all the ardour of true hearted salts,
We thought, no wonder that we did it
That we could raise a laugh when 'eer we bid it—
And as Time crept along, by slow degrees
We ne'er relaxed our Efforts, them to please,
Until at last, unto our sore dismay,
We found our themes wax scarcer, day by day
And we were forced to go out and solicit
Subjects, from friends around, whom we did visit
Now as in the end this poor resource had failed us
Our Chum grew wroth, and swore the D – l ail'd us
As in the "Retreat," one day we laid us back,
And for a Theme in vain our brain did rack
Our patience gone, while, plung'd in deep despair,
We heard a voice, from off the berth deck there
Cry out—Come "Peak"—come quick—come taste
What is't? D – l seize me if I know the laste
But's good—We jumped a rod, some more or less
Nor paused, till at 10– The Mizen Topmen's Mess
We stopped, and with a sigh of wonder
Viewed them; for they look'd as black as thunder—
Well; what's the row? Oh by the Lord said one quite moody
We recognized, at once, as that Loon, B – – – y^2
The whole of us poor fellows are at fault
Fore here's the beat of all provisions, fresh or salt—
Yes, chimed in another, we've sent for you, oer this 'ere trial
Now to preside—come, come, we'll no denial
And quick upon the mess chest, then and there
They elevated "Peak" and called him in the chair.
He went to work, instant, and nam'd a secretary
You know him well I think, one Thomas C – – – y^3
With pen and paper quick the chest was stowed
And mid the titterings of a gaping crowd
To business did proceed, and soon in court
The mute, confounded prisoner was brought.
What was't you ask? 'Twas not a man, woman or boy
On whom, their precious time, they did distroy

2. Alvin Boody, Landsman. Rogers, "Personnel of the *Portsmouth*."
3. Thomas Clary, Seaman. *Ibid.*

On whom, the fiat of such wisdom was at stake
No—No—it was no less an object than *that* cake—
But such a cake—Ye Yankee Pals, in pastry science read
Put up your Pans—your boasted art is dead
For if you strive till Gabriel's trump does sound
Another such upon the Earth will ne'er be found.
The witnesses were called, and in due order,
Ranged, toes in line, upon the Mess Cloth Border.
And each was sworn, upon a knife with blade off
That they would testify with truth what it was made of.
The first among this lot of clever fellows
Came up Brown Bess, that now is nicknamed B – – – s[4]
And with a squint, with him that's nothing new
Swore, that the principle *gredient* was glue,
Backed his assertions with this well known fact
That if you tried to bite, it stuck like wax—
The next appear—a dapper little man,
That some call H – – s, attached to Almoran[5]
Who with a face as long as any priest
Vow'd that what ever else, *was* there, there was *no* yeast.
For he with telescope had took a sight
And through the whole could find no ray of light.
He now fell back and with his thieving Irons
Pushed out, the blushing bashful Jerry L – – – s[6]
Jerry when brought up, and questioned by the Court
First hemmed, then hawk'd then spit, then stopp'd short
And stammered out, he thought twas plain enough
That twas composed of their old last week's Duff;
For now he recollected in good sooth,
In trying to bite it, he'd then broke a tooth
And probing well the cake, he now adduced it,
He'd found the piece and in the Court produced it
The case grew dark—"Peak" now in progress making
Next in an angry tone, bawled out for F – – – n[7]
Not the Old F – – – n, that's chroniclized by Boz

4. Charles S. Bellows, Ordinary Seaman. *Ibid.*
5. Almoran Holmes, Landsman. *Ibid.*
6. Jeremiah Lyons. *Ibid.*
7. Mathew Fagan. *Ibid.*

But, as true a lawyer as ere plead a cause
F – – – n began, and with much logic, he set forth
That it was made of flour, 'lasses, slush, of course
And he wouldn't mind, on it, his own head staking
The cake'd be well enough, with one more bakin'.
The Court all laughed, the Judge put on a frown
And quickly ordered Mr F – – – n to sit down—
Now in a trice, as neat as Tailor's bobbins
Popp'd up the pet—We'll call him Charley R – – – s[8]
And gave it in, at once, as his conclusion
That in this cake, they'd put some vile effusion
It was so weighty, that if a little lanker
'Twould for the Launch have made a fine Sheet Anchor
The Evidence was closed—the Chair now turned around
Emitting then, an awful, grumbling sound,
Slewed first to right and then to left, for ease
First gaped, then yawned, and then he gave a sneeze
And said he'd heard of cooks, by hundred or by millions
But never one could equal this George W – – – s[9]
Then slowly, rising, turned, and left the crowd
Amid their boisterous laughter, pealing loud
Gained the "Retreat" and put it in his book
And thus immortalized this *Pastry Cook.*

The Islands

IN MY PREFACE, I warned my readers not to expect anything like
an historical account of any thing, but merely the impressions made
upon my mind by the casual glance of a man of war's man. We sailed
on the 22nd of July, 1845, from Callao, bound down to the Sandwich
Islands, with a mail for the Ships *Levant* and *Warren*.[1] The latter
had sailed from Callao a month or more previous; the former had

8. Charles Robbins. *Ibid.*
9. George Williams, Seaman. *Ibid.*
1. The date of sailing was actually July 23, 1845. "Log of the *Portsmouth.*"

left but three days ahead of us. As she was considered the crack ship in the Station (before we came out) some little talk was made, as to the number of days we should beat her (for beat her of course we must). The most sanguine and unreasonable, would have it at all hazards that we should pass her in 3 or 4 days, but the sober set would be contented with 4 or 5 days beat in the run.

As to any matter of incident to be gleaned from the weather, this ocean (or at least this portion of it) is the most barren in the world. A ship being continually in the trades, must, being bound to the Islands, of course always have a fair wind. Now with a sailor, as with all other beings, "too much of a good thing is good for nothing," consequently too much fair weather beget's lazyness and lazyness begets growling, and growling causes ill humor all over the ship. I do not mean to be understood that Jack is particularly fond of bad weather, but variety is the spice of life, and he likes his spice, as well as any one else. But so it was, and as we were sailing along at the rate of 10 knots, day by day, never hardly touching a rope yarn, ill humor made his appearance, and a civil answer was a rare thing on board our once peaceful and quiet ship.

Seeing this state of things, some good natured young fellows to put a stop to it, set themselves seriously to work devising means, the sum total of which was, they determined to get up some sort of game that should at once give their surly shipmates some work and restore their lost humor. Accordingly one pleasant evening the two ring-leaders, both Yankees, and by a singular freak both nicknamed *Sal*, aided and abetted by a jolly Mizen Topman named Tobin, and last though not least by our Spouter, who was always on hand for a dance, a song, or a frolic of any kind, paraded themselves in the lee gangway, and gathering a gaping crowd, proposed the Game of Strongback.[2] I can imagine your surprise at the name and your wonder as to how it can be played. Wait a bit, and I'll tell you.

First of all, two leaders are chosen; these two toss up a hat for the Choice of men. Sides to the number of 8 or 9 now being chosen, the hat is again tossed for the Out or Inns. The out sides then place themselves in a stooping position, clinging closely to each other, with the Leader as a sort of stay to the whole, thus making a line of from 18 to 24 feet long, according to the number on each side. The

2. The two "Sals" and "Spouter" are difficult to identify, but the "jolly Mizen Top-man" was Thomas Tobin, Ordinary Seaman. Rogers, "Personnel of the *Portsmouth*."

other party now retire to a given distance and the leader running up places his hands upon the back of the hindmost one and jumps as far as he is able astride of this human horse; he is quickly followed by all his side. The game consisting in the party's being able to seat themselves firmly, and clap their hands three times before touching the deck. Should any of the Inns happen to fall or slide off, the parties change places, the jumpers going down and the downers jumping. I should not think it an interesting game to the players, but it is extremely so to the looker on, and ever and anon the loud peals of laughter would announce the discomfiture of one party or the other.

This game was carried on for several nights and was very successful in restoring harmony, but at last as the novelty began to wear off the old symptoms again appeared, and our worthy quartette set themselves to work to invent new ones, and new ones they were, and certainly some of the most grotesque ever beheld by any mortal. There was Foot and a Half, Hammer the Block, Cockfighting (by men) and Last, Rounding Cape Horn. These were brought out, as the Theatre Bills say, in succession and succeeded in driving all growling out of the Ship.

We held the SW Trades until after we crossed the line [the Equator], and then after 3 or 4 days of the Variables, struck the N.E. Trades and were balling it off to the tune of 10 knots as merrily as ever. On the evening of the 19th Aug. we discovered the land and to the great mortification of all, found the Capt. was going into Hawaii to water ship. Then all our bright hopes of getting to Honolulu before the *Levant* vanished, and many a wry face was put on in consequence, but 'twas of no use, we had to go, and it was as well to laugh as to cry. As it was too late to go in that night we lay off and on, and on the morning of the 20th stood in for the Land.[3]

I believe no man can ever fully appreciate the feelings of the first discoverers of these lovely Islands, but I do think a near approach can be made to them by the first sight of their green verdant hills and high mountains, after even the short passage of 26 or 27 days. Although we had been, in comparison with them, but an hour at sea, yet a more lovely and enchanting sight than Hawaii presented, I think I never saw. The land is very high and in a clear day can be seen at the distance of some 50 or 60 miles, and as we ran in, every moment disclosed new beauties. Jack is never much given to admir-

3. Downey's date is correct here. "Log of the *Portsmouth*," August 20, 1845.

ing the beauties of nature, and the land has but little attraction for him, that does not contain abundance of whiskey, but here, though it was well known there was no liquor on the Island, the prospect twas so tempting that I heard more than one say he should like to live and die there.

The Canackers (or Ka-nak-kas, as they spell it) are passionately fond of the beach, seldom residing far inland, consequently wherever a good fishing ground is to be found there may be seen lots of their little thatched houses, looking for all the world like so many hay ricks. It was abreast of one of these native villages, called Hilo, that we anchored, and in less than an hour were completely surrounded with canoes, containing from one to four of the half naked Islanders, each with some little thing for sale. They are a wide awake set of covies and up to all tricks in trading. Their dealings have for the most part been with Sailors and they have got up to the ways of Old Salts, and knowing that Jack when in want of an article is not particular about the price, each one charges what he pleases, or rather what he can get. Another of their tricks is never to bring off change, so if the purchaser has a whole dollar, he must either give that for what he could as well purchase for a quarter, or go without.

There is in this place most splendid water and the most convenient place for filling up a ship in any of this group, and as this is getting to be known, it will not be long before the town of Hilo will vie even with Honolulu as a place of resort for vessels trading or cruising in these latitudes. Fruit, fowls, and hogs are very plentiful here and though they will not, as in the days of Cook, trade for Old Iron Hoops, nor give a boat load for a Jack Knife, yet they are cheap enough in all conscience.[4] There are also some pretty shells of the cowrie kind, and fine specimens of Lava. The Missionaries have quite an establishment here. They are if one may judge from appearances, much beloved by the people and their labors seem to be appreciated.

Any person, no matter what his color or rank, (so he be a stranger) that sets foot on shore is at once surrounded by a crowd, who will follow you no matter where you go and are very troublesome. If you order them away they cannot understand a word you say, and thus

4. Here Downey has made a casual reference to Captain James Cook, who was killed in Hawaii during his stop there in 1779.

you are compelled to submit to their unwelcome escort. From the merest child to the old gray headed veteran each one has something to sell and I verily believe they would part with anything on earth for a little money. The canoes which surrounded us from daylight until dark, during the time we lay here, were filled with a miscellaneous collection of Fruits, shells, Hogs, Turkeys and Chickens, while Tara, Potatoes, and Yams, flew about the Ship in all directions. All hands had a regular bowse out here, and when money began to run short, a brisk trade was carried on for Jack knives, Razers, Scissors etc. After a tarry here of 2½ days we again hove up and proceeded on our course to Oahu.

After once making Land in this group you never lose sight of it until you traverse the whole length, and long before we lost sight of Hawaii, Maui burst upon us. After an uninteresting run of 24 hours, we found ourselves off the harbor of Honolulu. We made signal, and soon got a pilot on board, before which however we had made out the *Levant;* the growlers now had their fill and some of them wished our old man in—some place or other. As soon as the Pilot was over the Gangway, he was beset with inquiries—When did the *Levant* get it?—About two hours since—No more?—No—Hurrah—Hurrah. The word flew from mouth to mouth, we had beat the crack ship 5½ days. This satisfied all, and they went to work with a will and ere the sun had set, we were snugly moored in the inner harbor. When the *Levant's* boat came on board they looked both surprised and angry, but 'twas of no use, they were obliged to put up with it.

Honolulu is the great port of the Sandwich Islands; it is a place of considerable business at certain portions of the year and pleasantly situated, but I do not like it as well as Hilo. We went to work on Monday to take in provisions for a six month's cruise and proceeded rapidly but it was soon found that a great part of the provisions in the Navy Store were unfit for use and so a survey was called, which detained us some days and finally ended in condemning some $20,000 worth of provisions to be sold for the benefit of the U.S. We proceeded in our filling up but slowly and as the crew were in no hurry to leave the Islands, no one of them cared whether the survey ever concluded or not.

The following Sabbath after our arrival, instead of our usual *short* lecture from the Capt. when called as usual to muster, we were edified with a brief but excellent discourse from the Rev. S. C. Damon, the Seaman's Chaplain on the Island. Though his plain manner of telling us our faults did not please some, yet the great part of the Crew were pleased with him, and when in the evening our Capt. proposed a subscription to aid the Seaman's Friend Society, there were but few who did not throw in their mite. The above named gentleman is of a certainty a Seaman's Friend, which all of those who went on shore will testify, for upon calling at his study, he was always willing and pleased to receive them, and give them all the information in his power, in regard to any subject that might be broached. He always gave those who called papers, tracts and books, and sent a large quantity of each on board for gratuitous distribution.

I will mention one little incident that came under my notice, to show that half civilized as they are, they have not forgotten their ancient habits of thieving. The Ka-nak-kers were allowed on board at all hours, and one day while all hands were on the Spar Deck, there was one of them, a fine looking young fellow, sitting on a Mess Chest, busily engaged in trying to converse with the Ship's Corporal [Henry Osborne]. Some duty calling the Corporal forward, he left the Native sitting there, and he seemed to all intents and purposes to be only busying himself with the mastification of a piece of bread and meat which had been given him. All at once the Master's Mate of the Deck sung out for the Master at Arms [John Morgan] and told him to search the fellow as he thought he had seen him steal something from the chest and conceal it in his bosom. Jimmy accordingly overhauled him and from the bosom of his shirt, drew out an old Razer, which had proved too tempting for him—as a matter of course he was at once ordered off from the deck and with the utmost "sang froid" he picked up his traps and without a particle of shame on his countenance, wished us good day and trotted off.

While we lay in Honolulu the spirit of Mischief so constantly attendant on Jack gained the Upper hand and the first demonstration he made of his intention of holding a Levee, was in the shape of one of the Launchers who came off staring drunk and was as a matter of course consigned to durance vile. The convention having thus opened, the next member who took his seat was the Hon. Gentleman from London, who was so outrageous in his efforts to convince all

76

around of his sentiments of the rights of man, that "by and with the advice and consent" of the Officer of the deck, some slight but effective constraints were put upon him.[5]

Next morning as soon as the Hammocks were piped up, the Hon. Mr. Jobin [i.e., Tobin], the Member from Boston, presented his credentials and was regularly admitted; he made a few very pertinent remarks upon the occasion, but owing to the great fatigue he had undergone, having travelled all night in order to be in season, he begged to be excused for an hour or two and was soon in a sound sleep. The next upon the Carpet was the Delegation from the Emerald Isle, who having entered when the discussion was rather dull, soon followed the example of the Member from Boston, and when he awoke, found to his dismay that he had insinuated himself into a body where he had no business, and having by dint of argument convinced our 1st Luff [Missroon], who acted as Moderator on this occasion, that such was the case, he was allowed to retire, with a warning never again to force himself into this honorable body or else he should be compelled to enter into all their deliberations and to abide the result.

At or near 11 A.M. a loud flourish announced the arrival of the Hon. Member from N.T., who came in in great agitation, and being filled to the brim with indignation to think that the mind of man should be in any manner curbed, burst into an inflamatory speech, occasionally varying from the thread of his discourse to enquire if we were men. This seemed to be a point he was eager to have solved, and he continued to enchain the attention of his hearers, until he himself was enchained, and concluded by pointing out in his own person an example of what the Iron hand of the law could do. I have never been able to find out whether he had satisfied himself, as to our being *men,* or not.

Towards evening, the convention was completed by the joint arrival of the Delegate from the Mediteranean and the Hon. Member from Philadelphia, who had both undergone considerable fatigue and some hustling before, they considered themselves competent.

5. One assumes Downey is discussing the punishment of various members of the crew for drunkenness. The record is terse but quite descriptive: "Following 12 lashes: Timothy Whelan, drunk and insolent. Chas. Sangster, boring the working party. Thomas Tobin, drunkenness. John Pearsall, drunk on duty. Wm. Pendergrast, drunk and fighting. Daniel Smith, drunk and fighting." "Log of the *Portsmouth*," September 3, 1845.

Thus having a quorum, they proceeded to business in secret session, and although several persons arrived during the night who bore upon their countenances the private mark of members, for some unknown reasons they all declined taking their seats. Their deliberations continued the whole night, and until 9 A.M. next morning, when having intimated that they had come to a conclusion, they were forthwith mustered at the mast, where the Capt, who was "bona fide" President, gave them his opinion as to their proceedings, and after bestowing upon each one 12 marks of his approval [12 lashes with cat-o'-nine-tails], dismissed them "sine die." These sort of Conventions were rare however in our ship, and generally confined to a particular set.

After a tarry [of] 11 days, on the evening of the 5th Sept. we again unmoored Ship, and bidding adieu to the friends we had become acquainted with, shaped our Course for Monterey.[6] Our Ship has now made the shortest passage from the States to the Islands on record, having been at sea but 97 sailing days. Truly may we and all the Yankees brag on her.

A Sabbath at Sea

IT IS AN OLD SAYING, and often times a true one, that "there is no Sunday on board Ship." Among the greater portion of Sea going vessels, the Sabbath is only known by its being muster and duff day, or by the opportunity given on that day for the Crew to overhaul and mend their dunnage, without any interruption from Pipes or the Buffers, save such as is absolutely necessary for the working of the Ship. The Different Gangs that have been "hazed" throughout

6. The *Portsmouth* did not sail until September 6, 1845. *Ibid.*

the week are accustomed to look forward to the Seventh day, *not* as a day of rest but as *one* day to themselves.

On board all American Ships of war it is customary to read on the first Sunday of each month the "Rules and Regulations of the Sea Service" the first article of which enjoins upon all Commanders to have divine service performed on the Sabbath, and yet how few comply with this law. It has often seemed much like a farce to me, to see the virtuous indignation, which some officers show at the slightest violation from these Rules on the part of the Sailor, while they themselves are the first to disobey and disregard both the first and second articles.

It was our fortune however to have a Commander of whom it might be said, at least to outward show, "he feared God and honored the Congress." He never, from the first Sabbath we spent on board to the last (when the weather permitted) failed to read Divine Service, or to check any man who uttered any profane or obscene language in his hearing.[1] Sabbath was never with us looked upon as a mending day, but as one of entire rest. At sea or in Harbor, 'twas always the same, and on no occasion do I ever recollect any job of work being done on the Sabbath. The decks might be holystoned every day in the week, but on Sunday they, as well as those who operated upon them, had a rest, and holystoning decks on Sunday was no more thought of than a Militia Muster would be in one of the strictest of the Blue Law villages of New England.

I have said that the record of one day's proceedings on board Ship was a key to that of every day, but Sunday is an exception to this assertion. The very air seems redolent of rest, and from the time all hands are called in the morning until the watch is set at night, there is none of that extra noise generally heard about decks. If any person has occasion to pass a message, or call upon a messmate, it is done in a quiet orderly manner and not with loud bawling. Even the very calls when sounded by the Buffers seem to emit a smothered sound. Breakfast passes off quietly, and even Jimmy Legs on this day forgets to order "On deck all but the cooks," but if he has anything to say, does so in an easy subdued manner.

1. Montgomery has been described by all who knew him as an intensely religious man. See Theophilus F. Rodenbough, "John Berrien Montgomery," *Magazine of American History* (July, 1878), II; and Edwin Bryant, *What I Saw in California* (New York, 1848), p. 326.

When the word is passed to clean, out come the Bags, and one and all give their dunnage a thorough overhaul, selecting their best clothes, and rub and polish hats and shoes with more care than they would ever do on shore. There is no hurrying or throwing clothes on in a slovenly manner; every man seems aware that he has plenty of time and is determined to make good use of it, to dress himself as neat as possible. Bright work, that may have been neglected throughout the week, now receives an Extra Rub and long before the Drum calls to quarters, every thing is ready and every man by his looks seems to invite a close inspection.

As soon as the men are shifted and off the Berth Deck, the Cooks under the Superintendence of Jimmy and his aid proceed quietly to clean it, and as if conscious that the time is their own, they clean it much better and in less than half the time they would if they were continually driven. Chests are squared and opened, everything in the shape of Tin Ware brightened up, Mess Pans and Kettles shining like Silver are placed in the most conspicuous situations, Bibles & Prayer Books, of which every mess has a number, are neatly arranged on the Chests, and everything looks as tidy as if it were kept but for show. Around the Galley the Ships Cook and his mate, are seen with Rag and Brick in hand, polishing up all the Bright Work in his precinct—and Tormentors, Ladles and all the Paraphanelia look as if they had but just been drawn from a package in the Manufactory. The Range Cooks too meanwhile are busily engaged upon Kettles, Pots and Pans, and the array of shining utensils is enough to dazzle one's eyes. During the time consumed in doing all this extra work, no loud talking or laughing is heard, and though all are in good humor, they seem to have no inclination to spend any part of *their* time in retailing their feelings out. Long before the hour for muster the deck has undergone sundry sweepings. Every nook or corner, where dirt could by any possibility collect has been peered into and cleared out, and the cooks, decked out in their best, are lounging lazily around their messes.

Punctual to the hour of 10 comes the drum, and all silently wend their way to their respective Stations at quarters, and after a minute inspection from the Officers of the Divisions, are duly ranged "Toes to the crack" and reported ready for Grand Review. The Capt. and 1st Luff now proceed fore and aft, and having inspected the order and condition of things on the Spar Deck, descend to the Berth, where everything is overhauled from the Fore Passage to the Ward Room, and having finished this maneuver they return to the Spar Deck where the Retreat is beaten. After a delay of a few moments to allow the Carpenters to rig the Capstan Bars, open shot boxes to form seats, and the Quarter Masters to throw a Jack over the Capstan, the loud call of the Boatswain and his mates summons all hands to muster.

Upon arriving upon the Quarter Deck, we find it transformed into a Bethel and each and every one takes his seat as reverently as though he were in the most georgeous Cathedral in America. To one who may only have seen a Sailor during the brief term of his stay on shore, all this may seem but foolishness, for to them it appears as if any place but church would suit him. But—Stop—comparatively speaking you know nothing of the man—you have only seen him, when he has given way to the fun loving part of his character, when he has been released as it were from a long imprisonment, and well knowing he has but a short time to stay, he is determined to make use of that time to spend his well earned Whack, any way he can. His sole object is to get through with his money as soon as possible, and well aware he can spend little or none at church, he avoids that place with scrupulous care. But until you follow him in all the ups and downs, the inns and outs of a long cruise, you can know nothing of his religious feelings. I do not believe that there breathes beneath the broad canopy of Heaven a man who has a stronger veneration for, or a greater trust in the Magesty and Power of his Creator than your true sailor, and though his manner of showing it might not suit a Landsman, still it is there.

Isolated as he is from all but his own little world, he has a better chance to reflect upon God than a Landsman, who has the ever varying round of changes to employ his mind on Shore. During the long dreary look out, by day and by night, he is alone; and in communing with himself, when the humdrum tales of his life fail him, with the most wonderful of all works of the Creator spread out as a map before him, 'twould indeed be strange if he did not reflect upon that Maker, and learn to place confidence in him. This confidence it is that enables him, when called upon in the hour of danger, no matter how loudly howls the storm, how keenly blows the blast, or how awful the situation of his Ship, without a moment given to idle thought, to jump into the rigging, climb the dizzy height, and peril his life. Place a Landsman in his situation and he would hesitate long before he would brave the danger, and why? Not because he is physically incaple—oh no—but because he cannot trust to the Mercy of God to preserve him.

I have read an anecdote of an Old Salt who asked a Boy to loan him his Bible; the boy agreed, but said, "you must not make sport of it." "No," said the Old Man, "whatever else I do that is wrong, I never make sport of God Almighty." There is in this anecdote a true characteristic of Jack. He is a mirth loving individual, and the more sport there is in any argument the better it suits him. During my whole intercourse with Sailors, I have but seldom found one to whom this anecdote would not apply. They in their rough, off-hand way often argue about the reality of Religion in a manner that would lead a listener who is unacquainted with them to think they are making game of it, but to one who understands them it is plain sailing, for the only way of interesting them in any subject is to intersperce it now and then with something to raise a laugh.

This is a long digression from my yarn, but while you have been reading it, the Captain has assumed his post and opened the Book; look, every head is uncovered and every eye and ear intently bent upon him and a more orderly, serious and attentive lot of hearers, to my belief never listened to the word of God. The beautiful and impressive service of the Church of England is read, followed occasionally by a short and applicable sermon, and when the benediction is pronounced, every man silently and seemingly fearing to make the least noise, glides forward and the Crew are piped down—each one spending the balance of the Day to their own liking.

The libraries, of which we have two, the one furnished by the Government, the other bought by private subscription, are now opened, and the books consisting of Histories, Travels, Lives of Celebrated Men and other Sterling works distributed to all that call for them. The same orderly, quiet manner prevails and each one selects a place in which he may enjoy himself. Here and there may be seen groups of those who, unhappily unable to read themselves, are listening with greedy avidity to some more fortunate shipmate who amuses them by reading aloud. With a great majority of Old Salts who *can* read, the Bible is the favorite for Sabbath reading, and an old fellow who would growl at you, and almost curse you out of your shoes if he saw you with a book on week days, may now be seen attentively pursuing the word of God.

The necessary Ships work has to be gone through, but save that, no hand is laid to work on the Lord's Day. The same reverent feeling pervades through the whole 24 hours, and even after the hammocks are down, the influence of the Christian's God is felt. How different is [the] course of the following days; from the first peep of dawn, until 9 at night, all is noise, bustle, confusion and work, and so it continues until another Sabbath rolls round. These are the Green Spots in the Desert of a Sailors Life.

The First Death

[The delightful and often bibulous shore leaves in Honolulu marked the end of what might be called the "honeymoon period" of the *Portsmouth*'s first voyage. Almost as a symbol of less pleasant times to come, one of the crew was killed in an accident on the run from Hawaii to Monterey, California. If one is to judge by the increase of whippings with the cat recorded in the Log, it seems that not only was morale at a low point, but that a clique of hard-drinking salts with a flair for mischief and a touch of insolence harassed the officers daily and created a shipload of short tempers.

When the *Portsmouth* put into Monterey on October 28, the rumors of war with Mexico were so strong that officers and crew expected the excitement of action almost hourly. But weeks of waiting and sailling up and down the dreary western coast of Mexico from Manzanillo to Acapulco and back, in search of news, turned into months of frustrating inactivity. So numerous did the cases of desertion, disobedience, and drunkenness become on all the vessels in the Pacific Squadron, that the court-martial flag flew for three weeks at Mazatlan, whence Commodore Sloat had moved his base of operations in the fall of 1845.

In such an atmosphere the smart-aleck, rambunctious, and often insubordinate Downey inevitably came to grief. The entire ship now knew that he delighted in poking fun at certain members of the crew. They resented the select group who secreted themselves in the ship's storeroom to hear his compositions. Sometime in the late fall of 1845, four of Downey's enemies accused him of having unnatural relations with a cabin boy, Jonas Rhoades. While Downey was cleared of the charges, it became clear that he had violated orders to keep the storeroom locked. As punishment he was disrated to the rank of Seaman (November 11, 1845). But Downey's troubles had just begun. A few months later

(February 1, 1846) he was given twelve lashes for "disobedience of orders." Then in the spring of 1846 Lieutenant Missroon ordered Downey to write up a defense of certain men who had already been court-martialed. Downey at first seems to have refused to undertake this *ex post facto* task, but finally he consented (he had no choice) and produced an imprudent if not impudent defense of those who had been tried. Carried away by his own eloquence, Downey read his defense to members of the crew. Its fame spread, and Downey was soon in the ship's brig, having been charged with insubordination, suspected mutiny, and improper use of official documents. Thinking that Downey's notebooks contained evidence of mutiny, the officers attempted to confiscate them, but Downey and his friends hid them so successfully that they were never found. Again Downey was cleared of the charges, and since he was punished with but twelve lashes, it seems probable that the officers knew perfectly well that Downey was innocent of mutinous intentions and guilty only of insubordination. But after this experience Downey had an abiding hatred for all officers from Ship's Corporal to Captain.

Despite his personal difficulties Downey had also caught the war spirit of 1845–46. His sketches reflect the anxious waiting for news and show an increasing awareness of the role the Pacific Squadron must play in the threatened war with Mexico. Downey slowly began the transition from that of a shipboard humorist to that of an amateur reporter tracing the impact of Manifest Destiny upon that remote province of Mexico: California. The doldrums were ending; henceforth Downey would have difficulty including all the fast-moving events of the conquest of California which he so fortunately witnessed with his own eyes.]

OUR SHIP had been singularly fortunate thus far in her cruise, for though carrying upwards of 200 souls, and passing rapidly into all sorts of climates and weather from heat to cold, and on the coast of Chili and Peru exposed to the heavy unhealthy dews so common there, yet until now, we had never had a case upon our Doctors list— save that of colds, Dysentary or Rheumatisms, and all hands from the Commander down were boasting upon the health of the Ship and indulging at least the *hope* that we might be so highly favored as to return to the States without recording the loss of any of our Crew. This entire absence of sickness on board a Ship containing so many souls was almost unprecented thing, and this combined with the fact of our always making quick passages, gave us among all the name of the *Lucky Ship*.

I know not why it is, but with all the improvements made among Sailors in late years, it seems impossible to eradicate from their minds the firm belief they have in fate. There are some Ships that with them bear an *unlucky* name and for each it is almost impossible to Ship a Crew, while others again are never at a stand, because they are said to be *Lucky*. You may talk to them of the foolishness of the thing and they will laugh and joke about it, but you cannot shake their belief, 'tis firm as a rock. Among other superstitions prevalent among them is that some misfortune is sure to befal any Ship that sails from port on Friday. This day is in all their calendars put down as an *unlucky one,* and they will never sail on that day, if they can by any possibility avoid it, but as on board a Man of War the Commander reigns supreme, so when he says go, go you must, however much it may be against your feelings.

As I have before said, we have always made good passages, no accident ever occurred on board, but we also had never sailed on Friday. Once when coming out of Rio we had made an attempt to get under way on that day, but failed after nearly running down one half the vessels in the Harbor, and at last gave up the idea and again dropped our anchor. The Old Salts said that our guardian Angel was on the look out for us. Our *luck* was yet to be tried and a trial we had, the consequence of which was to confirm more strongly those who had faith in the superstition and almost to shake the minds of those who opposed it.

On the 5th Sept. at 5 in the evening we hove up our anchor in the Port of Oahu and with a fine fair wind stood out to sea; after we were fairly underway and time for conversation was gained, some of the Old Growls were bitter in their complaints of the folly of sailing on Friday, and prognosticated bad weather and a long passage if nothing worse. And sure enough, seemingly as if in fulfilment of part of their sayings, hardly had the Pilot left us when the wind died away stark calm, and for the whole night we lay rolling and tumbling like a log on the Ocean. Next morning however we caught a good breeze, and though for the first few days every thing promised fair, it soon left us and we had nothing but a succession of calms or light head winds.

The passage we were now making rarely occupies vessels of even ordinary Sailing capabilities over 15 or 20 days, and we had hoped to make it much sooner, but in this we were disappointed and as day after day rolled by and we still made no perciptible progress, the "Old Croakers" found plenty of food to growl on. Wherever you went about decks, and saw a group collected together, among them you would find one of these old fellows, who upon the least chance would declaim loudly against the hazard we ran of sailing on the unlucky day, and prognosticating that the long passage would not be the only misfortune that would happen to us. But few however of their young shipmates paid much heed to them and merely listened to the yarns they would spin about what had happened to vessels whose Masters had dared to sail on the forbidden day in times long past (of which they would retail a large quantity) to pass away the long hours of the watch. But strange as it may seem, as if to confirm their superstition and put to shame all unbelievers, an accident and a serious one too, did happen.

Among our Crew we had but few old men (a sailor is called old at 35 or 40) but prominent among these few was Jack Whelean, a native of Philadelphia, a thorough sailor, and as jovial a messmate as ever ate a scouse. Jack was something over 40, had followed the sea from his childhood, had been in the English, French, and Turkish services, and being of an observing turn of mind had collected a large fund of incidents that had happened to him, which in his own peculiar way, he would retail to the no small amusement of all that heard him. He was of a mild, pleasant disposition, ever willing and ready to lend a hand at work or join in a skylark, and in fact, to sum the whole in a few words, "he was a true Sailor." Somewhere near the hour of 1 A.M. on the 24th of Sept I was aroused from my sleep by hearing a cry, or groan from some person seemingly in great agony.

It is a singular thing, but no less singular than true, that a man may accustom himself to sleep on board a ship while all the noise and bustle consequent upon working ships is going on over his head, and even allow his neighbor to turn out and in, as the watches are releived without being in any way disturbed by it, yet still any noise out of the usual run will arouse him at once. This was my case, and starting up I listened for a moment, and hearing it repeated, I hurryed on my clothes, and seeing a light in the Sick Bay, ran forward at once.

As I opened the door the first object that met my gaze was my poor friend Jack stretched out upon the floor, surrounded by a pool of blood that seemed to stream forth from all parts of his body—his head was badly cut, his left eye closed altogether, while from the appearance of his legs I at once thought they were both crushed to pieces. I soon learned that he had fallen from the fore yard (where he had gone on duty) upon the Forecastle. It seems that after rigging

86

out the Steering Sail Boom, some part of the running gear had got jammed, and in endeavoring to jerk it clear, he had lost his balance and fallen the whole distance (about 40 feet), striking upon his left knee, shattering that leg to a mass of jelly, breaking his right leg, and cutting his head deeply.

Our surgeons were immediately in attendance, but it was almost impossible to ascertain at once the extent of the injury sustained. He was a very lusty man, and in falling from such a height it was but reasonable to suppose he must have jarred his whole system. Amputation was suggested, but such was his corpulency that upon consultation, they decided that it was more than probable that he would die under the operation, and he could *but* lose his life. At all events, of the two evils they chose the least. The weather was cool and favorable, and by arranging the limbs in the best possible manner there was a chance (if he was not inwardly injured) of his recovery, but still he would be a cripple for life. This plan was accordingly adopted, and his leg was placed in a fracture case, the broken parts arranged with care, and nature left to do her own work.

Two or more of his messmates, as duty would allow, were constantly with him, and go where you would about decks the first question that greeted the ear would be, how is Jack? is there any chance for him? and sorrow, deep heartfelt sorrow prevailed among all. The Old Prophets, though they were as much shocked as any one, would however point at it as a fulfilment of their augeries, and became if possible more strongly convinced than ever in the doctrine of fatality.

On the morning of the accident, group after group would collect around the Bay, all anxious to catch a glimpse at the sufferer or eager to assume the post of watcher by his side. One and another would now bring to mind little incidents that had happened but a few days before, that savored strong of presentiment—such as his saying that he should not go home with us but remain out here and join the *Shark,* and that but a few short hours before he fell, he had been conversing with some person about death, and had expressed a wish, that when his time did come, he might at least have his senses. Poor fellow, even this boon was denied him, and from his continued insanity the surgeon pronounced that a concussion of the brain, had been added to his other misfortunes, and that he could not long survive. The Bell, which hung under the Forecastle immediately above his head, was muffled, and the mournful sound emitted by it served to remind every one of the sad occurrence and its expected consequences and cast a deep gloom over every countenance. Orders were passed in a low tone, footsteps that always seemed unusually heavy, now seemed to fall noiselessly upon the ear, and all conversation in the neighborhood of the Bay was carried on in Whispers. He did not seem inclined to take any nourishment but water, and the Surgeons in vain tried to induce him to swallow an opiate; he would occasionally sink into a troubled doze, from which he would start and in the most pitious tones call upon his shipmates for aid, but poor souls, they could *but* pity him. Soon after 8 A.M. on the 25th he sank into a stupor from which he never aroused, but continued breathing heavily until 5 P.M. when he quietly breathed his last, without having had a sane moment from the time he was hurt. Upon a "post mortem" examination, it was found that a portion of the "frontal" bone had slivered off and entered the brain, which of itself alone would have caused his death.[1]

Early on the morning of the 26th the Body, after being sewed up in a Hammock and having a 64 Pound shot lashed at the feet, was removed to the Quarter Deck and covered with a Jack. At noon the call of "All Hands Bury the dead" summoned us on deck, where the crew were all assembled neatly in Blue. The Main Topsail was thrown aback, the colors half masted, and the body being lain upon a plank in the Lee Gangway, our Captain began the beautiful and impressive service of the Episcopal Church. Solemnity was stamped on the countenance of every one, and at the words "we commit his body to the deep" the Jack was withdrawn, the inner end of the Plank raised, the body slid off, a sullen plunge was heard, and the waters closed over the remains of poor Whelean.

During the whole of the ceremony a large Bird was seen hovering round the Ship and shortly after we had filled away, he was joined by a second, though from whence he came was a mystery. The two continued for some seconds to circle round the spot, and then majestically rose out of sight. Who then, after the seeming fulfilment of the prophecy before mentioned, would blame the Tar if he chose to think that it was the spirit of his deceased Shipmate, watching over the interment of his mortal remains. As soon as the Hands were

1. See entries for September 24 and 26, 1845 in "Log of the *Portsmouth*."

piped down, the gloom which had remained as long as the body was on board suddenly flew away, the usual noise and bustle commenced, and though the Sad fate of Jack was often mentioned, it was always spoken of as one of the things that have been.

Lines on hearing the Call of "ALL HANDS BURY THE DEAD"

> List Shipmates—List! that solemn Call
> Falls sadly on the ear,
> Tread light, ye who bear the pall
> A noble heart rests here.
> Now short the time since him ye bear,
> Neer thought of danger o'er his head,
> Whose hopes of long life, seem'd so fair?
> Yet now; alas! he's dead.
>
> *****
>
> Aye, place him on his lowly bier
> Around him Shipmates, crowd,
> A Sailors burial, he has here,
> His hammock, is his shroud.
> No proud display of hired mutes
> With wailing mock'ry pain the ear
> But o'er his corpse, with sad'ned heart
> You've dropp'd the bitter tear.
>
> *****
>
> The last sad rites are paid to him,
> The sea receives its dead,
> *The omen bird, with heavy wing
> Still flutter o'er his head.
> Tis past, tis gone, the waters close
> Around his senseless form,
> And onward still our good ship goes
> All heedless of the storm.
>
> *****
>
> His resting place, no stone shall mark,
> No foot ere desecrate the sod
> Down in the Mermaid's Cavern dark

*Alluding to the birds that hovered round the Ship

He waits the summons of his God.
On coral bed secure he lays
Beneath the blue sea's angry wave
It's been his home, since boyhood days
'Tis fit't should be his grave.

The Sabbath in Port

WHAT A DULL uninteresting world this would be were it not made
up of contradictions. These were my thoughts as laying in my hammock on the night of Sunday the 28th, Sept 1845, I compared the
manner in which that day had been spent with that of the previous
one. The former was at sea, where work was required to be performed to keep the ship in her proper station, the latter was in port
where one would have thought peace and quietness would have
reigned pre-eminent. We were lying in the port of Monterey, where
we had arrived the day before, from Oahu. The "green uns" judging
from the descriptions of the coast given by old cruisers, were all an-
ticipating very cold and disagreeable weather, where pea jackets and
flannels would be essentially necessary for our comfort. How were
we surprised then to hear the word passed to muster in white. Truly
the tales of travellers are not always to be credited. There were in
Port beside ourselves two Yankees, a French Whaler, and two Mexican Brigs. But as I intend to compare the manner of our spending
the two days, I may as well commence at daylight.

As the Report of the morning Gun died away in the mountains,
the Revilee was beat, and all hands called. I had scarcely got up and
stowed my hammock, when on going to the forecastle I espied two
large right whale, slowly cruising about in the Bay. As I paused for
a moment to watch them, an exclamation of "there they lower" drew
my attention to the French Whalers, who had lowered three boats,
and manning them they were soon skimming merrily through the
water in hot chase after the audacious fellows. It was a new and uncommonly interesting sight to me, who had never seen a whale taken,
but my feelings were not to be compared in intensity to those of
some of our old Whalers, who had got their adventurous blood up,

and appeared to share as deeply in the excitement as those in the boats. Foremost among these was Spouter, who perched upon the Cat-Head, became so wrapped up in the chase that he had eyes or ears for nothing else, but kept gazing steadily at the place where he last saw the whale, and muttering to himself as if addressing the Boats Crew "give way, give way, my souls" accompanying his words, with that see saw motion so common to sitters in a boat. He was ordered to move two or three times, but paid no attention, never moving from his position, until the harpooner in the headmost boat had risen to strike, when springing up, he grabbed a squilgee handle, threw himself into attitude and poised his weapon, keeping at the same time a wary eye upon the movements of him in the boat. As the Iron was darted, he too darted his stick and with the impetus lost his balance and fell headlong overboard to the infinite amusement of all the bystanders; nothing disconcerted however, he swam quickly to the Gangway, climbed up, and all dripping wet as he was, came forward and resumed his place on the Cat-head.

The whale as soon as he felt the iron, darted off like the wind, and towing the boats after him, swam with unabated speed for more than a mile. I have seen some tall travelling in my life on railroads, Steam Boats, and such critters, but I never before witnessed any thing in that line, that could begin to compare with this. There is nothing that will give any idea of it, unless it be the speed of a cat, tied to the tail of a sky Rocket. This race against time was too severe to last long, and as soon as his speed began to slacken, they commenced hauling up to him, and as soon as they were near enough lanced him. Hurra said Spouter—give it to him—that's your sort—once more —just under his fin—Hurra—there he spouts the claret—Mind your eye—Starn all for the Flurry; thus like a madman he continued to shout and dance around, heedless of the laughter of the crowd of gazers round him, and just as the whale turned on his side, he gave three hearty cheers, and continued capering and shouting, until a slap across the mouth from a wet swab, brought him off his fancy horse and down to the stern reality of a man of war, and washing decks. The whale being now dead, they fastened the three boats to him and commenced towing him in—But! you will say; there is no contradiction in this long yarn on your part—wait a bit—Every thing must be done by degrees and I have only now begun my story. The usual ablution of decks being over, breakfast was piped, the word passed to clean, and after the customary inspection, service was performed and every thing promised for the religious observance of the day to be strictly carried out.

But the truth of the Old Primmer song that

> "Satan always finds some work"
> "For idle hands to do"

was never more strongly exemplified than on this particular day. Some mischeivous fellow, not having the fear of God before his eyes, had dropped a fish line over our bow, and feeling a bite hauled in, and to his great joy discovered that he had captured a fine large mackerel—he said nothing about his good fortune but slily depositing his prisoner in the head, continued his sport, and in a very few moments, such was his luck, that he had forgotten everything about Sunday, Sermon, and everything else but fishing, and was as busily engaged as he could be, providing not for the welfare of his immortal but of his mortal part. Bye and bye, a second strolled up and catching an idea of what was going on had joined him, and a third, and fourth, and at last so great were the quantity of fish around the Ship, and so extensive had the mania for appropriating them become that fore and aft, forecastle, chains and even the sacred precincts of the poop, were lined with eager crowds and the cry was "still they come." Every soul was kept busily at work pulling them up, and in fact it seemed literally to rain fish so steady was the supply that came flying over the nettings. For a time all this was carried on quietly, and much care was taken not to soil the decks but no sooner did it become noised about that the Captain had given his permission for the crew to catch as many fish as they wanted, than all care vanished, every man who could not procure a line, out knife, and fell to work upon fish, and in an incredible short space of time, our once snowy decks, from the Knight Heads to the Taffrail on the Larboard Side, resembled a large slaughter house more than a man-of-war's decks, being covered from clue to earing, with blood, heads, and entrails.

Now commenced the true sport of the thing and order for the balance of the day was set at defiance, and though the scenes that presented themselves were at once laughable and agravating yet good humor prevailed. Some unlucky wight would attempt to go forward along the Gangway when slap alongside his head would come a mackerel and if he stopped to see whence it came, whack he would get another, and if he opened his mouth to growl at that, ten chances to one but he would get one right across his chops, until in sheer dismay he was compelled to scuttle out of the way as soon as possible. Every Tub, Bucket, Mess Kettle or Pan in the Ship was filled to overflowing, and fish lay about decks in all directions. When the harvest first began a number of Fore Topmen had stationed themselves between two guns and after some tall bragging about their experience in former times at mackerel hunting, ended by swearing roundly that they could clean faster than any ten men could catch and finding no one sufficiently at leisure to dispute them, fell to work on a very respectable pile that had accumulated before them. They did work smart and no mistake, but after two hours of excessive exertion, they one and all gave up the Contest, and lay back gazing upon the still growing pile in mute despair.

Nor was our sport confined to Mackerel alone, for some of the Forecastlemen caught a large skate, which was forthwith dissected, and others were amusing themselves with hauling in and maiming the Shark, Dog Fish, etc. One old Genius did nothing the whole afternoon but fish for them, and when he had hauled them up on the Forecastle, he would torture his brain to invent means to torture them, such as cutting off their noses, and unshipping their fins and then tossing them overboard. One poor Devil, after having a large stick of wood lashing to his tail, was returned to his native element; as soon as he found he was at home again, he wiggled away manfully to descend and succeeded in dragging his unusual appendage down a considerable depth, but its buoyancy proved to much for him and he soon slowly rose tail first to the surface, and though he made some desperate struggles, he was not again able to drag it down, but continued drifting about, occasionally casting his eye up towards the laughing crowd, as if to reproach them for their cruelty. Meanwhile the French Boats came in, and brought the whale astern, but so busily were our men engaged, that they could spare no time to gaze at them.

Amongst others who were as busily engaged as his Satanic Majesty is said to be in a gale of wind, was our old friend Brush, who was running hither or thither with a bucket in his hand, gathering fish wherever he could lay his hand on them, and paying no attention as to whether his messmates caught them or not. He had gathered a goodly pile yet still he paused not, until as he was grabbing a large fine fat one, he found himself grabbed by a burly Fore Topman, and from the expression of his countenance there were strong symptoms of an obstruction in his wind apparatus,—Hello, gasped he—I say, you've made a mistake here, I ain't a fish—I know that well enough, but you are a fish taker—well what of that? Why, merely they don't belong to you—How do you make that out said Brush? Why, easily enough, says his opponent, none of your mess caught 'em. I don't know about that, rejoined Brush, these 'ere fish all look pretty much alike, and are laying quite thick about here and I'm not judge enough of human nature to discriminate much about 'em, but you see I go on the same principle them fellers outside do, that is them as works smartest gets the biggest lot, but if you have any particular fancy to that fish, you can have it. But it aint that fish I'm talking about, says Ratlin, I've been watching you about an hour, and though at chucking them in that bucket, you're about Inkstand, still I haven't seen you catch any this whole day. Wal, I rather think you must have been asleep then, for I've been catching them all the while—I say there's a fine one let me git him and then I'll talk to you, so saying he screwed himself out of Ratlin's grip and seizing three or four that lay close together he ran forward, singing out, "You see, I'm there on appropriation."

He was a strict observer of the Sabbath generally, and seizing a chance when he was at leisure, I asked him how he reconciled this kind of work with the sanctity of the day—Why, said he, that's all very simple—Now I've argued the case with myself and have come to the Conclusion that it is a Dispensation of Providence—You see, we haint had a blow out of fish, since we left home, that's one thing; wal, fish is gittin too thick out here to be comfortable, that's another thing; then these 'ere natives are too ever-lasting lazy to catch 'em, that's another; then they wouldn't bite last night, and we are going away on Monday—Now puttin all these things together, you see we shant get another chance at them; now what's nourishment for the body, is good for the soul, and in consequence of all this it seems to me, as plain as the nose on *your* face, that they are sent here a purpose to be caught, and I should consider it downright sin if we didn't improve the opportunity—beside all the rest—what the rest was no one but himself ever knew, for a loud call from a messmate in the chains called him off, and away he went in hot chase of a fresh supply of fish.

94

By this time our decks between blood and slime had become as slippery as Glass, and it was a matter of great difficulty to stir about without falling. All Hands as before stated had cleaned in white in the morning and as it was against orders to change until supper time, they now looked like any thing else but white, so bedaubed were they from head to foot. Many very ludicrous scenes took place in consequence of falls, but foremost among the rest for the exercise of native wit, was that of a spruce little fellow who though he had only joined us in Oahu, yet such was his pleasant, jovial disposition that he was fast rising into the good graces of all, and bid fair to become a pet with everyone.[1] He was a Ward Room Boy, and having just eaten his dinner, and put things to right, he came running up on to the Forecastle to see the fun, but alas! hardly had he gained the deck, when presto! up went his heels and down came his stern plump on deck—he sprang up with a laugh, and though a little disheartened at the idea of having ruined his trowsers, was congratulating himself that he had not fallen on his back and thus ruined his frock also, when the Count, our Surgeons Steward, who though as true a son of the Sod as ever spoke the brogue, had always denied his country and sworn roundly that he was born in *Kentucky,* thinking to display his wit at the expense of some one, stepped up and said, "Look here my youngster if that's a way ye have of settling your dinner, I would beg leave in the quietest manner possible to advise you when you practice the move again to select a cleaner spot, for by the powers of decoration, but you've a fine map of the world on the hinder part of ycre trowsers now."[2]

This raised a laugh against the youngster, who was however, though unknown to the Count, a wit in a quiet way, so waiting until the merriment at his expense had subsided, Charley with a knowing leer, answered him with, "well, if it is a map of the world, just look and see if you can't find *Ireland* there." The Count was astonished to be bearded, beaten by his own weapons and by a youngster too was too much, but he knew better than to attempt to retaliate in any other way but words, and for once, being at a loss for them, he contented himself with casting a malignant scowl upon Charley, and

1. James Robinson, who had shipped on the *Portsmouth* as Ward Room Steward just as the ship was leaving Hawaii. "Log of the *Portsmouth*," September 6, 1845.

2. The "Count's" real name was John L. B. Connelly. Rogers, "Personnel of the *Portsmouth.*"

moved off down the Ladder, to the Spar Deck amid peals of laughter from the delighted crowd.

This however did not affect the fishermen who continued operations until the sun had set, when Old Knight-heads, (the Capt of the Forecastle) did by dint of hard growling knock them off, and it was long after dark before the decks assumed anything like their customary order.[3] Our Captain it is true did not entirely approve of this manner of spending the Sabbath, but willing to indulge the crew, he winked at it, and perhaps called it necessary work. In the end too, strange as it may seem, it proved to have been necessary, for though we lay two days at anchor, and all hands were on the "qui vive," there were not enough fish caught after this day to make a meal for all hands. As it was, we procured salt from a trading Barque that laid near, and every mess from Cabin to the Loblolly Boy's had fish enough salted down to last some weeks.

The Frenchman got his whale on board and started his tryworks and the last I saw of that Sunday's work or amusement, was, as I descended to my hammock at 9 P.M., the light of his fire. Now reader compare this chapter with the one headed a Sabbath at Sea, and then answer if you find any contradiction.

A Sad Mistake

ENVY is always a close attendant upon genius, be that genius large or small, and a man who has the faculty of amusement cooped up in his head, is sure, whenever he attempts to exercise that faculty, to offend some one or another of the would be somethings always found on board Ship. This was the unhappy case of Peak. He had no particular clique to whom he hung and by whom he allowed his productions to stand or fall, for fore and aft, athwartship or amidship he was always pleased and happy to collect a crowd of his Shipmates, and strive to the best of his ability to amuse them, and drive dull care away. He was always in good humor and was in sooth a general

3. "Old Knight-heads" was either William Griffiths or Joseph Senggie, both listed as Captain of the Forecastle. *Ibid.*

favorite with all—no, not all. There were a few who could not bear to see him pass an hour with ease—who could not endure the idea of allowing him to spend his time in peace, or amuse himself by instructing others. No, they were envious of him. They had some of them striven long to get a clue in him, by which they could compass his ruin. But thus far their efforts had been vain, he had too long a head for them. He would thus far and no farther go, and all their ingenuity could not suffice to torture any word or deed of his, into depravity enough to found the basis of a grand charge against him.

He was himself an impudent, headstrong fellow, and though he was often forewarned of the watch set upon him, yet he took no care to avoid the snare. There was a general order in the Ship to allow no person except the Yeoman to enter the Store Room, but Peak, whom some of the Boys had persuaded to learn them to write, in an evil hour broke through the restraint and opened a Regular School down there. From the moment they discovered this fact, they set themselves to work to torture something out of this Capital that should, at last, crown their hopes, and forever crush Poor Peak. Long, anxiously, and carefully did they watch and peer, and pry, and strive to get the required hold, for they knew he stood high in the estimation of the Commander, and that no common charge would throw him. Circumstances at last favored them, and their hopes were crowned with success—in prospective.

In Oahu among others we had shipped a youngster who had run away from a merchant Ship.[1] He was a fine open hearted jovial little fellow, of near 16, and his appearance was so prepossesing that for the first month of his tarry on board the breath of scandal or envy never fell upon him. But unhappily for himself he became attached to Peak, and that attachment drew down upon him the manevolence of Peak's enemies, and what he had hoped would have proved a source of happiness to him became one of sorrow. His intimacy was at once noticed, and spies were set upon them to ascertain how far they might go in a lie, and matters being in this train they soon amassed what they thought evidence enough to convict him.

They had however counted without their host. Peak was too strong for them, every charge was triumphantly refuted as brought against him, by the 1st Luff, and not content with that, he referred the mat-

1. Jonas Rhoades, who had shipped on the *Portsmouth* as a Cabin Boy when the ship was in Honolulu. "Log of the *Portsmouth*," August 26, 1845.

ter to the Commander who called thereon a Court of inquiry, who after a careful investigation gave as the decision that there was no charge, no suspicion, no breath of scandal upon the character of either of them. His having broken a General Order he could not deny, and as a punishment was ordered not to keep the Store Room opened except in case of actual duty and then to close it again at once. There was also an order passed that the Boy should not talk to Peak. This order was broken, and to the shame of the 1st Lieut be it said, he flogged the Boy for speaking to a Shipmate.[2]

What the crime alleged was, reader, if you are a Man-of-War's man, you know; if you are a Landsman, it is best not to disclose it to you, lest you surmise that "when bad begins, still more remains behind." If any of my Shipmates ever read these lines, they will have no difficulty in recognizing the characters described, or the circumstances which transpired to give this theme—It was however but the wonder of a day and was, after *its* day was over, as one of the things that have been. Should it fall into the hands of those who are depicted I beg of them a fair reading, and a serious thought of the annoyance they were to a Shipmate, and hope it will tend to guard them against such foolish ebulitions of feeling and dissuade them from any future attempts on an unoffending man.

THE CONSPIRATORS[3]

Come Shipmates, stop, here's something now quite new
I've got a first rate yarn to spin to you.
The subject's one with which you're all acquainted
'Bout how board Ship, our morals will get tainted,
How we will do in word or deed together
'Till some would think our virtue but a feather.
But avast a bit—you're getting on too fast

2. Downey was disrated to Seaman on November 11 on the charge that he had failed to keep the storeroom locked. Some months later (February 1, 1846) both Downey and Rhoades received twelve lashes apiece for "disobedience of orders." Downey probably wrote his "A Sad Mistake" sketch some months after the incident. "Log of the *Portsmouth*," November 11, 1845, and February 1, 1846.

3. The four men who testified against Downey are difficult to identify, so careful has the latter been in avoiding their names and rank. Downey suddenly stops friendly references to "Jimmy Legs" (John Morgan, Master at Arms), and to Henry Osborne (Ship's Corporal) whom he now calls "The Tool." Unless the officer whom he mentions as a conspirator was Lieutenant Missroon, very possibly it was Lieutenant Daniel C. Hugunin, for whom Downey had an intense dislike.

Suspicion may be strong—but cannot last.
Tis never safe to judge by outward looks,
In proof of which, I could refer to many books,
But will content myself, to while the time away
And tell an incident—on board our ship one day
That did occur—in which some four smart fellows
That often blew their own wind without bellows
Got awful suck'd—and fell far short their mark
Which was to stab a Shipmate in the dark.
Not stab him "bona fide" with a knife
And thus with one sure blow, rob him of life.
Oh no—such manly deed their noddles never entered
And if it had, their coward hearts would ne'er have ventured
But cherishing 'gainst him, some secret spite
A hellish charge at last they brought to light,
A charge, which would could they but prove it true
Forever damn him, soul and body too.
Who were this set? you ask that thus would bring
A shipmate up, for so abhorred a thing?
I'll tell you—One was an Officer—God forfend,
He called himself a *bully* from North End.
He called *himself* I say, or else I doubt
If ever mortal wisdom would have found it out.
For though he swaggered large, and cock'd his cap askew
'Twas whispered round that he was not "true blue"
One duty wa'nt enough for his good looks
So he crept in to drive the "birth Deck" cooks.
This much of number one; I say no more, for fear
That should he chance my compliments to hear
He might get wroth and growl about a libel
Though for their truth, I will be sworn upon a Bible.
Now number two, was forty times as bad
As number one, for all the sense he had
Was crowded into one small space, and there it staid
Despite all efforts to disloge it made
He was a *soger*—not a Soldier—mark me now
The difference is plain, as twixt a Bull and Cow.
For though a man may be a *Soldier* without blame,
As well as *Sailor,* for what is in a name?

Yet be a *Soger* sure he never can with ease
His Shipmates all will curse him when they please
And they're supported too in all attacks
For he is loafing, while they break their backs.
Then two I think you now will recognize
If not, in God's name where have been your eyes?
Now number three—great two fisted fool
That to rare villiany lent himself a willing tool
Would round the "Birth Deck" prowl and seek a chance
To nick poor devils, and their woe's enhance
This one alone of all this rare quartette
Had reason on his Shipmate thus to set
And such a reason—Oh ye sharks and fishes,
Oh! all ye little boys, who wash the dishes
Oh! all ye men, who watch at night do stand
Oh! Topsail Yardmen as ye gaze for Land
Oh! Cooks around the Galley sing,
Oh! Holders billow forth the awful thing
The man that in his duty thus was zealous.
A reason had—'twas this—dont laugh—but he was jealous.
Take all the sense away, these worthies might have had
Concoct the balance; evil disposition add
Give it the power to act, to see, to talk
Around the decks allow the thing to walk
Then just to finish it, add one thing more
The will, the power to lie—that's number four.
This was the set that now in conclave came
To swear on Peak a deed without a name.
Now number one had seen him motions make
And glances throw, known only to a rake
Had seen him answer when addressed, yes, yes, just-so
Knew that he'd gi'n away a thing or two
Some short, some long, some old, some new,
So taking all things in consideration
Thought if report was made 'twould save the nation.
He spoke his thought, and asked if they agreed
Then bade them say what they had seen, with speed,
Out spoke the Soger, I know you can't be wrong
But I have proof that is both sound and strong

100

I've had suspicion long upon the train
I've seen him sow, with all his might and main
Known him to give what he's refused to sell
As trowsers, kerchief, boots as well
As blankets, which he's yeilded up with joy
And slighted even me for this new toy
But stronger still, I crept the other night
And in his face, I sudden flashed a light
He started, sprang and stretching forth his neck
Exclaimed "come Charley, let us go on deck"
Combine these things, with what you too have seen
And tell me now in sooth what they can mean.
Poor number three, had set with eyes and mouth wide open
And gasped, and sobbed, and choaked as if his heart was broken
Now added that he'd tried from time to time
The charm to break, but found he could not shine,
That he had lain, and listened by the hour
In hopes some clue to get, that would have power
To break the spell, and bring the envied prize
Back to his home, to cheer his drooping eyes.
But, spite of all that he could do, or say
He found his influence failing fast, each day,
And feared unless some measures, were enforced
He'd be obliged to yield, and bolt the course.
Of course, he thought that Peak was very wrong
To step in, where he'd tried to shine so long,
And humbly hoped the accusation would be laid
When he would swear without remorse to all twas said,
Claimed as a boon while tears rolled from his eyes
If Peak *was* damned, that he should have the prize.
Now four stepped up, and having took a sneeze,
Told them to bring the charges as they please
Say anything, or every thing, say seduction
And he would swear he'd seen a close connection
Use every means, and never knock off trying
Depend on him, for he would do their lying.

* * * * *

The Club adjourned, and in high spirits too
To think on Peak, they'd gained so great a clue.

His ruin now they deemed as certain—sure
Grief to his heart that time could never cure
Shame to his brow; the Gangway for his back
A name accursed, his sorrowing brain to rack,
This was the tableaux of their damned play
They hated him because, he had more sense than they.
Then number one, bursting with news so loud
Sought the first Luff and to the ground he bow'd
Told a straight tale, and strong additions made
Urged, what he'd seen and heard, what others said
Wound up by guessing, with evidence so strong
'Twas plain enough, that there was something wrong,
He then retired, and straightway Peak was called
Who came with smiles, but with the charge was pall'd
Yet undismayed, and knowing his cause was good
He braced his mind, and a strong lawsuit stood
Scorned to deny each charge as brought to light
Admitted them in all their strength and might
Heard witness called, and at their stories smiled
Heard charge on charge, to deep damnation piled
When they had done, and knew no more to tell
With eye unblanched, pronounced them "false as hell"
Dared them to prove *one* overt act but true
This they declined, as it they could not do
To highest court the cause was now appealed
And scope for action given, in fair field,
The verdict's rendered, the quartette slink away
For Peak's fair fame is clear as broad noon day
And all the products of this well drugged cup
Were for a day to shut Peak's Store Room up.

Mansinilla

READER, if you were a Shipmate of mine in the *Portsmouth,* it is unnecessary for me to ask you what sort of a feeling the name of the place which heads this article brings over you. For myself, I can never even think of it without a certain horrid sensation and I verily believe the eternal buz of the Natives will forever ring in mine ears. But for the information of those, who have never visited this so much to be execrated place, I will attempt a description of our passage, the trouble we had in finding it, and the horrors of the dreadful night we passed there.

We had left Oahu on the 5th Sept bound on a cruise along the Coast of California and Mexico, and though we were delayed by light baffling winds, the passage was on the whole a pleasant one, and on the 26 we arrived in Monterey. Here the rumors of a war between Mexico and the United States were very strong, but to them we paid but little heed, boasting with all the vain glory of Yankees, that with our good ship alone we could take the whole coast of Mexico, and even daring to assert that there were not natives enough in the whole of the Mexican provinces, to drive us off, or prevent our landing, at our own good will and pleasure. How we were mistaken, and what a shameful defeat we suffered, this chapter will show, and also serve as a warning to all boasters "never to halloo till they are out of the wood."

As stated in a former chapter, we lay but a few days in Monterey, when we again hove up and proceeded on our cruise down the coast. Of all parts of the world it was ever my fortune to cruise in, this is the most uninteresting, there being no variety—in the shape of squalls or heavy breezes, nothing but a succession of light, baffling winds, and it growing daily more and more intolerably hot, as we approach the line. The temper of all hands became gradually soured; it is a rare thing to get a civil answer from a Shipmate until after sunset.[1] Then indeed they will collect in the Larboard Gangway and for the short time allowed for smoking previous to 8 Bells,

1. Downey reports the atmosphere aboard the *Portsmouth* during the days of great heat and slow sailing with great accuracy. Within four days after leaving Monterey, no less than twelve of the crew had received lashes for insolence, neglect of duty, for being drunk while on duty, and for "skulking." "Log of the *Portsmouth,*" October 1–4, 1845.

the Laugh and Jest will run merrily around, but it is plain to be seen "that times is not as they used to was." But our progress ever so slow if we get along at all (as Brush wisely remarked) we shall get somewhere, sometime or other; so in the course of time we arrived at the Port of Matzatlan.

There had been a flying report that our Old Man, placing great confidence in the war rumors, would lay off and on with the Ship and send a boat in under English colors, to see how the land lay. This report had kicked up a considerable of a growl among the Old Salts, who bitterly complained of such a maneuver, swearing it was a shame to put such a craft as ours under false colors, and when told it was policy and justifiable stratagems in war, would damn all such policies and stratagems up in heaps and bring up the Old Motto "that honesty is the best policy" in support of their side of the question. There was not however any occasion to try their patience further than by report, for when we came into the Anchorage, the Stars and Stripes floated at our peak, and over the head of the first Officer and Boats Crew that went on shore the same colors waved, thus entirely satisfying the Old Growls in every particular.

While the boat was absent, conjecture was rife, forming all sorts of yarns, and the coppers were filled to overflowing, but by dint of almost superhuman exertion Jesse prevented any of them from getting adrift. In due time the boat returned, and soon after through the listening ears and gaping mouths of Cabin and Ward Room boys it was generally known about that Texas was annexed, that Mexico had not a word to say (for fear of Capt Stockton's big gun, that was cruising in the Gulf ready to blow them up) that Genl. Jackson was dead, and that the American Consul was coming on board to breakfast in the morning. Combining all these things together, it was carried "nem con" that we should not lay long here, nor were our anticipations disappointed for in the course of the day, we hove up and proceeded on our way to the no small satisfaction of all the Jacks, who did not much relish the idea of laying so far from town.[2]

2. On March 1, 1845, Congress, by joint resolution, had offered to annex Texas. On July 4 Texas accepted and on December 29 following was admitted into the Union.

"Capt. Stockton's big gun" was Downey's reference to an enormous gun which Captain Robert F. Stockton had designed and installed in the Navy's first screw-propelled steamship, the U.S.S. *Princeton*. When Stockton's "big gun" was being publicly demonstrated for the first time in February, 1844, it exploded, killing Abel P. Upshur, Secretary of State under Tyler, and several other dignitaries. At the time of Downey's writ-

It had leaked out, that we were to proceed first to San Blas for wood and water, and if we should fail in procuring the necessary supplies there, we were to go on down to Mansinilla, and if fortune should be against us there, thence to Acapulco, and after having filled up, return again to Matzatlan and there await the arrival of the Commodore. We had the same monotonous time of it, the only change being that it grew hotter and hotter as we got to the Southward, and the patience of every one seemed stretched to its utmost tension; one strain more and it must surely snap.

In the course of time, we arrived at the place where San Blas should be, and great was the anxiety evinced, and awful the strain upon the eyes of the several look outs, to discover the locality of a celebrated White Rock. We knew it must be somewhere about the place where we now were, and spy glasses, eye glasses and all other sorts of Glasses, were flying fore and aft at a great rate and it seemed plain enough even to the dullest mind, that if said rock ever was to be seen, there was but small chance of escape for it now. Of course there was not. Why at 12M they had shot the sun, and by means of parallel ruler and compass, had brought the Ship right here and the rock right there. Now then could it happen otherwise, than that we should see it (when we got near enough)? Now all the Navigators had been gazing and peeping away for dear life, and yet when a little before sunset, it was discovered, they said it was just where they expected it would be and that they had only worked themselves into the state of anxiety, as a precautionary proceeding.

When at last we did see Rock No. 1 we ran boldly in for the land, keeping a bright look out for White Rock No. 2, which was said to be directly off the mouth of the harbor, or rather river for harbor there is none and were it not for the name of the thing, we might as well be at sea, as at anchor. We ran in until it began to grow dark, and as there were no signs of White Rock No. 2, our old man determined to heave her too and wait for the moon to rise. This was no doubt a very salutory measure, yet I heard not a few laughing at the idea, saying they had heard of heaving a Ship too for almost all sorts of things, and we had even in this Ship hove too when on the line for a squall to come up, and now to end all things, we were going to

---

ing, the *Princeton* was sailing in the Caribbean. See E. B. Potter, editor, *The United States and World Sea Power* (Edgewood Cliffs, New Jersey, 1955), pp. 263–265.

Andrew Jackson's death had occurred on March 15, 1845.

heave too for the moon. Growling was of no use. The Old Man had said, so, and so it must be, and though many a wistful eye was cast towards the hammocks and thence to the Officer of the Deck no such good news was heard. All hands were called to bring ship to Anchor, and stations you must keep until you are piped down, even if there were no chance of anchoring for a whole month.

In due time of course the moon did rise, and having risen, condescendingly threw her bright rays slantindicularly upon White Rock no. 2, who was now apparent Enough, to all who chose to look upon him. This was cheering and all sail was made on the Ship to beat up to the Anchorage, we having while lying too drifted far down to the leeward. Fate was however against us, the wind had died away almost stark calm, and after a deal of humbugging, we at last down Mudhook, and held on what we had got. We were at anchor it is true, but in port or near port we were not, and to add to our trouble, someway or other during the muss the White Rock had changed to a Brown One, and whether we were even here or not was almost a mystery. At all events we should have to lay where we were until a breeze should spring up and enable us to exert our propelling qualities.

Having come to a conclusion upon this all important point, hammocks were piped down and in a very short space of time, it had become a matter of no importance to a large majority as to where we were, they being busily engaged in balling off sleep. When day broke, and all hands were called, the rock was again changed and looked as blue as the most violent "Anti-Temperance" man, that ever swigged a drop of New England, but nothing daunted, the 4th Cutter was called away and taking the Stewards, shoved off, bound to Market, while the 2nd Cutter being hoisted out and manned, was soon despatched with the seine after fish. Poor fellows, the crews of both had a hard time of it; the 4th Cutter having to pull somewhere near 20 miles before she found the town, and the fishermen, who after pulling nearly the same distance returned after all with fishermans luck, (ie) naked posteriors, and hungry interiors.

Meantime the other boats were got out, and the Carpenter, mustering every axe, saw and hatchet, collected a volunteer gang and started ashore to procure wood and water. Late in the afternoon they too returned, having it is true loaded their boats with green wood, but seen no water. The accounts too that they gave of the quantity and ferocity of the natives (Sand Flies and Mosquitoes) would have deterred another gang from venturing again on such an expedition. There was not one among the whole crowd, who had escaped, and such another scratching, rubbing and cursing of Native Americans it was never my lot to hear before. Wood being bad here and water worse, no one was at all displeased to hear "in Boats and up Anchor."

Our next chance was Mansinilla, and though no one had ever been there, yet with the habit of hoping so common to the Sailor we all painted a bright picture for it, and were sure it must be a good place, and of course must abound with fish, and would afford us a chance to fill up our barrels which were now at a low tide. Thus in forming pleasant conjectures we passed the time away. It was but 180 miles from San Blas to Mansinilla and we had a fair wind, what there was of it, so we amused ourselves any way we could and hoped for the best. We had but very indifferent charts of the place and such was the sameness of the coast, that it was a matter of some difficulty to determine where the port was at all, so we were obliged to coast along and trust to luck. After a deal of discussion on the subject, it was decided one evening just as the sun had set, that it appeared that we had hit the place; a boat was accordingly lowered and the Master entering her she shoved off on a voyage of discovery.

In the course of an hour the boat returned and her crew, in answer to the many enquiries made as to what sort of place it was, seemed to exhaust their stock of good words (and they were not a few) in describing the beauties of the harbor. It was such a nice land locked place, such a fine landing, and as for fish, there was no end to them, the bay was fairly swarming with them, and in fact they could hardly pull the boat along they were so thick. Every body was in extacies at the description given of this beautiful place, and as the hour was too late for us to venture in, we stove off and on and felicitated ourselves upon the anticipated happiness of the morrow. As a matter of course, in due time as the Earth revolved, the day broke, and our head was again turned towards the land, and though our progress was but slow, yet 'twas sure, and we were all happy.

About 3 P.M. all hands were called to bring ship to Anchor, the usual bustle ensued and as our beauty shot into her berth all were lavish in their praises of the beauty of the place. The constant stir in which all hands were kept, furling sails and getting out boats &c. gave no one any opportunity of noticing that there were *small* but *strong* bitters among the sweets, in the shape of myriads of sand flies, who now paid their respects to us. They were the first native Mexicans that had visited us, and they came in the most unceremonious manner possible. For though they were all descended from a very high estate (ie, from the tops of the mountains) yet there was no show of side boys or piping of the Side for them: Oh no, they came on board, very quietly and the first intimation you would have of their presence would be in the shape of a severe nip, and if your eyes were not uncommonly sharp, ten chances to one, if you would be able to detect the offender.

As soon as the work was over, awnings spread, and the fishing gang, seine and all off, the few who were left on board repaired to the Top Gallant Forecastle, to catch the first breeze and loaf away an hour or two in exchanging opinions as to the state of affairs in general, the weather, the prospect of war, the quality of the land hereabouts, and in fact almost any subject that might be started. Now commenced the real sport (forgive me shipmate for calling that sport, which was such agony to you) but I leave it to yourself if the reminiscence is not laughable, for the gnats had rendezvoued on board in millions and as they of course, like all impertinent persons, took a part in the discussion, their remarks became so pointed and made such lasting impressions that in the course of an hour it was voted, "nem con," that however opinion might differ on other subjects yet upon that of the disagreeable companionship of these natives there was no room for doubt, and they were unanimously voted a great *bore.*

The fish lines having been dangling over the bows for near an hour, and even the most experienced of all our fishermen having failed in getting even a bite except from the gnats, a spirit of discontent broke out, which from suppressed murmers, and execrations, soon proceeded to loud cussing, and until this time unheard of anathemas, upon Mexico and all its inhabitants. Coming events they say cast their shadows before, and if we might call this first draft the shadow and judge from the trouble they occasioned what the events in the shape of hungry musquitoes would turn out to be, any person with even a *small* share of common sense might see that our future prospects were any thing but agreeable. 8, 1 2 & 3 Bells were struck and still no signs of supper, as there were so many men away in boats and it was useless to make a Dozen messes of it. Jack will growl heartily if anything occurs to delay his meal hour even for a short time, and now the delay extending to a most unreasonable length, connected with the Causes already mentioned, gave him as he thought cause sufficient to growl to his hearts content.

Somewhere near 5 Bells the boats having all returned Empty (the fishermen because there were no fish to be caught, and the watermen because they could not land for the surf) supper was piped, and during the mastication of that meal, the various discoveries made were retailed out, and the future prospect discussed. It was settled by a large majority that there were no fish to be caught here, but that as wood and water were plenty we might make some stay in fact the orders were passed for the launchers and 1st Cutters to stand by to go away at daylight in the morning. As one by one they finished their meal so also they silently repaired to the upper deck, leaving fair field for the Berth Deck Cooks to clear up, and hoping for some small relief from the heat by the land breeze.

The breeze came, but such a little one, could scarcely feel it, yet with it, oh horror of horrors, in close companionship came those most awful of all the awful plagues of a hot climate, the Musquitoes. They came in countless swarms first from the mountains and no doubt deeming any thing in their waters a lawful prize, they fastened on to us, nor could their hold be broken save by death, and even then the sting was left. They seemed to be half famished and in sooth, I believe that no one of them had ever had a meal of genuine Yankee blood in their lives, and we, being the first of that notable race that they had ever fallen in with, they were determined to rescue the name of Mexican from the stain which has rested on it since the battle of San Jacinto, and prove that cowards though they were, they would do their best to take our Yankee Man of War. Yes take us they did, and by storm too—they boarded us on all quarters, and though millions were sacrificed in the attempt, the cry was "Still they Come," and it really seemed that for every one killed, twenty fresh hands would spring up.

Hammocks were piped down, though but very few were foolish enough to take them, or even make an effort to discend to the berth Deck. The Forecastle, both Gangways, the Poop, Booms, Quarter Boats, and all three of the Tops were filled with panting crowds, all puffing and blowing, slapping and cussing, and truly so melancholy, and yet laughable sight, it was never my lot to behold. I am luckily one of those beings to whom these insects cause no annoyance, and though *they* could not prevent me from sleep, yet between the extreme heat, and the constant ire of hard words, odd expressions, and grotesque movements about me, I was unable to close my eyes for the whole night. It seems a cruel and I know by sad experience, that it is an aggravating thing to laugh at the misfortunes of others, but had even the benevolent Howard himself been on our forecastle that eventful night, I am sure he could not have forborne from laughing. Turn which way you would, the same song would assail your ears, and the slapping was as general and regular, as that heard in the pit of a crowded theatre upon the debut of a favorite. Ever and anon some poor fellow would poke his head above the rest of the mob, and beginning with a curse upon the musquitoes end with a prayer for a little, ever so little breeze, but before he could finish, his woe begone phiz would cause a roar of laughter from all around, even though they too were martyrs, which would so irritate him that he would with hopeless despondency, at last join in their mirth, and sink back in utter despair.

Native wit if any exists is sure to be brought out, on such occasions as this, and the outre expressions flying about our decks proved that we had no small share in our barky. Among so many it is almost impossible to select any particular ones, but for the sake of depicting as nearly as possible upon paper a scene, which I am sure will never fade from the minds of those who had the misfortune to be actors therein, I shall select one or two, as a sample of what was flying about decks. Very soon after 8 Bells, I could hear my old friend Ratlin, as he wandered to and fro exercising all his ingenuity in inventing outre cusses upon them. He had tried all means within the reach of his fertile imagination to keep them off but in vain, and at last, in utter despair, he had donned a suit of *white,* and in this rig, defied them to do their worst. He came to me about 10 P.M. and very gravely assured me, that being thin in flesh, he had a strong notion of hiring himself out for a Musquito Trap, for said he, when they light upon me and enter their bills, they go through the little meat there is there, and even into my bones and there they stick fast, so that when he had thus secured a lot of 'em he could roll over, and smash 'em by the million. He had often read about Samson, who killed the ten thousand Phillistines with a Jaw bone of an ass but always thought they rather stretched the yarn but now he began to believe it was true, for he, who was not half the man Samson was, had killed ten million mexicans with only one roll of an Ass (for ass I was ever to come here.)

Between 5 and 6 Bells I took a cruise round the Berth Deck, and the various sights and sounds that assailed my eyes and ears defied all description. You would hear some fellow at one moment snoring away lustily, at the next you would see his hand fall heavily upon some part of his naked body, and a curse upon all Mexico, and Mexicans as long as the Main Top Bowline would follow. In another moment, whap he would come out of his hammock on to the deck, and making a desperate dive for the hatch up he would go.

As I struck the deck I was somewhat startled by the appearance of Old Wheel the *windy* man, who notwithstanding he possessed an infinite quantity of good humor, had now found cause to exhaust his stock, and with a sweeping imprecation upon the heads of the enemy, had left his bed and board, and with no other covering, save a blanket, thrown round his shoulders, was wending his way towards the upper regions in search of some relief. I do not remember having ever previous to this occasion, addressed a question to Wheel without receiving in return a civil answer. But now the case was changed, and upon my making the inquiry as to "how he was," was answered only with a surly growl, and a heartfelt "Go to hell—don't bother me" Why Wheel said I "are they so bad?" "Oh by Heavens yes, they have taken me by storm, they have occupied every hole and corner of me—I lay there like a damn fool with my mouth open, and they have gone down inside of me, and filled me chock a block. I'm bound off for the scuttle butt, to drink a gallon or two and try if I can drown them out. If we stay here another night, I shall take a Boatswains Chair, and sling myself under water up to my chin."

One poor Dutchman who slung near the Galley, endured the torment in silence as long as possible, and at last in utter agony, groaning out—"Oh Mein Got—d – – n ze musquitoes—I would ten time rather sleep in Hornets-nest," evacuated the premises. But there was no cause to complain about fair play, for the groups of Officers who were sculling round decks proved that they were no respectors of rank or dignity. The Forecastle was crowded with a group smoking and slapping, while now and then a heavy curse upon native mexicans would be heard loud above the other conversations. The Poop had a number laid upon it, both quarter boats were full, and to crown the whole our Old Man was up and off, pacing the quarter deck with the speed of a Quarter Horse. Skizics who had heard from some person that if you greased yourself, they would not trouble you, called upon his body servant and stripping himself caused said servant to take a pound of butter and slush him fore and aft.

Such was the state of affairs, when at Midnight a boat was manned with a volunteer crew, with the avowed purpose of hunting for turtle; they returned at an early hour of the morning, and though they caught no turtle, 'twas evident from their looks and actions, that they had found something equally as strong—

At daylight more for the sake of form, than use all hands were called, and the Launch and 1s Cutter ordered away for water, cusses began to reign predominant when—hark what sound is that belay—belay—belay—that augers well—Strike the Casks in board—Stand by to Hoist in the boats. This was good news, and we could have given three cheers with hearty good will, the yard and stay were manned, and never did the boats seem half as light as on that eventful morning—

As soon as the sea breeze set in, we got underway and though a large number of the varmints still hung on board, yet by dint of a thorough fumigation, under the direction of our Medico, and a wholesale murder, wherever they were seen, aided by a strong breeze, we at last got clear of them. The Horrors of that night were however long after talked of, and many a joke cracked at the expense of the USS *Portsmouth* which with her smart crew was fairly beaten off by Musquitoes.

Mazatlan

THE READER must not suppose by the heading of this article, that I am about to give any detailed or geographical description of this Port—No, far from that—my Book only purports to be a detail of Incidents that occurred on board Ship, and as such, I shall confine myself to the Ship board altogether. In my last chapter, I had brought my readers to the verge of a Court Martial and before however, the Court had been called, another victim was added to the dish, and in this wise—The Launch had been ashore watering, and most of her crew had of course moistened their clay, even to soaking: Among the rest was one, who had long been an object to *pick* upon, and of course when he came over the Gangway he was forthwith marshalled at the Mast, and after a severe inspection Legs and the Corporal of the Guard were ordered to convey him to the Brig.[1]

Jack felt quite lively and during his progress forward, cut up some extra shines in the Gangway, which somewhat daunted the worthies who had charge of him, and, sad to relate, as he passed the forward Bitts, the Lanyard of his Knife caught the end of the Bitt Pin, and drew the Knife from the sheath. Poor Legs, in an agony of fear flew back, the Corporal drew a Cutlass and the pair of them sung out for help at the top of their lungs. Jack, too drunk to notice their dismay rolled along and fell at full length in the Brig. and there remained as quiet as a Lamb. Legs ran aft and made his report, that, "the sanguinary Tar had attempted his precious life" and the Autocrat then and there preferred charges of "Mutiny" against the poor devil. This completed the number of cases from our ship at the coming court. Meanwhile, matters went on much the same as before, annoyance was the order of the day, and all Hands were as unhappy as the man in the power of the Autocrat could make them.

At length the court went into session, and for three weeks, day after day, the court martial Flag was displayed each day from the foremast head of the *Constitution*.[2] One day, after the trial of one of the poor fellows from our Ship, Peak was summoned to the presence of the Autocrat; and then and there ordered in the most peremptory manner to procure materials and write a *defence* for those who had already been tried. It was in vain that he protested against such a proceeding, saying that as he had heard none of the evidence he could not be supposed to be in any manner conversant with the merits of the case, and consequently that he would be unable to do justice to the accused. He was told that his excuses were of no use, that it was the Captain's orders and that write he must. Finding all remonstrance useless, he prepared for the task, and having been

1. This was undoubtedly James Welch who was consigned to the brig and later court-martialed. "Log of the *Portsmouth*," November 4, 1845; March 6 and 12, 1846.

2. The United States frigate *Constitution* (44 guns) served as the headquarters for the court-martial mentioned above.

allowed the privilege of communicating with the prisoner, he gathered as much of the evidence as the prisoner could recollect, and then clothing the prisoners own ideas in language of his own, endeavor his best, to produce a defence that should influence as much as possible the members of the court in his favor.

As a matter of Course when anything of this sort is done on board Ship all hands are agog to see the production of a fellow tar, and, after a fair copy was made and dispatched to the Court, the original was read and re-read to many admiring audiences. However small its merit might have been, it was sure to come in for a full share of praise from the Jacks, and from them its merits were soon blazoned forth. The Warrant Officers requested a perusal, and at last it found its way into the Ward Room. No sooner had it been perused in that apartment, than outward signs of a blow up were discovered. It contained too many home made truths to be easily swallowed, and a scheme was laid at once to ruin the innocent author thereof by fair means, *or foul*. It was well known throughout the Ship, that he had been, during the whole cruise, keeping a series of sketches of any Incidents of note that occurred, and it became at once a desideratum to procure his papers.

His good Genius, however, did not fail him at this critical moment. One of the Boys had heard an order given to search for the Papers known to belong to *Peak* and straightway came forward and informed him of the fact, so that he had a chance of securing them before the search continued. Every nook and corner where papers could have been concealed, was carefully overhauled, spies were set, and all means devised to discover where they were secured, but to no purpose; nothing could be discovered. At the close of the first day, it was rumored about that various and many conferences were held between Legs and the Autocrat, and soon after, first one and then another were seen to dive into the Ward Room, and, after a short conference, the whole of which was committed to paper, to slip mysteriously out again.

Legs, the Ship's Corporal, and one of the Marine Sergeants too, were engaged might and main in the cause, and could be seen, from morn till night, sculling about decks, peeping and prying into all corners, and stealing up, when a Knot of two or three were talking together, endeavoring to pick up something with which they might hurry off to their Patron. By dint of hard raking and scraping, they at last gathered a mass of something, which they thought would answer their purpose and at the close of the second day, Peak was summoned to the Mast, and thus addressed by the Autocrat— "D – – – I have been informed that you have taken certain papers, said to be defences, which were in fact, libels upon the Officers of this Ship, and, before they became Public Papers, by being accepted by the court, you have read them to various portions of the Ship's Company, thereby tending to throw much discredit upon the Officers, for which I am going to try you by a Court Martial."

"Very good, Sir," said Peak.

"I repeat—I am going to try you by a Court Martial—your intentions in reading the—"

"Stay, Sir," said Peak in a respectful manner, "you cannot know what my intentions were, you only know my actions—let the court judge of my intentions."

"Confine him."

Peak was at once conveyed to the Brig, and then commenced one of the most curious series of actions ever transacted on board any ship in the service. The Brig was under the Larboard side of the Top Gallant Forecastle, and as soon as Peak was incarcerated, the Upper and Lower Ports were shut in; all passing to and fro on the part of the Crew on the Larboard side was forbidden. No one was allowed to speak to or even look [at] the Prisoners. Nothing, even Bags, Hammocks or Grub [was] allowed to be passed to them except through the Corporal [of] the Guard, and strict orders were even given to allow of [no conversation] between the Prisoners, and the Corporal was ordered to take a position underneath the Hammocks and report any conversation which might take place between those confined. In spite, however, of all their efforts, they did not discover any thing which would assist them in their *holy* purpose, and consequently determined to go forward upon the capital they had amassed, and do their best. Consequently, the charges were fully made out and forwarded to the hands of the Commodore for his approval.

Meantime the sentences of the Court upon those who had been tried were sent to our Commander, and he resolved to have them carried into execution one at a time. One evening Legs came to the Brig and handed a paper to one, which upon opening proved to be the sentence. His punishment was to be *100 Lashes* upon the *Bare*

Back with the Cats. On the following morning, at 2 Bells the awful call of "all Hands Witness Punishment" was heard. The Prisoner was taken out, and after a long Preamble his sentence was read in a formal manner, and he was ordered to strip.[3]

From time immemorial, when a man has been condemned to such a punishment as this, custom has allowed that it be laid on in as light a manner as a decent regard for the Court would allow, or in other words that the sufferer's back be mangled as little as possible. In pursuance of this ancient and honorable custom, when the Boatswains Mates commenced their work, they of course favored him as much as possible. What was then the astonishment and dismay of all Hands when our Christian-like Commander ordering them to stop, marshalled them before him, and addressed them in this wise "I know that the punishment is painful to you, and torture to the Prisoner. But still the Majesty of the Law must be upheld, and I require of you to inflict upon that man as heavy a punishment, as if he were to receive only *one dozen*. You must not, shall not, favor him; if you do, I shall punish you in the same manner I am now punishing him. Go on now, take your time—Clear your Cats—and do your duty." After such an admonition what could they do? They obeyed orders and the back of the wretched victim, when taken down after having received the One Hundredth Lash, was one mass of raw flesh from his neck to his waist. Isnt this a libel upon the Christian Character?

Two or three mornings after the imprisonment of Peak, the Autocrat came forward, and stationing himself on the starboard side of the Forecastle, gazed upon him, and audibly grinned his satisfaction, at having trapped him. Peak however, conscious of his own innocence [mutilated] a moment betrayed by nod or look that he saw him, but continued to pace up and down in the Brig in an animated conversation with his fellow prisoner. This seeming indifference cut the Autocrat to the quick and one morning, after a longer survey than usual, he walked Aft and sending the Corporal forward, paraded poor Peak at the Mast and thus addressed him:

"For two or three mornings past I have observed that whenever I have come forward, you have commenced walking in the Brig and have put on an insolent, impudent look."

3. This was James Welch, earlier accused of attacking Master at Arms, John Morgan, with a knife. The Log reads: "Punished James Welch (O. Sea.) with 100 lashes of cat by order of court martial." "Log of the *Portsmouth*," March 12, 1846.

"Why sir," said Peak, "my looks must belie me sorely, for I have no such feelings. I know that I am innocent of the crimes charged against me and consequently cannot, merely because I am confined, put on the look of a criminal—I look pleased because I feel happy."

"Well Sir," said the Autocrat, "if I see any more such looks upon your countenance, I will make them another charge against you, and moreover will put you in Solitary Confinement."

What small, what petty means, did not this man descend to in order to annoy one, who was in *rank* so much his inferior. Thus time rolled on, and for two weeks was his victim confined awaiting patiently the trial; but it could not last forever, and at the expiration of the fortnight, one bright Thursday morn the prisoner was called to the Mast and then and there the commander read to him a letter received from the Commodore enclosing the Charges, *unsanctioned,* in which he informed him that he had perused the Charges made by Lt. M against D – and that *he* could not discover in them sufficient cause to bring him before the Court. Moreover that the exigencies of the service demanded the departure of our Ship, consequently there would not be time to try the case. He therefore authorized him (the Commander) to investigate the case himself, and if *he* found sufficient cause, to remand the Prisoner to confinement until the Squadron should meet again, or otherwise, to punish him at his own discretion.

Having gone through with this ceremony, he then went on to read the charges which were to all outward appearance heavy enough to have hung poor Peak. They consisted of "Mutiny," "Insubordination" and "Lying." The Autocrat read them over in a very pompous manner, and then began saying that he could prove the first Charge by such and such witnesses, naming over a sufficient number to have demonstrated the case as clear as noon day. Peak, though somewhat astonished at the serious turn affairs had taken, was nothing daunted. He knew that he had read the papers as charged, and he also knew that his intentions in doing were not to excite Mutiny or Insubordination, but merely [mutilated] those of his Shipmates who had curiosity enough to listen to them. He therefore told the Captain that there was no necessity for examining any witnesses. He did not deny the specification, which was, "having read certain papers" but he did most solemnly deny the intention imputed, *viz.* "Mutiny," and that all the evidence in the world could only prove a man's actions, not his intentions. This was a sort of *poser* and consequently they allowed this charge to go by default, and changed it to that of *Disrespect*.

The second charge was a very unexpected one, *viz.* "Lying." This was attempted to be proven by one of the Marines, a poor pitiful thing who had willingly lent his services to involve one who had never injured him. This man it seems, had upon learning, that witnesses were in great requisition, had volunteered his information which was found to be of a very important nature, and it consisted of this—He had been on post one day, and while *diligently performing his duty,* had heard the Prisoner (previous however to his confinement) in conversation with some messmates, say that "he (the 1st Lieut) had sent to the Prisoner for a copy of the papers, and that the Prisoner had refused to send them to him."

Oh monstrous Offence—Peak had said he would not allow the Autocrat to see certain libellious papers. Here was evidence enough to hang him instanter. This charge was a clincher, Peak could not in good faith, deny the charge, because he knew nothing about it. He might have said so, or he might not, he had said a great many things he could not remember and as in his humble opinion, *Instant death* would not follow a confession, he allowed the charge, and gave the Autocrat the full benefit of it.

Having thus plead guilty to at least one of the mighty charges alledged against him, it now remained with the commander to decide whether they were in his opinion of sufficient importance to warrant him in keeping Peak a Prisoner until the Squadron should meet again. Here again the Autocrat, who had seemingly forgotten the virtuous indignation he had exhibited when he confined Peak, and whose view upon the enormity of the Offence had warped most awfully since the Commodore had said he could not see sufficient cause, put in his oar, and suggested that he thought it was not worth while to keep Peak confined upon Pay and that he should like to see the case disposed of.

"Oh Yes, Oh Yes," said the Old Man, "we will dispose of it—he has now been confined 2 weeks—if there is not sufficient cause to bring the case before the court, it appears to me that he has been suspected wrongfully, and consequently we will discharge him and send him to his duty with a reprimand."

"But," hinted the Autocrat, "if *we* let him go thus easily, the whole ship's Company will laugh at us, and it will bring much discredit on us—we must punish him in some manner, and for some Offence."

"Oh Yes, Oh Yes [mutilated] *we* will punish him," said Capt M –. "Call all Hands to witness Punishment." The Hands were accordingly turned up, the grating rigged, and Peak received a round dozen, which was duly logged as being for "Insubordination and Lying" but which was in truth for no other Offence than that he was in the Brig, under heavy charges, a great deal of fuss had been made to get him there; much time and paper had been wasted in forming a set of charges sufficiently strong; the Spies had been busy in spreading the news fore and aft, that he was at last caught foul, and that nothing short of 200 would be his doom.[4] The majority of the crew not knowing the true state of the case, had begun to think there was some truth in the yarns, and so, if they had let him go scott free, the Ship's Company would *laugh* at the Autocrat. But the infliction of the dozen did not save him, for all hands were aware that he must have been outlawed in some way, or else he would never have let Peak off so easy, and in consequence when the facts of the case became known, the laugh was against him, and Peak was looked upon as a sort of Martyr, who had suffered for the good of his fellow Shipmates. Thus ended the famous attempt to try a Man, for having literally obeyed orders, the manner of whose obedience, showed to the world more of the internal machinery of the Ship *Portsmouth* than suited the views of her rulers.

Peak had heretofore written the Ship's Log, and kept the key of the library. Now, however, these were taken from him; he was positively forbidden to touch pen or pencil to paper, for himself or anyone else in the Ship, and the *Tool* and his *myrmidons,* Legs and the Ship's Corporal, were ordered to keep Peak forward of the Mainmast on the Berth Deck and to watch him closely, and if he was seen with pen or pencil in his hand to report the same forthwith. They had him down to a small helm, but still he held his own; despite all their watchfulness, they could never catch him foul, or discover where those mighty papers were secreted.

Previous to this scrape, there had been quite a correspondence or war of words carried on between Peak and a Fore Topman, belong-

4. "Joseph T. Downey—12—lying and insubordination." "Log of the *Portsmouth,*" March 26, 1846.

ing to the *Levant,* in which the wit of both was often much drawn upon, and so caustic had their effusi[ons] become, that these "jeu d'esprit's" were most anxiously looked for by all parties. In the search for Peak's papers they had come across a Blank Book, which contained a number of these things done in a rough manner, but so guarded that they could not torture them into any offence. They were read and re-read, sworn at, and laughed over in the Ward Room, but the hidden meaning could never be fathomed, and consequently they were given over, but the copies were retained in the possession of some one of the Gentlemen. The embargo upon Literature of course put an end to all [mutilated] pleasantries of this kind. The Autocrat was aware of this, he knew it was a source of amusement, and in pursuance of his system of annoyance, he issued the order which stopped it forever.

About this time rumors of the coming war passed thick and fast upon us; every day brought some new yarn, and mystery was the order of the day. Visions of hard fought battles and lots of Prize Money began to flit before our eyes, though one half of the sad realities we afterward experienced never entered the noddles of any one. The *Constitution* was about to sail for home, and many of our Lads whose times were out, or nearly so, and some, who had gaind the name of hard cases, applied for permission to exchange with some of her men, who preferred remaining on the station. Permission was granted, and in consequence a great exchange took place—some of which were for the better and some precisely the other way.[5]

Amongst others who were exchanged off was one of the unfortunates, whose age alone excused him from trial by court martial—he had always been a trouble to our Autocrat and I verily believe he was glad to get rid of him, especially when he saw the heavy two fisted fellow who was to be sent in his place. But awful was his disappointment when he found that the substitute was as bad as his own man. He loved liquor a deal better than Johnny P – – – – and

5. By the time the *Portsmouth* had reached California the previous fall, it was obvious that a distinct clique of hard-drinking troublemakers existed among the ship's crew. Among them were Daniel Coakley, five times whipped for various offenses in the past eighteen months; James Welch, who had been guilty of desertion, fighting, and drunkenness; and George W. Adams and John Pearsall who had similar records. Montgomery and his staff must have been greatly relieved to learn that all of these men, and some eight others, wanted to return to the States by transferring to the *Constitution.* "Log of the *Portsmouth,*" March 22, 1846.

was more trouble when under its influence.[6] He was about to refuse to receive him, but the pleadings of poor *Nation* and his solemn promises of reformation, so operated upon the feelings of the Autocrat that he at last consented that he might come, but he must promise that he would turn over a new leaf. "Nation," "Chimes" or B – – – –, for by either of these cognomens was he known, would have readily sworn to turn over anything in the world to get out of that ship, and having faithfully promised to reform, was at length transferred bag and hammock, and speedily became a great favorite with our mirth-loving customers.[7]

Ah Chimes, many and many a poor devil's side have you caused to ache, with laughter, as you have bewailed your unhappy lot and spun yarns of former life in the gangways. Wherever the crowd was large and the laughter most voiceferous, you might be sure that "Chimes" was there, holding forth most eloquently. Truly to use your own words, you did "lead a miserable life" on board this barkey, and though many of us missed you much when you left, yet all were glad for your sake that you escaped from the clutches of our Autocrat.

And Sergeant Slim too—he came with this exchange—Oh! you fund of amusement—you ghost of an antiquated Brown Stick Squilgee Handle or Bean Pole, in what quarter of the world [mutilated] you roost now.[8] Shade we cannot call thee—for there is not enough of thee to make a shadow. Dost thou remember that eventful night you first joined us? when thy hammock did play thee such a trick and explose those *Canes* of [mutilated] an unreasonable manner, when thy awful plight drew down upon thee the caustic tongue of our Jack Ratline, whose remarks thereon caused a roar of Laughter from one end of the Birth Deck to the Other, when even the "Mokes" in the "black sea" caught the infection, and laughed so long and strong at thee, as to raise thy Ebenezer, and almost provoke thee to go forward and chastise them? Oh Sergeant, Sergeant, the memory of that night will never fade from our mind, and ever and

6. This was undoubtedly John Pearsall.

7. "Nation," "Chimes," or B – – – seems to have been James Brown. "Log of the *Portsmouth*," March 22, 1846.

8. Although Sergeant Slim comes to figure prominently in various of Downey's sketches, it has been impossible to identify him with absolute certainty. He appears to be Sergeant George Miller, of the Marine detachment aboard the *Portsmouth*.

anon, as we recall the past, our cachinations are long and loud, and our side aches, in retrospection. We introduce you to the reader now, and shall in the course of our Cruise have many happy yarns to relate of you and your adventures.

Our exchanges however were not all happy ones, and we lost many a sincere friend, and good shipmate by it. Often and often have we sighed in vain for the cheerful voice of Charley R – – – – and his volatile chum W. H. P – – – – many and many a night have we walked the Lee Gangway and ever and anon, while wandering in the fields of fancy, imagine that we heard the well known voice of Jesse B – – – –. Even thee, Lawyer F – – – –, we have wished for, but wished in vain. You had your choice to go or stay, and we fondly hope you were satisfied.[9]

After all the exchanges were made, things soon relapsed into their own quiet way again, and war became the order of the Day. It soon was noised about that we were (that is the Squadron) to take the Port and town of Mazatlan. How the report came no one knows, but it gained great credence among the Country people, and the Consequence was they began to leave in crowds, and the poor city was nearly deserted. Every little craft that could steal out to sea did so, and those which could not be gotten out were warped into the inner Harbor, and even high up the little river where we were accustomed to fish. The whole squadron was now gathered together and lay waiting orders from home.

Towards the last of March something came, what we Jacks never knew; but on the strength of it we, the Portsmouth's, were ordered to be ready for sea in a few days. All was now conjecture as to our probable destination, some had Callao, some the Islands, some Columbia River, while a few, and very few too, predicted that Monterey would bring us up. Monterey, Oh! Blessed Monterey! the visions of Mackerel that the mention of thy name brought up, caused thy champions to carry the day, and some days before we sailed it was voted "nem con" that we should proceed to thy longed for waters. Fish Lines were hunted up, hooks sharpened, and every

9. "Following transferred off ship—W. M. Wood, James Welch, Thomas Jones, Jesse Balcorn, James Pearsall, Mathew Fagan, Chas. E. Robbins, Daniel Coakley, James E. Conway, Daniel Mahoney, George W. Adams, Augustus Stevens (Went to *Const.*)." "Log of the *Portsmouth*," March 22, 1846.
"W. H. P." is not identifiable.

exertion was made to put ourselves in a complete state of preparation [mutilated] a war of extermination against the Californian fishes—alas how little did we suspect that our expedition was to end in prosecuting the war, against men, not fish. No matter, we were in happy ignorance, and on the night of the 31st of Mar., 1846, we weighed our anchors and stood out to sea, to the great relief of the whole Squadron, who had named us the "Court Martial Ship" from the fact that we had never, so far, fallen in with the Flag Ship, but what a Court Martial ensued, and to the great satisfaction of ourselves, for when we were away from the Commodore we had only our own humbug to annoy us, whilst all the time we lay within signal distance of him, we had not only our own but his to put up with.[10]

The Sch*n* *Shark* had sailed some hours ahead of us, bound for the Islands for repairs, and as we slowly dropped out of the Harbor, the Band of the Flag Ship, struck up a lively tune and off went *Old Poverty* on her weary way, leaving the rest of the Squadron to devour as much of the Mazatlan Beef as the commodore might see fit to order. We had lain in port nearly 4 months and right glad were we to get to sea once more. Time flies so much quicker at sea than in port, and there is always some change, if it is only that of the watch. Behold us, then, reader, on a bright April morn, out of sight of the Land, in a taut boline, running 9½ knots, air clear, pure and warm, every body contented and pleased to see blue water once more. The *Shark* is on our Lee Quarter, booming off for the Islands, we have got new Officers in place of 2 of our drunken Growls, and right pleased are all with the Change.[11]

Our passage up was short, and marked with no particular incident save one, and that was a mournful one, viz *death*. The grim monster crept in among us and picked out one of our youngest, and most beloved Shipmates. He was an apprentice, named Wm. H. Marshall, a quiet, goodnatured, persevering young fellow, just budding into manhood. Enemies he had none; all, all were friends to him. His complaint was a mystery to us; he went on the list after having eaten

10. The *Portsmouth* set sail April 2, 1846. "Log of the *Portsmouth*."
11. On February 15, 1846, Lieutenants Woodhull S. Schenck and Richard Forrest were dispatched from the *Portsmouth*. Their replacements were Lieutenant Joseph Warren Revere and Passed Midshipman (later Acting Master) Napoleon B. Harrison. "Log of the *Portsmouth*," February 14 and 15, 1846.

his breakfast, and the first news we had next morn, he was a corpse. So sudden was his death, that even the doctors thought he might be in a trance, and he was kept for some days, in the vain hope that he might revive.[12] But no, his time had come and we were to hear his voice no more in this world.

There seemed a sort of fatality attached to Monterey; both times we had sailed [for] this port had happened to be Friday, and both times we had [lost] a Shipmate before arriving. The weather being cool, the body of our Shipmate was kept for interment on shore. About a day subsequent to our arrival it was carried on shore, and buried in a romantic spot, 'neath the shade of some beautiful trees, there to remain till the trump of Gabriel shall summon his spirit to the Bar of God. Peace be with thee, poor Marshall—thou wert an agreeable shipmate, a dutiful son, and a fond brother. May God temper the news to the bereaved ones at home, and be this some comfort to them, he was beloved by all who knew him.

Now kind indulgent reader, I have brought you through all our little trials and troubles back again to Monterey, but sad to relate, d – – – d the fish can we find here. All, all are gone; scared no doubt by the prospect of *war*, which now seems inevitible. Here we are to water ship, get General Liberty, and wait for orders from the Flag Ship. If we receive none for a month we are to proceed to San Francisco, a port some 120 miles to the northward of this.

Here we first heard of Capt Freemont and his quarrel with Gen[l] Castro.[13] The knowing ones predict a skirmish from this, but Liberty is over, the Ship is watered, Castro has visited our Ship, the *Barnstable* has arrived from Boston in 120 days, and yet here we lay all at peace safely moored in Monterey—[14]

12. See *ibid.*, April 21 and 24, 1846.

13. Captain John C. Frémont, leading a surveying party of U.S. Topographical Engineers had come to California late in December, 1845, reaching Fort Sutter on January 15, 1846. Short of supplies and horses, he received permission from General José Castro, Commandant and Acting Governor of Northern California, to refit his forces at Monterey. Frémont, whose official purpose was merely to find a short route between the United States and the Pacific Ocean, lingered in the area so long that the suspicious Castro ordered Frémont to leave, charging that he had come to California to incite revolution. Approximately a month and a half later (April 23, 1846), the *Portsmouth* arrived at Monterey to learn of this difficulty. Allan Nevins, editor, *Narratives of Exploration and Adventure by John Charles Frémont* (New York, 1956), pp. 464–475.

14. The *Barnstable* arrived on May 8, 1846. "Log of the *Portsmouth*."

San Francisco

I GIVE THIS ARTICLE this heading, because while in this bay we transacted some of the most important acts of our cruise. It was here we first heard of war, here we hoisted the Yankee Flag—and here we won a name among Californians which will long be our boast. A new era seem'd to dawn upon us, and after the time of our arrival in Monterey, some good spirit took possession of the body of our Autocrat [Missroon], and he became another man. As I have before stated, we were to lay a month in Monterey, and then if no other orders arrived to proceed to San Francisco. We lay out our allotted time, during which Liberty was given, the Ship watered and nothing else of interest occurred, and on the 1st of June we up anchor and left that harbor bound for the North.[1]

The evening before, a fine Ship called the *Barnstable* of Boston, upon whose sailing qualities great wind was blown, had sailed for the same port, and our fellows, who wanted no better fun, had joked her crew long, and loud upon the start we would give, and beat them at last. We also took on board two passengers this trip, one of whom was a Dutch Tailer, who had emigrated to this country, but who, in his travels south in search of a location, had lost his horse, and was furthermore in deadly fear of Castro, who had by this time issued his famous proclamation against all foreigners, and had for those reasons solicited a passage to Yerba Buena in our Ship.[2]

The other was Jimmy Neal, a perfect specimin of a genuine Backwoodsman, one who had been for years in the country had ridden all over California, and could spin all sorts of yarns about Indians,

1. Downey's cheerful attitude belies the fact that on the day of departure from Monterey he received twelve lashes for being drunk on duty. *Ibid.*, April 27, 1846.

2. For the Proclamation of General Castro issued March 13, 1846, see H. H. Bancroft, *History of California* (San Francisco, 1886), v, pp. 19–20.

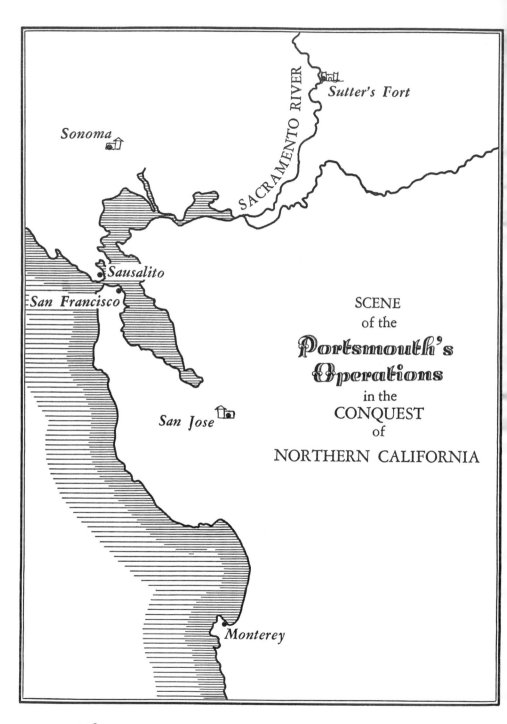

SACRAMENTO RIVER

Sutter's Fort

Sonoma

Sausalito

San Francisco

San Jose

SCENE
of the
*Portsmouth's
Operations*
in the
CONQUEST
of
NORTHERN CALIFORNIA

Monterey

Bears, and Buffaloes.[3] He was dressed in a very primitive manner, and obtained from our men the sobriquest of "Leather Legs," by which name he was known ever after during our stay in California. Jimmy had a quick perception of the ludicrous and soon found out, the foible of the Tars was to believe any thing he might relate be it ever so improbable, and taking advantage of this, he would gather a gaping crowd round him, and retail out all sorts of improbable yarns for their edification.

At, or about noon of the day on which we sailed, the *Barnstable* was descried right ahead and before 3 P.M. we had overhauled and passed her, promising to leave the news at Francisco, that she was coming—before sunset, we were off the mouth of the Harbor, but it being rather an ugly looking place to venture into by twilight, our old man hauled her off, and we stood off and on the whole night. Early next morning however, we ran in, and before 8 A.M. were snugly and safely moored at the Best watering place on the whole coast, *viz* "Sausolito" or the sweet water. The Town of Yerba Buena was on the opposite side of the Bay some 9 or 10 miles off.[4] What our future destiny is no one can tell, but at all events we must make the best of the present.

New and startling rumors now began to spread about. Capt Fremont had returned to California, had been joined by Lt. Gillespie, who was on a secret mission from the States, and was determined to

3. Samuel Neal, Downey's "Leather Legs," was a messenger entrusted with letters from Frémont and Gillespie (encamped on the Sacramento) to the U.S. Consul, Thomas O. Larkin and to Commodore Sloat at Monterey. After being detained by high water Neal reached Monterey on May 31. One of the letters requested that supplies be sent up from Yerba Buena to Frémont's forces. Consequently, on the evening of the thirty-first, Neal came on board the *Portsmouth*, which sailed the next day for San Francisco Bay. Although he arrived on June 3, Montgomery did not send supplies until June 11, by which time he may have heard of the first activities of the Bear Flag rebels, for they had stolen General Castro's horses on the morning of June 10. See T. O. Larkin to John B. Montgomery, May 31, 1846, in George P. Hammond, editor, *The Larkin Papers* (Berkeley, 1951–5), IV, pp. 406–07; Bancroft, *History of California*, v, pp. 77–187; and for another description of Neal by Downey: Fred B. Rogers, editor, *Filings from an Old Saw: Reminiscences of San Francisco and California's Conquest, by "Filings"—Joseph T. Downey* (San Francisco, 1956), pp. 25–26, 162.

Neal left the *Portsmouth* for Frémont's camp on June 3. See Fred B. Rogers, editor, *A Navy Surgeon in California, 1846–47: The Journal of Marius Duvall* (San Francisco, 1957), p. 12.

4. Sausalito actually meant "little willow." In the course of the next six months Yerba Buena comes to be called San Francisco.

chastise Castro for his insolence. In furtherance of this plan, he had sent down to us a requisition for money, stores, and ammunition, and our Launch was forthwith to be fitted out, and proceed up the Sacramento River, with the necessary supplies.[5] These rumors coupled with the great movements of cleaning, caulking and watering Ship fully occupied our time. There for the first time this cruise we had a general wash. All of the Starboard Watch were sent on shore one day, Bag and Hammock and each individual stitch of clothing and bedding was subjected to a severe ablution, and when night came all returned on board, clean and sweet from top to toe. The following day, the Larboard watch went through the same maneuver.

We had not lain here over a week when we received from the most authentic source the news of the revolution which had taken place in the upper country, or as it is properly called the Sacramento Valley.[6] As we were of course, non-combattants, and the Insurgents mostly composed of Americans, we soon had a deputation from the Californians proper, praying for our interference in the matter; and, slap upon the back of this came an emmisary from the opposite side, entreating our Old Man, if he would do nothing else, at least to re-

5. It is probable that Frémont had originally intended to come down to Yerba Buena to outfit his men directly from the *Portsmouth's* stores, but the uneasy state of things on the Sacramento demanded his presence there. Thus, after waiting some days for Frémont, Montgomery dispatched a launch on June 11 to take supplies to the Captain's camp. The launch was commanded by Lieutenant B. F. B. Hunter and he was accompanied by Purser James H. Watmough, Assistant Surgeon A. A. Henderson, and thirteen men. For a thorough account of Frémont's activities at this time see Allan Nevins, *Frémont: Pathmarker of the West* (New York, 1939). See also "Log of the *Portsmouth*," June 3 and 11, 1946.

In his "Filings from an Old Saw" Downey gives the impression that he was among the thirteen crew members who went to Frémont's camp, and he even quotes the greeting passed by Hunter and Frémont upon their meeting. Why he omitted this highly interesting episode in his original sketch is unknown, but one suspects Downey was never on the trip up the Sacramento, but got the details from a crew member who did make the journey. See Rogers, ed., *Filings from an Old Saw*, pp. 29–33.

6. More properly the revolt had occurred in the Sacramento and Sonoma Valleys. On June 10 Frémont had allowed Americans to steal horses from Castro near Sutter's Fort. A day later they seized the village of Sonoma and sent its wealthiest citizen, General Mariano G. Vallejo, off to Frémont's camp as a prisoner of war. By June 15 they had proclaimed that California was a republic and had raised the "Bear Flag" in Sonoma plaza. It was the news of these events which brought deputations to Montgomery. Ray A. Billington, *The Far Western Frontier* (New York, 1956), pp. 165–167.

main neutral.[7] This latter proceeding, to judge from appearances, was the most congenial to his feelings, and though to use his own words it was "Highly important" that he, being a Government Officer, should know something about matters, yet, as the people did not seem inclined to be communicative, it was much more important for the sake of preserving his $2500 per year, that he should not embroil himself in party affairs, he contented himself, with sending the Autocrat to Sonoma to survey the premises, and report to him how matters stood, to promise to both parties his powerful protection, and thus secure himself a seat on the fence, from which he could at any time descend, and aid the predominant party.[8]

The Autocrat accordingly started on his mission, and in due time arrived at the before mentioned place, and found the Bear Flag raised, and, barring a few prisoners who had been removed to Fort Helvetia, no further damage done.[9] Having accomplished his mission, he forthwith returned to the Ship, and we remained passive spectators of revolution, to join which, the blood of every one fore

7. Among those who were urging Montgomery to act was W. A. Leidesdorff, U.S. Vice Consul at Yerba Buena. Montgomery refused the Consul's proposal that the *Portsmouth* support the Bear Flag rebels, saying: "My position you know is neutral; I am a mear (sic) observer of passing events—looking out solely for the security and interest of our country and countrymen in an honest way." Montgomery to W. A. Leidesdorff, June 20, 1846, in the W. A. Leidesdorff Papers, MS in the Henry E. Huntington Library.

8. Here Downey revealed a complete lack of understanding of Montgomery's position. He was under the strictest orders from Sloat to maintain a neutral stand until further developments. Yet he had not only made effective efforts to remain informed, he had continued to supply Frémont on the Sacramento, by sending "carbines, cutlasses, 2 pistols; powder, ball and caps . . ." to him on June 28. And while he refused to supply the Sonoma rebels, he sent Lieutenant Missroon to Sonoma to learn of the progress of the rebellion. "Log of the *Portsmouth*," June 28, 1846.

In his 1853 "Filings" Downey was more appreciative of Montgomery's role, noting that ". . . Lieut. Missroon, was despatched to that place (Sonoma) to ascertain the truth and particulars of the story for the old man (Montgomery) was totally ignorant;—oh yes, the sly dog, he was ignorant." Rogers, ed., *Filings from an Old Saw*, p. 27. See also excerpts from Montgomery's journal as quoted in E. A. Sherman, *The Life of John Drake Sloat of the U.S. Navy* (Oakland, California, 1902), pp. i–xii.

9. If Seymour Dunbar's interpretation is to be trusted, Lieutenant Missroon arrived at Sonoma on the evening of June 16 to find the Bear Flaggers dispirited and about to call off their rebellion. The sight of his uniform, and his air of authority saved the day for the rebels. He read their Proclamation and terms of capitulation and thus raised the group from a "band of horse thieves" to the status of "revolutionaries." Seymour Dunbar, editor, "The Fort Sutter Papers," MS in the Henry E. Huntington Library.

and aft boiled. In this position of affairs we remained during the whole month of June, occasionally "sub rosa" giving a passage across the Bay to some Express rider connected with the Revolutionists.

At, on, or about the 1st of July we up anchor and stood across the Bay to the Port of Yerba Buena, where we moored ship, and made preparations to celebrate the glorious 4th. Preparations did I say? and such ones too. I was never before on board any Public Ship where the memorable anniversaries of our country were not celebrated in some unusual manner, but here save in the fact of cleaning in white, with the thermometer at Zero, and firing a salute at Meridian, no one would ever have suspected that any unusual day had rolled round.

Matters now began to wear a serious appearance; rumor upon rumor of war on the other side of the Land reached us and all communication with Monterey by Land, where we were informed the Commodore was, was denied us. We fitted out our Launch to proceed outside, and communicate with him.[10] The Launch had been gone some 4 or 5 days and we were beginning most anxiously to look for her return, when on the night of the 7th a few minutes before sundown, the Gig which had been on shore came alongside, and the Old Man his face all beaming with smiles, and his hand full of papers, came dancing over the side, and quickly himself and the Autocrat were pacing the Quarter Deck, laughing and congratulating themselves highly upon something.[11] Presently the Autocrat, popping his head down the Ward Room Hatch, said something to the Officers below, which was responded to by a Hearty Cheer. All the Jacks were Agog to find out what this good news could be, but as the Gigs crew were busily engaged hoisting up their boat, nothing could be found out from them, and such rumors as flew about decks were most outre and laughable. Some had one thing, and some another; and amongst others Sergeant Slim hazarded the remark, that

10. Commodore Sloat, aboard the *Savannah*, reached Monterey on July 2, 1846. Sherman, *Life of Sloat*, p. 71.

Four American vessels, fearing capture in case of war, anchored near the *Portsmouth* for protection on July 2. The next day Montgomery dispatched the launch under the command of Acting Master Napoleon B. Harrison to Monterey for news, and on July 5, Marines were sent ashore to protect Vice-Consul Leidesdorff and other American citizens. "Log of the *Portsmouth*," July 2–6, 1846.

11. Downey has the wrong date. News did not reach Montgomery until the evening of July 8. *Ibid.*, July 8 and 12, 1846. For a description of the effect of the news on the officers, see Rogers, ed., *Journal of Marius Duvall*, pp. 30–32.

he thought perhaps "Pork might have ris" and as the Old Man had a good supply on hand, it was likely he was going into speculation.

As soon however, as the Gig's sails were belayed the mystery was solved, for as each one of the Crew came forward he was pinned by a gaping crowd and such was the eager curiosity to hear the news that they were not allowed to get forward of the Gangway until they disgorged the whole. Out it came; and joy, patriotism and pride glowed upon each countenance as the tale was unfolded "War had at last commenced." Genl Taylor had given the Mexicans hell and taken Matamoras, Commodore Sloat had hoisted the Stripes and Stars at Monterey, and a courier had come through with orders for us to do the same here.[12]

Sleep was voted a bore, and all over the Ship might be seen knots of 8 or 10, discussing the news just received and planning out events for the future. We were well aware we should have no trouble with this port, for most of the Californians had run away when the Revolution first broke out. But how would it be in the Country? How would the Bear Flag Men like this? Capt Frecmont however, had joined and took command of them and as he was a Government Man, they would have to submit any how. The 4th Cutter was ordered to be ready to convey an officer to Sonoma to hoist the flag there, and then they were to land a party of Marines, and Carbiners on the morning of the 8th, and to hoist the Stripes and Stars upon a Flag Staff in the Public Square at 8 A.M.[13] Conversation could not

12. On May 31 Sloat heard rumors of the battles of Palo Alto and Resaca de la Palma. The rumors were officially confirmed on June 5 but he hesitated to leave for California until June 7, hoping for further confirmation and naturally for some indication that war had been officially declared. After Sloat reached Monterey he still could not bring himself to seize that port. This decision was the more difficult to make since Consul Larkin urged him to postpone action and to let the Californians invite the Americans in. Sloat's officers, full of fire and patriotism, urged taking Monterey on July 4. Finally the news of the Bear Flag Rebellion and Frémont's assumption of leadership, plus a fear that the British might seize California, forced Sloat to take Monterey on July 7. Justin Smith, *War With Mexico* (New York, 1919), I, pp. 335–336.

13. Lieutenant Joseph Warren Revere, a direct descendant of Paul Revere carried news of the declaration of war to Sonoma, and there on July 9, 1846, hoisted the American flag. "Log of the *Portsmouth*," July 9, 1846.

Downey's remark "on the morning of the 8th" is incorrect. Montgomery did not receive news of Sloat's action until the evening of the eighth when the news came overland from Monterey to Yerba Buena. Downey later corrected himself in his "Filings" articles (pp. 34–35). Lieutenant Harrison did not return with the *Portsmouth*'s launch until July 11.

however last forever, and towards midnight the several groups retired, and at last all was as silent as the grave.

Next morn at daylight, a busy scene presented itself. All Hands were ordered to clean in "White Frocks, Blue Jackets & Trowsers, Black Hats and shoes" and the Call of All Hands to Muster even collected every soul on the Quarter Deck; when the Autocrat, all smiles and bows, read the Proclamation of the Commander in Chief, as also the General Order, and then proceeded to pick out the landing party, who were to guard the Flag to its destined place.

By 7 Bells matters were all arranged, and the party of Marines and Carbineers landed on the Bank, and after being marshalled in due order, the Band, consisting of one drum and one fife, struck up Yankee Doodle, and off we marched keeping time as best we might, to conquer the redoubtable town of Yerba Buena. As we had anticipated, there was no foe to dispute our right of possession, for, save here and there a stray female face peeping from an Adobe wall, no living thing did we see, always excepting those invariable appendages to a Mexican Town, the Dogs, who looked on in mute astonishment and forgot in their wonder even to bark at us. On we went then in all the pride and pomp of Martial Array, over hill and dale, through sand and some little *mud*, until through the skillful pilotage of our Old Man, we at last found ourselves brought up all standing in a hollow square, round the Flag Staff.

Here, had time allowed, our Old Man would no doubt have inflicted a speech if not a sermon upon us, but Fate decreed to the contrary, consequently the Flag was bent on to the Halyards and by a flourishing and patronising invitation, the whole of the male population of Yerba Buena, comprising, dogs and all, some 25 or 30 souls were called into the Square. The oration was delivered, the Proclamation read, and then the Autocrat with his own hands hoisted the Colors, while three hearty cheers from the bystanders, a prolonged howl from the dogs, and a salvo of 21 Guns from the Ship completed the Affair.[14] A party of Marines was now detatched and ordered to occupy the Custom House as Barracks, and the remainder, with the Jacks, marched off for their boats in the same order they came up, the Band in the mean time making the air resound, for the first time in California, with the soul stirring melody of "Ole Dan Tucker," "It will never do to give it up so" and such like mar-

14. For the proclamation and oration see Sherman, *Life of Sloat,* pp. ii, iii, and xxii.

tial tunes. We now returned on board, and so for our part ended the first day of occupation of the town of Yerba Buena.

Not so, however with the party on shore. The Foreigners in town, consisting of some 20 or 30, formed themselves into a volunteer company, elected officers, and putting themselves into a drill school swore to defend that Flag to the last drop of Blood. By dint of hard talking and much imbibing of "Aguadiente" some of them became great warriors and, foremost among the rest stood the Dutch Baker, who was a strong admirer of the "Star Bangled Banner" as he termed it, and so deeply had he fallen in love with it, that he could not tear himself away from a Grog Shop that fronted the square, but there he remained the whole day, never stirring further from the counter than to the door where he would take a look at our Flag, and bawling out "Dat Star Bangle Banner, Oh long may it wave" return in pure desperation and take another drink. He continued at this until the drink so far overcame him that he could not utter a sound, and then, sinking on the floor, he rolled his carcass to the door, pointed up with his hand to where it flew, and in this position quietly sunk into the Arms of Morpheus. Nor was he alone in his adoration of the Flag and Bottle, but his case is noted as being the most glaring one. Every body seemed to rejoice at the change of affairs, and even the very dogs, in the course of a few days, put on a much more Christian like look.[15]

The Boat which was dispatched with the news to Sonoma reached that place at 4 P.M. and found Capt Freemont and his party there; no sooner was the news spread that the U.S. had taken possession, than all hands gave up to an excess of joy.[16] Bells were rung, guns fired, Whiskey Barrel tapped, and hiliarity became the order of the day. The Bear Flag was deposed, that of the Union taking its place, and free and independent citizens might be seen in all directions, wending their various ways and some of them making awful deviations

15. For another amusing account of this historic event see Downey's version in Rogers, *Filings from an Old Saw*, pp. 37–38. See also Rogers, ed., *Journal of Marius Duvall*, p. 49.

16. Revere left the *Portsmouth* at 2:00 A.M. and arrived at Sonoma before noon. After raising the American flag he sent news of the war on to New Helvetia (Fort Sutter). Montgomery placed Revere in command of the American forces at Sonoma on August 1, 1846, a position he retained throughout the fall of that year. See Seymour Dunbar's introduction to volume XIII of "The Sutter Papers," MS in the Henry E. Huntington Library.

from a straight course, all in consequence of their great love of liberty having overcome them. An express was forthwith despatched with the news and a Flag to New Helvetia, and in less than 48 hours from the first hoisting in Yerba Buena, the Yankee Colors were flying at every important post in Upper California and the U. States in bloodless possession of that beautiful Country.[17]

We had remained in quiet possession for near week, when rumors strange and startling began to be started among us. One of these was that Castro with 800 men was coming in to run us out, another, that the English fleet was on their way to compel us to haul the Flag down. The latter yarn gained by far the most credence, as growing jealousies had long been known to exist between the two Governments about movements in this country, and the English Admiral had kept a strict watch upon us for some months past.[18] Every nerve was now strained to put our town in a state of defence. A code of signals was concocted and a staff being erected on a Hill, two of our youngsters were sent on shore each day to keep a look out and telegraph any sail that might come in sight.[19] Night and day signals were established between the Barracks and ship and "Betsy Baker" as our Launches Gun was named, was landed and planted in the square at the foot of the Flag Staff.

The Old Fort at the mouth of the Harbor, was in a ruinous state, but there were in it some valuable pieces of ordnance, (which however were most unfortunately all spiked) that only required drilling out and remounting to be very formidable. We could, at a very small outlay of Labor, have repaired the Old Fort, but to man it would require more men than we could spare, so after much consulting, planning and laying out, a party was sent a-shore to dig out the Hill side and construct a Fort, that should hand down the name of the Founder thereof with immortal honor to posterity. It was a sort of half moon shape on the back side, and a kind of Lozenge shape in front, in fact it was a "Chef d'Ouvre" of engineering, and would bother any mortal to give a clear view of what its real shape was. But no matter, it was a Fort and all hands from high to low, were des-

17. Reports of the flag raisings at Sutter's Fort, Bodega, San Jose, etc., can be found in the official correspondence of Montgomery to Sloat printed in Sherman, *Life of Sloat*, pp. ii–xi. See also Rogers, *Filings from an Old Saw*, pp. 38–39.

18. Admiral Sir George Francis Seymour, commanding the British Pacific Squadron, had followed American naval movements closely.

19. Origin of the name of the now famous "Telegraph Hill" in San Francisco.

tined to supply their quantity of Labor upon this redoubtable defence.[20]

After two weeks of the hardest kind of digging, blasting and a sufficient quantity of cussing, the excavation was finished and all was in readiness to build up the front wall or parapet. Here again the all subduing ingenuity of the Autocrat aided him. About 5 miles above where the ship laid was a large bottom of salt grass, the roots of which were long and tough, the foundation of it firm and solid like turf. Here then was Adobe's [sic] ready made. A small craft belonging to the enemy was taken possession of, and forthwith commenced carrying Adobe's for the furtherance of the grand plan. They were brought down, landed on the Bank and thence transported on the Heads of Jacks, to the top of the Hill, where they were received by the Brick layers, and soon the wall began to assume a ferocious appearance.

The Old Fort, and mission, were now torn down to furnish timber and Plank to floor the new redoubt; Carpenters, Blacksmiths and all other sorts of Mechanics, were busily engaged, and in the space of 3 weeks behold our Fort, bristling with Cannon, and alongside of them a due quantity of shot. But not an ounce of Powder was deposited there, to be in readiness in case of need, nor was a single man detailed to man the Guns. The Fort was there and was sufficient, without Powder or men.

It was a source of great debate, as to what should be the name of this peice of human ingenuity. Some called it Fort Montgomery, some Fort Missroon, a large majority—Fort Folly—but Sergeant Slim hazarded an opinion that it should be called Fort "Pick and be d – – – d," for, said he, "twas the hardest place to pick dirt out of that ever I saw." It was eventually I believe called Fort Montgomery, though it never was made any use of while we lay there, and when the Commodore came, to show his appreciation of our work he took all the wheels off our Cannons and propped them up with sticks. This was a death-blow to the Autocrat who forthwith hauled down the Flag Staff he had erected there, and left the Fort alone in its glory.[21]

The Fort being finished, some new work was projected—what should it be? Various secret conclaves were held between the Auto-

---

20. For another account see *ibid.*, p. 40.
21. For mention of the fort see "Log of the *Portsmouth*," July 15, 1846.

crat, Boatswain, Carpenter and Fling *Sailmaker,* all tending toward some definite object. At last this mystery like all the rest was solved. A bright idea had struck the Autocrat, he would build a Block House, which should command the Town even if his redoubtable Fort should be taken by storm. The Sch^n *Dobey* was accordingly dispatched over to the Widow Reed's and soon returned with a full cargo of Logs, and Chips and his gang were sent on shore to build the War Aparatus. Meanwhile the Old Commander had resolved to establish a Civil Law in part, on shore, and a circumstance occurring about this time, which required the intervention of the Majesty of the Law, he seized upon *it,* as a favorable chance to put his resolve into execution.

It was in this wise—some time in July, one fine Saturday evening we were most agreeably surprised at seeing a large Ship stand into the Harbor, wearing the Yankee Flag, and crowded with men. This was cause for conjecture; what could she be? where could she be from? and what did she contain? The first question was easily solved, but, the two last were posers. The knowing ones had exhausted their guesses, when in popped Sergeant Slim, and with his peculiar nasal twang "guessed" that she was sent out by Government, to relieve this Ship, and that the heads we saw, were those of the "Cruities" who were to take our Ship, while we were to go home in the *Brooklyn* for that was the name observed by the Long Coat Gentry, aft, who had the sole use of the Spy Glasses.

This idea coincided so perfectly with the wishes of by far the larger portion of our crew, that it met with many supporters, but as she drew near, it was silenced by the sight of some Females among the crowd. "Oh you be d – – – d," growled an old Sheet anchor man, to whom the Sergeant was spinning this yarn, "if them is our releif what the h – – l are them wimmen doin there?"

"Oh! is there wimmen there, too?" said Slim—"well now that is what I call comfortable—Dont you know what they are there for? Well I pities your ignorance, and I'll tell you, I expect Congress has took the case in *con-*sideration, and thinking them poor fellows may have to stay out here a long while, have allowed them to bring their wives along with 'em. Nice aint it?"

As soon however as she was to anchor, Slim and his fancies were lost sight of, for the real square truth burst upon us from one of her Boats-Crew, who had come alongside to bring the Capt. She was a

New York Ship, six months from home, and had brought out 200 Mormon Emigrants to settle in California.[22] Poor fellows, we thought their lot a hard one, but they seemed satisfied with it. When these facts were made known to Slim, he said with his accustomed good humor "Oh very well, I knew it was something of that kind."

The following Sabbath, some of the new comers visited our Ship, and attended Divine Service. Great curiosity was evinced by most of our men as to what sort of people *Mormons* were. Various were the ideas formed, and as the boat which brought them came alongside, every neck was stretched, and every eye fixed upon the gangway to catch a glimpse of the animals. But when they appeared, great was the disappointment of the mass to find they were like other people, "bona fide" flesh and blood, and not bearing upon their countenances any mark of ferocity or blood thirstiness. Yes, there they sat before us, a fine looking set of men, and some very pretty girls, and with one look all the wonderment passed away. The next day, by request of the Capt. of the *Brooklyn,* our boats and men were dispatched to assist in landing the Mormons and their effects. They had come prepared at all points, to withstand the fatigues and privations of a new settlement, and from all appearances bade fair to live prosperous and happy in this (to them) Promised Land. All the vacant houses in town were soon tenanted, and a good row of snow white Tents were erected for the accomodation of those who were not otherwise provided for.

But a few short weeks passed, however, when the circumstance mentioned, as calling for the Strong arm of the Law occurred. It was in this wise A number of families had domiciled themselves in a large Adobe House, that had been formerly occupied as a store, and in leaving, the owner thereof had allowed some articles in the shape of certain trunks and callico curtains to remain in the House for safe keeping. Well, these said articles captivated the fancy of one of the sect and, thinking the curtains would be excellent for his bed, and the trunk handy to contain his clothing, he had forthwith appropriated them to his own use. Now, as long as he remained in the house all this was very well, but having found a small tenement,

22. The *Brooklyn* arrived on August 1, 1846. Washington A. Bartlett wrote that there were some 240 Mormons on board under the guidance of Elder Samuel Brannan. Bartlett found Brannan to be a shrewd but uneducated man whom he suspected was "playing a deep game for his own benefit." Bartlett to Edward M. Kern, August 6, 1846, "Fort Sutter Papers," VIII. MS in the Henry E. Huntington Library.

which suited his convenience much better, he determined to remove his bag, baggage and worldly goods into it. In putting this design into execution, he did not only move his own, but also the goods above mentioned which belonged to another, he neither knew or cared who. This appropriation was contrary to all Law except Mormon Law and, had it been allowed to pass over, would bring the sect into disrepute, consequently when the matter was reported to the Head of the Society, he went straightway and lodged with our old man a complaint of a Theft against the delinquent.

Here then was a chance to show authority, and well was the opportunity embraced. Our sometime 4th Lieut [Washington A. Bartlett], who was now by the change in affairs rated as 3rd, him whom we have heretofore mentioned as the Tract Man, was constituted, duly appointed and sworn in as Alcalde, or Justice of the Peace, empowered to try this individual charge, and all others that might come before him; your humble servant the author, appointed as his clerk and scribe in general; and one of our Marine Corporals commissioned and sworn as High Sheriff and Constable of the Town of Yerba Buena and district of San Francisco.[23] Behold us now kind reader with a full head of steam, loaded to the Brim with Gas and Law; the last bell has rung, the cars are closed and off we go at a rattling pace on the straight track of the Civil Law. Officers, Books, Pen, Ink and paper are prepared, the Criminal is arrested, and brought before us, and after a careful reading of the charge, pleads 'not guilty.' All this preamble consumed the first day, and here we must pause and blow, for we are utterly overcome, with the vastness of Power vested in us. After a nights rest, we are about to proceed again on shore, when ship's news assists our Law overburdened ears —"Timoty—Timoty" said a son of the Emerald Isle, rejoicing in the name of Mc (guess the rest) "did ye hear the news of the marning?"[24]

"Ah," says Tim, "What is it Mc—?"

23. The Alcalde was Lieutenant Washington Allen Bartlett, Master of the *Portsmouth*. Since he could speak Spanish he was a logical choice for the job involving dealings with the local citizenry. Montgomery seems to have appointed Bartlett primarily because Mexican alcaldes and magistrates had fled or had refused to do their duty. Montgomery to Joseph B. Hull, November 19, 1846, in the W. A. Leidesdorff Papers, MS in the Henry E. Huntington Library.

Downey became the town clerk of San Francisco and Sergeant George M. Miller of the Marine Corps detachment aboard the *Portsmouth* was appointed constable during the period of Bartlett's administration. Rogers, *Filings from an Old Saw*, p. 62.

24. Philip McGowan, Marine Private. "Personnel of the *Portsmouth*."

"Oh by the Powers, quare news indade—By J – – s they are going to thry a Moor-man, in the Coort ashore, thry him for his life, too, poor divil—Oh Wirra, with that Judge, and that Jury, its myself that wouldn't give a rapparee for him. What wid Law and Religion and Thracts and Steering Sails, and Passarees, that man aint fit to thry a still boorn Lamb—Bad luck to him I say, may everh hair in his head, turn to a faggot, to burn his sowl in H – – l and that is too good an end for him too."

"But what has he done?" says Tim.

"Oh by the Powers, a mere bit of a mishtake he made in calculation, more's the shame to his schoolmaster, who eddicated him. You see the man has such a lot of things of his own, that his head is bothered entirely with taking care of them, and in removing his goods, he took a wee bit of calico, and a dirthy owld thrunk, that belonged to nobody as you may say, just to take care of and preserve them, and now by J – – s they accuse him of staling and are going to *thry* the case—I dont know what the Divil they have that word *thry* there for at all, unless it manes, they will *thry* how much they can punish the poor man. This case is a bad one and if he gits off wid hangin, in that court he may thank the Lord, that he may."

This incident is related, to show how fair the character of he who was to act as Judge stood in the estimation of those who knew him. But all their criticisms were of no avail, and ashore went the Judge and his posse to sit in Judgement upon the poor Mormon. The court was opened, the Charge re-read, the witnesses examined and the D – – – g charge indellibly stamped upon his name. In his defence, he stated that he did not mean to steal the property, and then went on at a great length, to quote from the Books of Jael and Hael and many other books contained in the Book of Mormon as translated from the veritable Golden Plates found by the Prophet Jo Smith, all tending to prove, that, in the promised Land, all that they found belonged solely and wholly to them. That it was a gift from the Lord, and consequently he was right in taking them. He finally wound up however, by saying if the Court was of a different opinion from him, he would confess the charge, and appeal to the Mercy of the Hon. Judge. He was convicted, and sentenced to Labor on the Public Works for 30 days, and pay a fine of $10.

This sentence was sent to the Governor, our *noble* Captain for his approval; of course he sanctioned it, and then by a marvellous stretch of the pardoning power vested in him, he quashed the whole proceeding, and allowed the Criminal to go scott free, rejoicing in having gained a Land, where he could steal to his hearts content, go through a trial, be condemned, sentenced and pardoned, all in one breath. Very like impartial justice this.[25]

The Court being now in full Blast, laws had to be made, in order that folks might break them, and so give some employment to His Honor and the Employees about his person. It was forbidden to fire a Gun within the precincts of the *city*—forbidden to slaughter in the streets (Cattle not men) and lastly, and to crown all, the sale of ardent spirits was put under strict *Taboo*. A poor apprentice Boy belonging to our Ship who knew nothing of the Law, was arrested, and brought before His Honor, under the severe charge of having wilfully and maliciously broken the Law, by firing a pistol in the Public Street, although there was not a house within 1000 yards of him. He was found guilty, and fined $2. There was no pardoning power for him— oh no—he was made an example of for the terror of all evil doers.

Fines, costs and penalties now began to pour in, a Calaboose was erected, and spies sent on shore, expressly to tempt some poor devil to sell them a Glass of Aguadiente, in order that they might go at once to His Honor, and inform upon them, and thus by their fines, add to the accumulating fund required for the support of the Supreme majesty of the Law. All these things were done, with the aid, abettance and advice of our Autocrat, who, when he had got the trap rightly fixed, began to allow the men to come ashore on what he termed Day Liberty—well knowing that if there was any rum in town Jack would have it, and having it, would of course get drunk; by getting drunk he would get into the Calaboose where he would remain all night, and next morn be mulcted by His Honor in a fine of $5 and sent on board Ship. Then he was in his glory—he could parade them up to the mast, and upbraid, and tantalize them, call them drunkards, beasts, brutes, this, this, was fun to him. Oh perversion [sic] of Justice! Oh most strict observance of the Articles read to us, 12 times each year; one article of which expressly states that "no person in the navy shall make use of provoking or reproachful

25. Edwin Bryant was as skeptical as Downey about the quality of justice rendered in Bartlett's court. His own comments on the case are revealing: "The proceedings were a mixture made up of common law, equity, and a sprinkling of military despotism." *What I Saw in California* (New York, 1848), p. 328.

language to any other person in the navy." A good Law for the curbing of the Jacks, but not binding on the Officer.

On the night of the 12th Aug. an incident occurred at once laughable, and showing to what a pitch of discipline these defenders of a conquered territory were brought, and what our resources were in a state of revolt. First let us premise, that Soldiers as well as Sailors love liquor, and will drink whenever chance offers. Also that Soldier Officers, and ours in particular, are very fond of Ardent. Secondly, there was lots in town, for those who knew how to procure, and our Jollies had their skins well saturated the major part of the time while their valorous Commander [Watson] had never less than 15 or 16 inches of raw Brandy imprisoned under his Jacket. Having established this fact, the reader will be prepared to understand more fully what follows.

On the night above mentioned, many of the soldiers were well corned, more especially those who were detailed for Post on that eventful occasion. The Gallant Captain [Watson] had swallowed his accustomed quantity, and in staggering across the square to regain his quarters, suddenly comes to a halt and peers sagely into the Darkness—what is it that he sees? Something, which bodes no good to the peace and harmony of Yerba Buena. With his eyes, blinking and twinkling like glowworms, he sees right before him, and bearing directly down upon the spot where he stands a band of Horsemen, armed "cap a pie." His soul burns with valor, or Aguadiente (most probably the latter). He shouts to the sentry on Post—"Fire—Fire— God – d – – n you—dont you see the enemy?"

The Sentry [Philip McGowan], like a good soldier, fires when he hears the stentorian voice of his commander ordering him—the garrison is aroused—Hurry, skurry—every one jumps to his feet—drunk and sober, are armed at once—What is the matter? bursts from every lip—no one can tell. At last, in rushes the valiant officer, breathless, and *fatigued*. By G – d, here's a pretty state of affairs—100 mounted Mexicans in the very square, and no alarm. Turn out—to arms—to arms—keep within the shade of the house—give me my carbine— Burns—Burns! Sir? says Burns—Take charge of the artillery—Mc- G – – [owan] assist Burns.[26] Where's the Dog? His last question caused a laugh, the dog mentioned was a little Californian puppy he had adopted, and a shrewd wag not having the fear of the cats before

26. Peter Burns and Philip McGowan. "Personnel of the *Portsmouth*."

his eyes, suggested that perhaps the reason he asked for him, was, he was afraid the dog might turn *traitor*.

All was breathless silence for a few moments—still the expected attack came not. After a lapse of a quarter of an hour, all Hands retired to their Beds again—they had not lain long however when Bang went another gun—the same farce was enacted. All hands were called. Burns and Mc ordered to stand by the Artillery and the Dog again enquired for. The Corporal visited the Sentry who had fired, and came back with a report that he (the Sentry) had seen a Body of Horsemen and fired at them. Still the attack did not commence.

Our Old Commander [Montgomery] who lodged on shore now appeared, his cloak streaming behind him, and carbine in hand, he charged upon the Barracks. He said it was evident that the Enemy was concentrating his force, and that it was "highly important" to be on the alert, yet not wishing to fatigue the troops, he suggested that they should lie down on their arms, and thus be ready for any emergency. This suggestion was acted upon, and for a short time the Barracks were again silent—presently the report of a third gun is heard —to arms—to arms, resounds through the House, Burns and Mc fly to the Artillery, and the Dog is searched for. This time the sentry saw both Horses and Men plainly, and counted 80 or more. The time has arrived for action. We must have reinforcements from the Ship, says the Commander, Yes, says the Soldier Officer, make the signal, Fiz, Fiz, Fiz goes a Sky Rocket, a blue light is burned.[27]

We will now step on board the *Portsmouth*. No sooner was the signal made and reported, than all was Hurrah Boys on board. The alarm was given on the Berth Deck—Hurrah Hurrah. Turn out— the Mexicans are charging on the town—up you go—trowsers or no trowsers—sang out the *Tool,* Legs and his aid. Such another mess. The Old Gunner and his crew running hither and thither. Bring the Carbines here! says one. Bring em here! says another. Where's my musket? Call away a Boat! shouts an officer, Call away all the Boats! says another. Give me a Cutlass! Get off my toes! You've rammed your bayonet in me!—Get out of the way there! Give me

27. "An alarm was given on Shore by the firing of muskets, and burning a blue light. Sent a body of men under the command of Lieut. Missroon.—at 2:30 (A.M.) the men returned, leaving a guard on Shore of 25 men under charge of Mid. Bell." "Log of the *Portsmouth*," August 14, 1846.

For a similarly amusing account of this incident see Rogers, *Filings from an Old Saw*, pp. 70 ff.

some powder! Give me some Balls!—such were some of the cries, amid the confusion that reigned for a few moments.

After a short time they got in the boats, and all armed—but such arms—some had Muskets, and no Bayonets, some Bayonets and no Muskets, some had Cutlasses, Powder and Balls, and some carbines and no ammunition—one man had a musket with no lock—while another had his lock tied on to a cutlass, and one fellow, a wild rollicking Irishman, having run fore and aft the decks to get a shooting iron, in vain, at last seized a quilgee handle and jumped in the Boat, twisting it by the middle and exclaiming, "By J – – – s I will fight them Irish fashion."

The debarkation was a difficult affair; the water was low and the boats could not get close to the shore. However this was no stay, overboard they went and fell into a sort of line as they reached the shore —Fall in! says one—I've lost my powder, says another—My cartridge Box has capsized and spilt my caps and balls!—Never mind, fall in!— and they did fall in, and marched up, falling out with each other every step of the way.

One party was marched down to where the enemy had been last seen—and made a grand charge up a pile of shavings; another party charged on a little house and found the *enemy* there in the shape of certain barrels of wine. Oh, how brave they were; they rushed in, fell to hand and hand conflict with him, and soon his destruction, if not total defeat, was certain. The destruction came, but the defeat was on the other side altogether, for no sooner was he imbibed than he assumed the mastery, and Poor Jack, arms and all, was completely at his mercy. Nor was the enemy slow in taking advantage of this mastery for he threw him on his back completely "hors de combat" and played all sorts of antics with him.

As soon as the first fright of the attack was over and our Autocrat who was in command of a party, ascertained how matters stood, he pronounced the whole affair a humbug, and after detailing a small party to remain on shore, ordered the remainder to return on board. As luck would have it, the party detailed to remain were those who had made the aforementioned assault on the Liquid Enemy, and consequently their deplorable condition was not discovered by his *Majesty.* Foremost among this valorous gang was Legs [John Morgan, Master at Arms], who as has been before stated, was a very Christian Like Man and *Loved* all his *Enemies,* particularly that

143

Arch Enemy, Alcohol and all his *satelites.* Such was his love for this Gentleman, that it almost amounted to *Idolatry,* and yet such was his strict regard for duty that animal passion could never overcome it. He well knew it was wrong for the Jacks to get hold of the stimulant, and consequently when he found the insiduous gentleman was roaming at large, he strove to fulfill the trust confided in him by putting him out of sight as soon as possible, and not being able to find any more secure place for him, out of pure zeal for the service, he stowed away an immense quantity under his Jacket. Of course he was but a man, and Stimulants showed as soon on him as on other men, and the next morning when he and his gang came on board they looked to use the expression of one of our Old Salts "as if they had been dragged through hell and beat with a soot bag." This was the end of the tremendous night attack upon the town of Yerba Buena.

The affair was wrapped in mystery for some days, but at length like all other mysteries it was solved, and turned out to be this: a gang of stray horses and wild mares, not having the fear of the Laws, Civil or military, which then ruled the environs, before their eyes, had chosen this eventful night to have a ramble and a race round the town. The Soldier Officer had first started the idea that they were mounted, and the Sentries, half drunk and half asleep, had seen double, fired at them, and thus caused all this row and trouble. This was the first and last attempt made during our stay by the Mexicans to regain possession of Yerba Buena.

Things now went on swimmingly with the new Government. Our Alcalde, was not only constitutional Judge of the District, but he was Collector of the Port, and had various other cognomens attatched to his Official signature, which no doubt added greatly to his dignity in his own eyes, but not in those of many other people. Sailors have from time immemorial been in the habit of running away from Ships when displeased or dissatisfied with their lot. A great many whalers came into Port about this time from the North West Coast to refit, and as a matter of course, numbers of their crews, taking advantage of the times, ran away. The Masters of such vessels as had lost men would come over and lodge their complaints with the Judge, who forthwith issued his proclamation, forbidding all persons under severe penalties from harboring or aiding such runaways, and dispatched his emmisaries in all directions in search of them, with the promise of large rewards should they succeed in capturing them.

But few however were brought in, yet among these few were two whose case demands a place in this record. They were the 4th Mate, and a Boatsteerer belonging to a Bremen Barque, who had one night instigated, as was stated, some 4 or 5 of the crew to desert, by lowering one of the Boats, and, after providing themselves with arms, ammunition, food, water and lots of Clothing, put off for parts unknown. $300 reward were offered for their capture, and after a week had elapsed, a man came in and said he knew where they were secreted, and, if he could have a sufficient party to aid him, he would lead them forthwith to where they were. He was accordingly furnished with a sufficient escort, and off he started and at the end of 3 hours returned in triumph, bringing his prisoners with him. They had it seemed proceeded directly out of the Bay and then stood to the Northward, until they found what appeared to them a secure place, and had there landed, and colonizing, formed an armed camp of their own.

The two ringleaders were forthwith handed over to the Civil Law, to be dealt with according to their *mis-deeds*. The charges against them were heavy, being no less than *Piracy, Grand Larceny,* and a number of other high sounding crimes. For this case a Jury was to be empannelled and the summons was accordingly served upon 12 of the principle men in town. The case was opened, a counsel and interpreter was allowed them, and all the witnesses "pro and con" examined. The Judge made his charge and the Jury retired. But strange to relate, there were two Dutchmen on this said Jury, who did not mean that their Countrymen should suffer any more than any other men; consequently, they could not be brought to understand how they were pirates—of Larceny they were willing to convict: of Piracy *no,* so at last the Jury came in, and announced to the court, that there was no chance of an agreement, so they were discharged and a new one empannelled. When however the case was again brought up, the Prisoners plead guilty to the whole charge. This changed the aspect of affairs. The Judge now had the matter in his own hands. Every one thought they would have got at least 5 or 6 years hard labor on the Public Works, but there was a Wheel at work we little dreamed of, and when they were sentenced it was for only 2 years. They were accordingly sent to the Calaboose, and in a few days were seen parading behind the Public Cart, with a sentry at their heels. No sooner, however, had the Bremen Barque sailed, than presto, out came the convicts and a few short days saw them both shipped in the service of Uncle Sam, on board our Ship. Our Autocrat had marked them, they were two strapping, strong young fellows, good seamen, temperate and above all Dutchmen. He could mould them to his will, and he determined to have them. The Charges, Trial and Sentence were but a Sham, and as soon as their Ship sailed, they came aboard of us, as good Yankees, and as free from *Piracy* as any of the rest of us.

Nor was this the only farce enacted under the name of Justice. The Commander in Chief, "pro tem" Governor of the Territory, had issued his proclamation, ordering an election for Alcalde's in the several districts. Now if the People had their own way, our Naval Judge would lose his office and well he knew it, so he laid a plan with some of the "big bugs," whom he could of course favor, to call a meeting, and nominate him for Alcalde. This was accordingly done, but the rival party saw through the scheme, and nominated their candidates and bid fair to run him off the track. He was not however to be daunted; he kept his Clerk up the whole night, writing tickets to be distributed and was himself, and friends, fully occupied in canvassing with all the Election Tactics he could muster.[28]

The morning of the Election came on, the polls were held at the Barracks, the Alcalde "pro tem" himself presiding, and examiners chosen by himself, two of whom were Yankees and the others Mexicans who favored him. As the voters severally came up, it could plainly be seen by the color of the Tickets who they voted for, and any doubtful vote, having a *white* Ticket was sure to be challenged by the Soldier Officer, who stood by, while any attempt to the part of any Bystander to challenge any *blue* Ticket was put down in a summary manner. A number of the *Whites* were compelled to take the oath of Allegiance, and go through various other forms, before they deposited their Tickets, while the immaculate Blues passed unscathed. Even the Soldiers, our own Marines, were marshalled by their worthy and valorous commander, and voted the Blue Ticket with flying colors.

28. Montgomery had ordered an election to be held on September 15, 1846. Alcalde Bartlett naturally hoped to succeed himself. Downey apparently resented having to stay up to write the tickets or ballots.

146

[If Downey's 1853 account is to be trusted, he as clerk of the election got gloriously drunk and stuffed the ballot box with votes for himself. When they were counted, Downey had 38 out of the 64 votes cast. Downey was hauled off to the ship's brig and punished with twelve lashes while a new election was held. This time the somewhat miffed Bartlett carried the day.[29]]

After the Polls were closed and the vote counted, there appeared a clear majority for the Naval Candidate, upon which the Minority party prepared a protest for the Governor, praying, that as he (the Candidate) was not a Citizen of the Country, that his election might be null. They furthermore added, that our Ship might be called away at an hour's notice, when, if he fulfilled the Duty for which his Government paid him they would be left without an Alcalde, and forced to go into another election. But our Old Fox, (the Alcalde elect) was not to be caught thus. He went to work and framed a petition, counter to that of the minority, in which he set forth the great advantages that would accrue to the town by the retention in office of one who had so great a knowledge of the affairs of the District (a knowledge gained in 3 weeks) that he would not cause another to be held, and they should make no other choice, but that he would appoint a Judge himself (well knowing he had no one else to name but the present Incumbent) until such times as more emigrants should settle in the Town, from whom they could choose one to suit their own views.

This paper was copied, and signed by the Gentlemen Friends of his, who had aided and abetted his Election. How then, could our poor Imbecile old Captain act? Why of course he confirmed the Election, and the next week the returns were paraded in the "Californian" (a paper just started in Monterey) as the choice of the free and Enlightened inhabitants of Yerba Buena—Oh Purity of Elections! how are thy rights twisted and turned to suit the views of Politicians.

But of all the Farces acted in California, the most laughable is yet to be accorded, and for bombast and toadiness, beats all that is recorded in the Books of Jael or any other Book ever printed. It was getting late in the season, and the Southeasters were coming on, rendering any other harbor on the Coast unsafe, and the news soon spread that the *Savannah* and *Congress* were coming to San Francisco to winter. They were both at this time lying in Monterey, and

29. Rogers, *Filings from an Old Saw*, pp. 53–54.

a Courier came through one day bringing news of the sailing of the *Savannah* on Tuesday, and the *Congress* would sail on the following Thursday; consequently they were both hourly expected. Friday came and passed, and no signs of the Ships, and the yarn began to grow stale, but on Saturday a fine Breeze gave great hopes that we might see them that day—sure enough, at noon the signal on the Hill gave notice of the entrance into the Mouth of the Harbor of an Am. Man of War, in a few moments it said there was another. Now—now we were sure.

Shortly the *Savannah* came booming in, and in an incredible short space of time the battery was cleared for a salute to the Am. Commodore—as soon therefore as his Blue Broad Pennant was seen above the Hills—bang, bang—went 13 Guns, and every body felt some pounds lighter, to think the Commodore [Stockton] had come.[30] We knew that we had lain here so long only to protect the town and Bay; now that he was come, he would assume that duty, and we were in strong hopes that we should be allowed to take a cruise to the southward. Prospects seemed to look bright upon us. As each one of the rest of the Squadron came in, they were growling about the short rations and the small allowance of everything they had been on, while we were all the time rolling in plenty. The Store Ship *Erie* had made this port on her trip from the Islands to report to the Commodore, and we had the first slap at her and filled up, chock a block, with provisions and clothing.[31] Small stores were plenty with us, Tobacco we had lots of and that of the best, and we were all agog to be off.

It was but a short time before we had a taste of the Commodore. He had gone down with his Ship to San Pedro and from thence marched to the Puebla Los Angeles and taken bloodless possession thereof. He had left the place in charge of Lt. Gillespie and some 40 or 50 Volunteers. After he had left, the Californians had risen "en masse" and surrounded Gillespie and his party and prevented him, so far as lay in their power, from communicating with the American Party. However, by dint of the promise of a Great Reward one of the Volunteers [John Brown] had run the risk, and after having two horses shot under him, had reached San Francisco with a pressing

30. Commodore Robert F. Stockton had been ordered to take command of the Pacific Squadron. He arrived aboard the *Congress* in July and relieved the ailing Sloat on the fifteenth of that month. After occupying Los Angeles, which he left under the command of Lieutenant Archibald Gillespie, he sailed to San Francisco.

31. "Barque *Erie* arrived," "Log of the *Portsmouth*," August 27, 1846.

call for aid from the party surrounded. With the promptitude characteristic of his character, the Commodore had ordered the Frigate *Savannah* and our Ship to be ready for sea at 4 hours notice. At 8 A.M. preparations commenced, boats came in, and by 12 M we were ready for sea.

Suddenly the Commodore changed his mind, and ordered us to belay all, for he was going himself. Here we were jammed again. But, before he went, he must of course, visit the town of Yerba Buena. Here was a chance for Toadyism not to be neglected. Handbills were accordingly printed, setting forth the Programme of the proceedings to be carried on the following day. The Marines of Both Ships were to be landed, the Band in all the Glory of Red Jackets and Brass Instruments were to flourish out also. His Excellency was to land under a salute of 17 Guns from the Public Square. He was to be received at the landing by his Honor the Mayor [Bartlett]; he was to be addressed by the Hon. Somebody, then he was expected to reply—then the procession would form and there he would be presented to the Ladies—then he would mount, and with an escort, proceed to inspect the environs—then he would return—then there would be a collation—after which the ceremony would close by a grand Ball.

Well, the morning came out, speck and span new, had its best jacket and trowsers on. The procession formed, the Marshall, mounted on smart Horses, with Blue Sashes waving in the Wind, rode to and fro getting every body in place. First came the Band, then the Marines, then the Naval, then the Civil Authorities, then the late Civil Authorities, then the late Californian Officers, then the Orator of the Day, then the Citizens then the stragglers, Indians, and Dogs, and the whole wound up by our old Chips [Wisner] wagging along, grinning for Dear Life with his memorable Pea Jacket and white trowsers on. They arrived at the Landing, got into a Line, His Excellency shoved off—Bang went the Guns, Hurrah sung out the crowd, and his Excellency walked ashore. Oh, What a proud day for Yerba Buena! Here was a real live Yankee Governor on "terra firma." The speeches were made, 9 cheers given, the Band struck up and up one street and down another they marched, Old Chips and the Dogs bringing up the rear. The Ladies were presented, blushed, giggled, and laughed at his Excellency, who joked with every body, and told them what he was going to do for them. The Band blowed till they were almost blown away, the Marines shouldered, presented and supported arms. The Dutch Baker got corned, and Old Chips took to hard Drinking and Danced a Bolero with the Dogs out of doors of pure joy. Oh what a happy day![32]

But the crowning event was yet to come off and that was the Ball. Talk of your Dignity Balls, your Ball en masque, your Fancy Balls, and your 4th of July Balls—Pshaw. There never was a Ball given since Noah first landed from the ark that could compare in all its details with the "Reception Ball" at Yerba Buena. The Large Dining Room of the largest house in the city was most brilliantly illuminated, and shone forth in all the blaze and brilliancy of 100 Spermacitte Candles, which reflected from some 30 or 40 mirrors. The resplendant countenances of all the assembled beauty of the District of San Francisco. There was the fine open countenance of the Russian Brunette, which seemed to say, "love me if you dare," there was the happy round smiling face of the Dutch Frow of the Cigar Maker, which said "I know you like me" and there was the pretty faces of all our Yankee Mormons, blushing and blooming like full blown peonies, and there was also a decent and rather numerous sprinkling of the dark hued daughters of California, who would dance no matter who feed the Fiddler. These were the occupants of the Dancing Room, and hovering round them were the Beaux, from Dancing S – – l, the most graceful performer upon the heel and toe principle, I ever saw, down down a long row from the grave citizen to the Lace and Epaulette bedizzened Officer of the Navy and winding up with Old Chips, with his beautiful teeth and snow white pants who stood at the door, grinning from ear to ear.

In the next room however were the sterling attractions of the evening. The first sight that struck the eye upon entering was the long table, spread over with an abundant quantity of the good things of this life—and then immediately in the rear was the *Bar;* not the Bar of the Law, but the Bar of the Law's particular Friend—Mr. Alcohol. Here he lived in all his splendor with all his multifarious names and cognomens. And the old round, chubby faced decanters stood so lovingly side by side, seeming to invite the bystanders to

32. Downey describes the whole celebration in greater detail in his 1853 account. Rogers, *Filings from an Old Saw*, pp. 61–65.

Edwin Bryant, another eyewitness, also commented upon the occasion in his *What I Saw in California* (New York, 1848), pp. 330–331.

partake, and hard indeed must have been the heart of any one who could have withstood the temptation. Certain am I, that few if any of that crowd, stood immactulate on that eventful night.

When the Ball first opened, all was joy and merriment, but as Alcohol began to obtain the mastery, strong symptoms of pugnacity showed themselves. Some old grudge had existed between our Purser and one of the Dignitaries of the Town and high words ensued, but suddenly, slap, bang, went a blow and down went the dig.[33] Now then all was hubbub, noise and confusion—"Struck, in my own house," says the Dig, "Give me my pistols." "Pistols be d – – d," growled the pugnacious man, "if you stir from that spot I'll brain you." "Peace—Peace or order Gent—Gentlemen," hiccupped the Soldier Officer [Watson], who had on this occasion raised his dose from 20 to 24 inches—"I demand, and command silence," sung out a short, fat red faced Lieut. from the Flag Ship. "Silence yourself," muttered the Soldier, "I am Commanding Officer here—you be d – – – d if you open your mouth again." "Well sir, what then?" "Why I'll sew it up for you, that's all!"

Bottles, tumblers, canes, and all sorts of missiles were flying about the room. Old Chips was in the thickest of the fight, striving as he in his drunken mood thought, to preserve the peace, or the Liquor (most probably the latter) until at last he found himself most unceremoniously pitched out the window, and landed on a dung heap in the back yard. Being nearly overcome with his exertions during the day, and finding his bed a soft one, he at once resigned himself to the arms of Morpheus, nor did he again open his peepers till the hogs rooted him out, and he found it was broad daylight.

Meanwhile the Row within doors was carried on in full force, and there was a fair chance for murder till some one who had not lost his wits ran to the Commodore with the news, and his appearance and commanding voice put a stop to all belligerent proceedings. By dint of loud talking, some small cussing and lots of knocking on his own part, he at last arrived at the merits of the affair, and having consigned some of the most unruly to durance vile, in the Calaboose, and sending others on board their own Ships, he at last restored order, and at an early hour in the morning the Ball broke up, and the Belles retired to dream of conquests made, while the major

33. James H. Watmough, Purser aboard the *Portsmouth*. See *Gen. Nav. Reg.* (1882), p. 749.

portion of the Beaux if they slept at all, awoke with such awful feelings in their heads as would cause them to remember for some time the Reception Ball at Yerba Buena, the latter part of which was not announced in the Programme.

The next day a large number of volunteers under Capt.—now Major Freemont arrived from the Sacramento and being put on Board the Ship *Sterling*, she, together with the *Congress* got underway and stood out of the Harbor, leaving us poor devils once more alone in our glory.[34] How we got along this time, how we enlisted volunteers of every hue, and nation, at $25 per month how we shipped them off, and how the Lord assisted in delivering us from a plague that had long haunted us, how we gave up the Governor Ship of the Territory, to Commod[r] Hull, and sailed from this port for San Diego, paying all debts as we went, is it not recorded in the next chapter, which you must read if you wish to know these things.

In Which the Fore Topsail Squares All

IT WAS a comparatively happy day for us, when we saw the Blue Broad Pennant disappear behind the hills of the Point, off Angel Island, bound out.[1] Ever since the hour we first received the news of his expected arrival, we had been busy, scrubbing, scouring, holystoning and cleaning. Touch her up a little here, and touch her up a little there was the order of the day—clean in White and clean in Blue, run here and run there, and above all, watch the motions of the Commodore. Now in the common course of events we had humbug enough of our own, but to have in addition to be harrassed about for a Commodore was always our lot when his pennant flew in our waters. Now, much as we had rejoiced at seeing his Ship, that

---

34. Frémont and his men, whose numbers had been augmented by the recruitment of American immigrants arriving at Fort Sutter in the fall of 1846, were on their way to Monterey. There they were to pick up horses gathered by Charles Weber, and to proceed overland to Los Angeles.

At this time Stockton impressed the whale ship *Stonington*, the *Julia*, and the hide ship *Vincennes* into service as transports for the new recruits. Rogers, *Filings from an Old Saw*, p. 68; Bryant, *What I Saw in California*, pp. 332-33.

1. The *Congress* sailed October 13, 1846. "Log of the *Portsmouth*."

joy only arose from the hope we had of leaving port soon, on a Cruise. But when we found we were to remain, the sooner he was out of sight the better for us.

As soon then, as he *was* out of sight, matters began to go on in the old way, and we set to work with a right good will to prosecute the work he had lain down for us. First and foremost then, the redoubtable Block House was to be garrisoned. This was easily done, and at the same time our marines were re-inforced by a band of Blue Jackets, who were most unceremoniously transformed into Soldiers.

The Block House gang was composed of some of our choice spirits, and from the mysterious noises emmitted therefrom nightly, a hearer might be led to suppose that whatever other care rested upon the mind of the inmates, they cared not for the Mexicans. There were some 15 or 20 of them domiciled in a little place some 40 feet square, and there they pigged in, eating, drinking and sleeping in one great hall. This sort of soldiering was rare fun for the Jacks, as when they were off Guard they could roam at large, all over town, and by their good conduct, ingratiated themselves into the good graces of the townspeople, and, as the sequel proved, something to their sorrow.

It being war time, of course money was scarce and as Jack was in want of many articles both in the eating and *drinking* line, they, the townspeople, reposing especial trust in their integrity—and honor, did for a long time allow them to procure what they were in need of on *Tick,* being well assured that they would be paid before the ship sailed. Well on the strength of this said *Tick,* Jack lived long, and strong, during his short tarry on shore, and many and many an hour has been whiled away during the watches at sea, in listening to the yarns of "Mr. Bye the Bye" of occurrences which took place in the old Block House and its Environs.

The season was now far advanced, and that continual plague of Upper California in winter, continued rain, began to annoy us on board, as well as those on shore. In order therefore to while away the long evenings, various were the games gotten up and uprorious was the glee occasioned by them. None, however, were more successful in interesting all hands, than one invented by the same "Mr. Bye the Bye" which was known as laughing by note. This was a game in which all were compelled to participate, for if you began as a spectator you were forced by the curious faces and woe begone phizes which assailed you on all sides, to join, and soon all were employed in one general laugh. The Mormon Girls too, being fond of society, soon scraped acquaintance with the most sociable of the Tars, and nightly jaunts and sundry walks into the country on Sundays, were the natural consequences of said acquaintance.

Certain it is that had the service allowed of it, and our stay had been prolonged much longer, some of the most susceptible of ours would have been seduced from their duty and joined "giblets" with some of these Yankee Mormons. Oh, the Misses Kettlebottoms, and Misses R – – s and Miss P – – h have many a sore heart to answer for, to say nothing, of the destruction among the hearts of some reefers, made by the E – – r family.[2] "No importe," we are clear of you now, and perhaps it is better for all hands, for had matrimony ensued from any of those flirtations, somebody would have been made unhappy for life.

Thus much for matters on shore. On board all was hurry and bustle from morn till night: we had received our orders from the Commodore to enlist all the emigrants who should come over this year to serve as volunteers for 3 months at $25. per month, and boats were despatched every day up the Sacramento, to bring them down to the General rendezvous as fast as they were enrolled.[3] And they did come down, and such a mass was never seen before by mortal man. They were literally the rag tag and bobtail of all Creation. Here they came, some with coats and some no coats—some with deer skin trowsers and some with awful looking things in the shape of trowsers, some with moccasins, some with Boots, some with shoes, and a great majority with no covering to their feet. In one thing however they were uniform: they had good rifles and shocking Bad Hats. They had all come across the mountains, and could blow awful strong wind about the way they could shoot, and what they could do to the Mexicans.

They were, to say the truth, among such a crowd some rare characters, and afforded much amusement to us during their tarry on

2. Downey's thin disguise for the Misses Kittleman, Miss Patch, and the Eager family. Miss R – – s is unfortunately not identifiable. The editor is grateful to Colonel F. B. Rogers of San Francisco for these identifications. See his notes on *Filings from an Old Saw,* pp. 140–141.

3. Downey is right here. See the letter of Montgomery to E. M. Kern at Fort Sacramento for the fall of 1846 in the "Fort Sutter Papers," xviii. MS in the Henry E. Huntington Library.

board, and from them I shall select two, who will be recognized by any one of the Old Stock who may read this book. The first among these rejoiced in the name of Savage, although among us he was better known by the "Soubriquet" of Oregon, from the fact that he had when coming on board, painted in large letters upon the Back of his only Coat (and an awful bad coat it was) the following advertisement—For Oregon—This announcement caught the eye of Sergeant Slim [George Miller?], and of course lost nothing in his hands.[4] He went up to the new comer and in a very serious manner asked him if he had not made a mistake or been put in the wrong bag by that Post Master at the Cross Roads, for said he, I perceive by your label that you were intended for "Oregon."

"Oh yes," replied the stranger good humoredly, "there was a small mistake there; you see, long fellow, when we came through, there was such a lot of us to sort, the man was *rayther* puzzled, and as you will find out, if you and me are long acquainted, that I dont stand still long at a time, so when he was counting out the Oregon parcels, I was dodging about trying to get some thing to eat, and so he missed me; however it dont make much odds, the news I carry (pointing to his rifle) will be as good in California as Oregon, and when the war is over, I can get re-mailed and be sent back safe and sound to my anxious friends up there."

"Oh yes, of course," said the Sergeant, "but then you see I only asked you for information, you know, as I am a Government Man and like to see things carried on in a seamanlike manner, and if you were not satisfied with the way you was served, you see I would write to the Secretary about it and have the Post Office Man overhauled and perhaps you might make a spec out of it yet."

This was a little too much for Oregon, who saw the laugh was going against him, and being a wag in his own way, he quietly replied, "I feel very much obliged to you, for your kind enquiries, and now I look at you again, you do look like a Government Man; why what a stout fellow you are; have they got a great many like you here? If there are, I think this ere Ship ought to be double jointed for fear you might break her up."

4. James D. Savage, who is more completely identified in Rogers, *Filings from an Old Saw*, p. 69, and in Bancroft, *History of California*, v, 713. See also Annie R. Mitchell, *Jim Savage and the Tulareno Indians* (Los Angeles, 1957), for an account of his later career.

"Oh! no," replied Slim, "there aint no more than me here; you see there wasn't but a few of my breed in the States, but the Government took 'em all up as soon as they came into Market and sorted 'em out among the Ships, just to show the world what a stout race they grew down east. They dont allow me to put my whole strength out here, because you see they want to keep it for particular occasions."

"Well that is a sensible idea," said Oregon, "for you look as if you would be sudden death on Pork and Beans if they did let you out."

"Good on your head," says Slim, "I guess you aint behind hand at that game; any how, there goes 8 Bells, now when we have got our grog you come down to our mess, and I'll run you a race at that." No sooner said than done. Aft trotted Slim and his new found friend to the Grog Tub, and from thence to the Jolly Starboard Fore Top Mess, where Oregon paid due justice to the Beans, and speedily by his quaint sayings became a favorite with all the Mess Mates. Oregon was never daunted at a war of words and he could at any time gather a crowd around him to listen to his wonderful yarns about his adventures coming over the mountains.

Next upon the list of characters came one who was nicknamed by his comrades, "Old Grizzly"—he was to use one of Chimes favorite expressions "some relation to Bear" for of all the appetites with which mortal man was ever gifted, afflicted or whatever else you like, he certainly had the most ravenous.[5] He was also most awfully subject to the cholic and when he had crammed his bread bag to the utmost tension he would be seized with sudden pains and down upon the broad of his back he would lay and bellow like a bull for aid. Common remidies were of no use to him, and as uncommon diseases require uncommon means to rout them his comrades had found out one for him which was "outre" enough.

Whenever he was attacked in the manner before described, Oregon and one or two more would mount him, and planting their feet in the pit of his stomach, thus literally tread the pain out of him. This process had to be repeated at least 2 or 3 times every day, for no sooner was the pain gone, than back came his appetite, and after he was stuffed on came the cholic. Poor "Old Grizzly," many was the laugh the Boats Crew had at you and your misfortunes, until one

5. "Old Grizzly" was possibly Isaac Graham who later settled at Santa Cruz, California, and ran a sawmill. Rogers, *Filings from an Old Saw*, p. 15; Bancroft, *History of California*, iii, pp. 762–3.

unlucky day the sight of their empty Bread Bag, the contents of which you had devoured, elongated their faces and caused curses long and loud to be showered upon you and your appetite. Nothing was said about his failing, and when dinner time came, Brush, who was rather late, invited the Old Fellow to dine with him. Grub invitations never came amiss to "Grizzly"; accordingly down he went with Brush, and as most of the Mess Mates were finished they two had a clean field to work upon. There was in the mess an old fellow who officiated as Steady Cook and who was eternally studying navigation.[6] At sea or in Port, 'twas all the same to him, the Book and slate were at work—ask him any time how the Ship headed and it was sure to be Northwest. By being steady cook he had a goodly supply of Pork, Beef, Bread and Beans on hand. Well, he gave a friendly greeting to the new comer, handed him a pan of Beans, and introduced him to the Knife and told him to cut for himself and be at home. At the grub accordingly "Grizzly" and Brush went, and famously did they get on.

Brush, who was no fool of an eater, had finished his meal, picked his teeth, and being too much of a gentleman to rise before his guest, now amused himself with watching his motions. Slowly and surely "Grizzly" went ahead, and the pile of Bread and Pork grew smaller and smaller every visit he made to the Pan. Now the Pork vanished and he attacked the Beef. Closer and closer did Brush and the cook watch his moves, showing by sundry winks and nods how well they enjoyed the joke; now the Beef has all disappeared. Slowly turning towards Brush, "Old Grizzly" put out his hand, when with a shout both Brush and the Cook cleared the Berth Deck, and so eager were they to get up the hatch that they jammed one another in the attempt.

"Help—Murder!" roared Brush. "Ready about Stations Maintopsail Haul," gasped the Cook. "What is the matter?" sung out a number of voices. "Oh by the Lord," says Brush "if we haint got the Devil in our mess I never see daylight, he's eat 14 Pound of Pork and Beef and now wants to go down on me and the Cook." "Yes," said the Cook, "I saw him licking his chops at me, and then I thought it was time to put her about." "How does she head now Steve?" sang out a mizen Topman. "Oh by Heavens, Sou West with a hell of an appetite!"

6. Probably Andrew Nutter, Cook. "Personnel of the *Portsmouth*."

Several men now interfered and "Old Grizzly" came up. Brush and the Cook kept at a respectable distance from him. Upon investigation, "Grizzly" said he was done and was just going to return thanks when them fellows ran away. When Brush was informed of this he shook hands with the Old fellow but at the same time, told him, "I swan to man I was never so scared in my life, I thought I was a gone one, you did look so awful savage at me. If you are took that way often, and will just look round you'll find a heap fatter fellows than me and the cook in the mess."

Nor was this the only eating feat accomplished by "Old Grizzly," his appetite continued so enormously large that a famine was dreaded in the mess, and Old Steve affirmed if he did not soon top his boom, he must apply to the Purser for two or three extra rations for him. And then at night too! Oh what a mess on our Berth Deck; we had such a lot on board there was no room for them to hang up, even if they had hammocks, and as they had no other resource, they were compelled to bunk in lump on deck, and as "All Hands" was called at daybreak, and the light had not yet had time to get below, the noise and confusion that there reigned was never equalled, no, not even at the Tower of Babel.

After they were regularly enrolled they were allowed to draw such articles of clothing and small stores as they required from the Purser. Here too was a Laughable Scene, for to encase a Landsman in a pair of short trowsers is to put him out of his element any time, but with these 'twas the worst job I ever saw. Some drew Red and some Blue Flannels, and it was no odds to them which, on it would go over all, and such a motly group as they were, would have puzzled Fallstaff himself. Trowsers over Buckskin Breeches, and a taut strain on Suspenders to keep them up. First a Red, then a Blue Flannel, outside of this a White Frock with a Blue Collar while overall some would sport a Pea Jacket. Black Silk Handkerchiefs, intended for the neck, were converted by some into Hat Bands and by others into sashes for the waist. Shoes were the only article they could not go amiss in, and luckily, we had but few pairs of them, or the Lord only knows what purpose they would have put them to.

During their stay on board the Autocrat was in an awful way. He could not keep his decks in order, and as for the Volunteers, his commands were no more than wind to them. They would sing out to one another from one end of the Ship to the other, and the hubbub they occasioned was agony to him. All things however must have an end, and at last the order came for them to move.[7]

The Schooner *Dobey* was fitted out, and in her they were packed to the number of 60 or 70, and shoving off gave us three cheers and with a fair wind wended their way to Santa Clara, a port some 60 miles up the Bay, where they were to be mounted and from thence proceed to join Maj. Freemont at Monterey. They all went but one, a long, slim, bean pole looking chap, who bore a strong resemblance to Sergeant Slim, whose carcass was encased in a suit of Linsey Wolsey, and who had jammed his Legs (or rather the things that were hung to his body in the place of those articles) plumb up to his knees in a pair of Boots. He was, or pretended to be, afflicted with dysentary and the doctor detained him until he should recover. He too, like the rest of the gang, was an awful eater, and could and would devour at any one sitting as much eatables as should in common times have sufficed for Three Common men. He was an inveterate [enemy] to exercise in any shape and would take his position stretched at full length, Boots and all, upon an Arm Chest that was standing in the middle of the Berth Deck, and for the whole 24 hours would never rise except to get his Grubbins, which having swallowed, he would down again, and sleep till next meal time.

Thus some 3 weeks rolled away in the same monotonous manner. Naught broke the routine of our every day life save the occasional despatch of a boat up the Sacramento. The Mormons had settled down into quiet life ashore, and the Law Business began to flag. An incident however turned up at last which gave cause for merriment for some days. Our 4th Cutter was the regular Mail Boat from Yerba Buena to Sonoma and the Sacramento Valley, and during her trips her crew were accustomed to while away their time and provide for the inner man by shooting Wild Geese, numerous quantities of which were found in the Upper Bays. So successful were they, that many of the Ships Company, whose mouths watered for a bit, had bought Powder and Shot for them, and went shares in the game killed. Never a trip was made but that more or less of these Geese decorated the mess tables.

Amongst the rest our Gunner's Mate [George Baker], who was a dear lover of any thing good, and withal quite a sportsman, thought

7. The *Portsmouth* took on some 37 volunteers from the Sacramento Valley. "Log of the *Portsmouth*," November 1–10, 1846.

he would have his share of the Geese as they were travelling about, and accordingly furnished his quota of ammunition, and for many trips regaled his chops with the game that fell to his share. One return trip his lot amounted to one fine, large fat fellow and he proceeded in the morning to divest his prize of his outward covering, preparatory to consigning him to the tender mercies of the cook, who was to do him up in style. Having picked and singed him clean and neat, he laid him on one of the Larboard Guns, while he went below for a moment for something he required. . . .

Now there was a standing order from the Autocrat, that the Midshipman of each division, should take the rounds every morning after quarters and pick up all articles such as ditty bags, jackets, books or shoes, that might be left about the Guns or decks, and consign them to the Lucky Bag, from which they were never recovered except by a drill of from 3 to 4 days upon "Charley Noble" as the Cooks funnel was familliarly called. Well, the Midshipman of the 1st division, where this goose lay, was at this particular moment going his rounds, and his eye chanced to fall upon this article which was, in positive contradiction of the Article before mentioned, laying "bona fide" on a Gun. He was a great hand for strict obedience of orders was this same Reefer, and such was the habit he had acquired of peering about, reporting and getting things in said Bag, and other mean tricks that, go fore and aft the Ship, you would not find one person, from Officer to Boy who would speak well of him.[8]

He saw the Goose, and no sooner did he see than he acted. He seized it, and marching aft ordered a Boy to deliver it to Legs [John Morgan] and order it to be placed forthwith in said Lucky Bag. Legs and the Boy both enjoyed the Joke, and immediately the Goose was delivered over to the Captain of the Hold, and by him consigned to the place thus designated. The Reefer walked aft, and the bystanders who had witnessed the transaction remained to see the fun. In a few moments up comes the owner and after looking where he left it, began to make strong enquiries after his property.

Scarcely had he ejaculated the question, "Where's my Goose?" than a dozen mouths were opened, and the answer burst forth—"Where? Why in the lucky Bag!"

8. Downey referred to Midshipman Daniel C. Hugunin who later was lost in the *Warren*'s launch. See below, p. 163.

"In the Lucky Hell," said he, "now you all see I want no fooling, where is it?"

"Why in the Lucky Bag, I tell you," said an old Quarter Gunner, "Tommy Roundhead just come round and, seeing it on the Gun, sent it down to the Master at Arms."

"D – – n Tommy Roundhead, and you too," says Lockstring, and down he dove to the Berthdeck and enquired to the Captain of the Hold [John Stinchfield] if his Goose was there.

"Yes," says Ullage, "and here it will stay till I get an order from the 1st Luff to give it up."

Aft bolts Lockstring to the Wardroom, where the Autocrat and the rest of the Officers were sitting. "If you please Sir," said he, "can I have my Goose?"

"Your Goose," says the Autocrat, "what do you mean? what do I know about your Goose?"

"Why sir, you see Mr. H – – – [Hugunin] has put it in the Lucky Bag."

"In where?" says the Autocrat, while a roar of Laughter resounded through the Ward Room, "put it where?"

"In the Lucky Bag," says Lockstring, with a face as demure as a Parson.

"Well, by heavens," says the Autocrat, joining in the Laugh, "this does beat all. A Goose in the Lucky Bag! Was it dead or alive?"

"Oh twas alive and all picked and cleaned, ready for cooking, and a nice fat fellow it was too."

"Well, well," said the Autocrat, "I have been to sea in a Man of War 20 years and this is the first time I ever heard of putting a goose in the Lucky Bag, and a dead Goose too."

"But Sir," said Lockstring, "can I have it?"

"Have it? Yes, to be sure, go and get it, but dont tell the wags of it, or they will be raising the devil with Mr. H – – –."

Lockstring got his goose and said no more about it, but the wags were about, and the affair soon spread about the Ship. And that night when Hammocks went down, nothing could be heard fore and aft, but cries of Goose—Goose—some fellow chock forward would sing out, "Who put the Goose in the Lucky Bag?" Another chock aft would reply "Tommy Roundhead"—and athwart ships and amidships the same cry was re-echoed, till the Deck sang with shouts of Laughter. The occupants of the Steerage and Ward Room heard it and though bursting with laughter, ordered silence but 'twas of no use. Jack would disguise his voice and still sing out. The row was kept up till one bell, and some affirm that it was sung out by more than one fellow in his sleep, but at all events with the first pipe of the Boatswains Call in the Morning came the same old question, "Who put the Goose in the Lucky Bag?" The Autocrat ordered the Buffers to pass the word, that if he caught any man at it, he would punish him, yet as it was well known he enjoyed the joke, but little heed was paid to the order, and the fun lasted some days when like all other things in a Man of War it wore away.

Madame Rumor who was always adrift now came in with a new yarn: the *Savannah* had gone down to San Pedro, had landed a party of men who undertook to march to Los Angeles; they had been met by a party of Californians, and in a field fight on the plains of Domingo [actually Rancho Dominguez] had been whipped and forced to retreat with the loss of 6 men.[9] This news was too bad to meet with many supporters, and was for a long time disbeleived but at last it came with so many convincing proofs that we were forced to swallow the pill bad as it was. The Battle was fought over and over about our decks, and many a would be warrior offered his opinion as to how matters should have been conducted.

The next item was the arrival of the Brig *Malek Adhel* [Mexican], a prize to the *Warren*—she had been cut out from the Harbor of Mazatlan and sent up to report to the Commodore. By her we received news from home of the progress of the war in Mexico and official accounts of the Battles of the 8th and 9th May.[10] Patriotism glowed in every body's breast and the War Fever ran high. The Berth Deck Politicians waxed warm, discussing the probable proceedings of Congress in the affair, and any poor wight who had by chance picked up a stray piece of newspaper was soon surrounded by a gaping crowd, and compelled to read the contents thereof aloud, for the benefit of all parties. Battles were fought, fields won, and

9. When Stockton learned that the Angelenos had revolted and driven out Captain Gillespie and his men, he ordered Captain William Mervine, in command of the *Savannah*, to sail south and to come to Gillespie's aid. Landing at San Pedro on October 7, Mervine and a portion of his crew joined Gillespie's men and advanced on Los Angeles only to be defeated by the Californians at Rancho Dominguez. John W. Caughey, *California* (New York, 1940), p. 280.

10. The battles of Palo Alto and Resaca de la Palma.

Charley May, pronounced the "neplus ultra" of all Dragoons that ever had or would exist.[11]

To see the prizes of other vessels of the Squadrons coming in engendered a spirit of discontent, to think that we, whose souls were burning with arder should be compelled to lay with one of the finest, and in fact the finest vessel on the coast in comparative idleness while all the other old butter boxes were sent to cruise and signalize themselves. We strove to content ourselves however with the hope that our time would come, and one dare devil, said at a hazard, the Congresses would never take the City of Los Angeles, until we went down to assist them. How much this saying was like prophecy? A few short weeks elapsed and we were up to our eyes in soldierizing.

Shortly after the arrival of the Brig the *Warren* herself made her appearance, and now things began to look as if we were in short to be off. The Governorship was turned over to Capt. Hull, and the men and marines from the *Warren* took possession of the Barracks and Block House ashore, while ours returned on board.[12] At last the cheering news came. The Commodore had ordered our old man to settle up all his business and proceed at once to San Diego, a port some 500 or 600 miles to the Leeward, and join him.

There were some men to be paid off in New Helvetia, an armed post some 120 miles up the Sacramento, and in order to complete this affair, and at the same time give the Officers of the *Warren* some knowledge of the navigation of the Bay and Rivers, the *Warren*'s Launch was to proceed up, under the Pilotage of one of our own Reefers, the before mentioned gentleman of Goose Memory.[13] He had by some means persuaded our Old Man that he was well acquainted with the rivers, though twas shrewdly suspected by the Jacks about decks that he overrated his powers in this instance, yet nothing was said, and he was bid go and Godspeed him, with many a hearty prayer that he might never return.

The Officer in Command of the Launch was our Old Man's Eldest

11. Captain Charles A. May, who commanded a squadron of Dragoons at the battle of Palo Alto. At Resaca de la Palma he had led a dashing attack at the center of the line against Mexican batteries. Justin Smith feels that May's reputation was undeserved, calling him "essentially a cowardly sham." See Justin Smith, *War with Mexico,* I, 164, 168, 174, and 467.

12. Joseph B. Hull, Commander of the U.S. sloop-of-war *Warren* (20 guns) succeeded Montgomery as governor of the "Northern District" of California in 1846–47.

13. Midshipman Daniel C. Hugunin.

son, the Sailing Master of the *Warren,* and his second son who was acting as his Clerk on board our Ship, had persuaded his father to let him go also.[14] Behold the Launch then, ready to start with the 3 Officers above named (not one of whom was liked by any Jack who had ever been shipmates with them) and a crew of 8 or 9 men. They had on board 12 days provision and some 8 or 900 dollars in specie. The wind was fresh and fair and off they started one Thursday afternoon with the prospect of a pleasant and speedy trip before them.

We were to start as soon as they returned, and we waited with patience the allotted time—12–14 and 16 days had passed and still no news from them. Dark rumors began to fly about decks that they were capsized, or made prisoners—perhaps worse than all that the crew of the boat, incited by the sight of the money, had risen, murdered the Officers, and taken to the woods. Whatever it was, a majority were satisfied that something had surely happened to them, for no boat had ever been known to be delayed so long before. After the 17th day a boat came down from San Joaquin, a river running into the Sacramento; they had seen nothing of the Launch. The next day another came from New Helvetia direct, she had neither been up to that port, nor had they seen any signs of her in their track down.

This settled the affair in the minds of many. There were two large bays to cross, before they entered the mouth of the River. It sometimes blew very hard in squalls in these Bays; it was most likely that she had been capsized in one of these squalls and as the shores were for miles nothing but swamp and Tula Grass, where no living thing could travel, they had either all perished by drowning, or worse, by starvation, cold and thirst.

This was the conclusion come to by the knowing ones, but the Old Man would not give them up; he still clung to the idea that they were made Prisoners by the Enemy. A boat was fitted out, and an experienced pilot in these waters employed to go in search of them, and he declined leaving the Port until he got some news from them. His feelings were natural—to lose two sons by such a chance was a heavy blow. He clung to one idea, we had formed another, and the sequel proved ours the most correct, for nothing was heard of them for many months, and at last the news that did come was meagre but

14. S. W. L. and John E. Montgomery, passenger and clerk respectively aboard the *Portsmouth.*

conclusive—some oars and bodies had been found which corresponded with those lost, and he gave them up with a heavy heart, as gone forever.[15] Poor Old Man, there were but few who did not feel for thy agony of mind at such a loss, and yet the remark was often passed that it was a retribution from God, for some of the cruel acts which had transpired under your Command.

During the time we lay waiting for the return of the Ill-fated Launch, the Shore people, who had allowed Jack so much Tick, getting wind that we were outward bound, began to stir themselves to procure payment for value furnished. Jack was willing enough to settle up, but he had not the wherewith and our Autocrat decidedly put his face against all such proceedings. His motto was that the Sailor had no right to ask for, and the Landsman no right to give credit, and if they were foolish enough to do so, they must get their pay the best way they could. Such coaxing and praying, such cursing and swearing as was done by the afore mentioned creditors, and such condolences as were offered by Jack, were never heard before, and ought not to be heard again—but of no avail. The Ship must sail, Jack could not, and the Autocrat would not, pay and so the wo-begone Landlords were fain to content themselves with the promise of a speedy return and sure pay at that time.

After all the Jacks were not to blame, because they had ration and grog money due them (which should be paid by regulation every three months) to settle all; the Landlords were not to blame, for tis the way they make a living, and they must take the chance of profit and loss; the Autocrat was not to blame, for money was so scarce that our Purser had paid as high as 20 per cent for money to defray the expenses of war, and thus no one was at all to be blamed. We settled matters by laying the blame on circumstances and squared all accounts for this time with the Fore Topsail. But for the honor of the Ship's Company be it said, that when we returned to this port after an absence of 6 months, to water previous to going home, all these accounts were paid to the last cent, and we came away with an honorable name from San Francisco.

The Old Man hung on and hung on, hoping every day to hear something from his sons, for anything was better than the dreadful

15. What happened to the launch and its crew still remains a mystery. It is very possible that the crew was attacked by bandits and murdered, for it was known that there was a large sum of gold aboard with which to pay troops on the Sacramento.

suspense he was now in. The *Savannah* came up from the Leeward to refit for home, the *Cyane* also came in to water and recruit, the orders from the Commodore were reiterated and at last not daring to tarry any longer, the welcome sound was heard of "All Hands up Anchor," the Capstan was manned, every body worked with a will and soon our Anchor was raised from where it had lain 6 long tedious months, and the Pride of the Pacific was once more underway.[16]

When I speak of the eagerness of "All Hands" to get clear of this place, I do not wish to be understood, that any one was tired of the people, or glad to leave for any other cause than this; we had lain inactive too long, we yearned to go below where soul stirring scenes were being enacted, in which we could play our part, and add more Laurels to the name of the Gallant *Portsmouth*.

As I have before stated, we got underway, and from my station on the main Yard, where I had a good view of the town, I saw many a Hat and white Handkerchief waved as an adieu, and though I was as pleased as any one else at the prospect of a cruise, could not help feeling some little regret at leaving those in whose company I had passed so many happy hours.

Our passage was but short, and the third day out we spoke the *Sterling* bound up with despatches for us, and learned that the Commodore was at San Diego, had landed all his men and was only waiting our arrival to commence a marching campaign in search of the Enemy. Enthusiasm now ran high, we should have a chance and already were the Enemy beaten in prospective.

I had almost forgotten to mention, that we left our "Tract Man" [W. A. Bartlett], now metamorphised into an Alcalde, behind us, to the great joy of all the crew, who had been sufficiently humbugged with him thus far in the cruise, and to the manifest discomfort of the townspeople who hated him as cordially as we did.

16. The *Portsmouth* sailed December 5, 1846. "Log of the *Portsmouth*."

San Diego and Soldiering

IN THIS CHAPTER I shall be compelled to depart in some manner from my original design of confining myself to shipboard affairs, and the reader will soon perceive the reason why I do so. As mentioned in my last, when we met the *Sterling* and got the news it was generally known about decks, that the Commodore [Stockton] or "Fighting Bob" as he was familliarly termed, had landed a large portion of his Ship's Company, and fortified the town, and was only waiting our arrival, and to complete the necessary preperations to march the Jacks some 150 miles into the interior, and retake Los Angeles.

Setting aside the bombast and wind blowed by the Sailors themselves, and looking seriously at the affair, it seemed shrouded with difficulty. Impediments sprang up at every step of the way and a mind less strong than the Commodore's would have quailed at the prospect before him. In the first place, provisions were so scarce that, in the article of Bread especially, all the Squadron with the exception of ourselves had been for some time on one half the usual ration.[1] Then the difficulty of procuring the means of transporting the artillery (as the Horses were mostly run off by the Californians) and oxen could not be procured for love or money. Then we had no carts for the conveyance of Baggage or Wounded, and at last but not least the trial of a novel experiment, of forming a lot of Sailors into a Battalion, and with the few short days allowed, of bringing them to the necessary state of discipline to ensure success seemed almost impossible.

The sequel however proved that what had appeared to be the strongest was the easiest impediment to overcome, and proved con-

---

1. Montgomery wrote Larkin on November 11, 1846, that "I feel it to be all important to the public interests for me to sail from this port at the earliest practicable date—which I cannot do until supplied with bread. . . . I . . . request that you will use your utmost efforts to have forwarded to Yerba Buena with the least possible delay all the bread which may be now ready for delivery." George P. Hammond, editor, *The Larkin Papers* (1951 ff.), v, p. 273; see also Montgomery to Larkin, November 12, 1846, *ibid.*, v, pp. 274–275.

Montgomery did not receive the much-needed bread until two weeks later. Montgomery to Captain William Mervine, *ibid.*, v, p. 287.

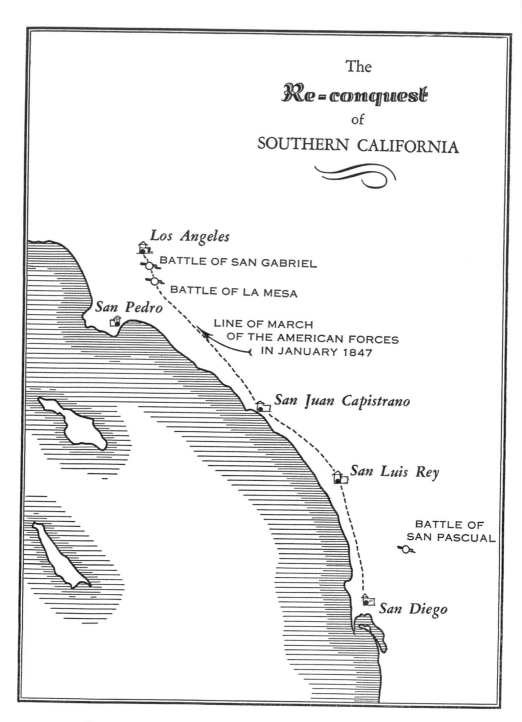

The

Re-conquest

of

SOUTHERN CALIFORNIA

Los Angeles

BATTLE OF SAN GABRIEL

BATTLE OF LA MESA

San Pedro

LINE OF MARCH
OF THE AMERICAN FORCES
IN JANUARY 1847

San Juan Capistrano

San Luis Rey

BATTLE OF
SAN PASCUAL

San Diego

clusively that, the old maxim that a "Yankee can turn his hand to anything" is no slur upon the nation, but an undeniable fact.

The Sailors were formed into companies and with the aid and instruction of such of the Officers as were at all "au fait" in the common field maneuvers of the Day, speedily became very expert at drill. I do not mean to say that they could go through the Manual or Marching Drill as readily as the Volunteer Companies of our Cities, but that their performance was much better than I have often seen among Militia Companies in the States. This proficiency is easily accounted for as they one and all entered into the matter heart and soul, and strove their best to understand and carry into proper effect all the orders which were given them. They knew that Regular Soldiers were on their way from the States to occupy California, and they considered the Honor of the Flag and the branch of the Service to which they belonged required that they should retake what had been lost and prove to the Californians that because they had gained an advantage over a few of our Ship's Company, they must not boast that Sailors could not stand in a Field of Fight.

But I am getting ahead rather too fast, and if you please, we will return on board the *Portsmouth* who we left outside the Harbor of San Diego.[2] We made port in the forenoon of the day succeeding the one on which we had spoken the *Sterling*, but as the wind was light and baffling, we had but small prospect of getting in this day; however we managed to keep her head in the right direction and made some little progress.

Just after dinner a light wind sprang up, and as we were passing along under its influence, the man at the Mast Head reported a Boat coming out to meet us. Now we would get the latest news, and all were agog to catch the first sound of the voices of the Strangers. In the course of an hour she came alongside and proved to be one of the *Congress*'s cutters with a Pilot for us. No sooner was he over the gangway than over came the Boats crew, who were quickly surrounded by a gaping crowd all eager to know what had happened and what was to be done. It was news too, and such a batch of it as to cause lots of speculation and afford plenty of chance for the Politicians to detail and enlarge upon until the cry of "All Hands bring Ship to Anchor" dispersed the crowds which thronged the Lee Gangway.

2. The *Portsmouth* reached San Diego, December 9, 1846. "Log of the *Portsmouth*."

Gen¹. Kearney had arrived in the Country accompanied by only about 100 Dragoons.³ Lt. Gillespie had been despatched by the Commodore with some 30 or 40 Volunteers to meet him, and after they had effected a junction [December 5, 1846] the whole party was attacked by a body of Californians under Andreas Pico, and though the Americans had remained masters of the Field, yet they had suffered a loss of 2 Captains, 1 Lieut. and 14 or 15 Privates killed and some wounded. They had been compelled to encamp upon a Hill some 40 miles from San Diego and were now surrounded by the Enemy in a starving condition, having lost most of their Horses, and had no means of conveying their wounded even had the Enemy allowed them to march unmolested.⁴

An expedition for their relief had been ordered to march that morning but when we hove in sight it had been countermanded and ordered to wait our arrival for reinforcements.⁵ The circumstances under which Genl. K. had fought were of themselves disheartening enough. His command had marched from Santa Fe, and were worn out and exhausted. Their animals, the most of which were mules, were broken down and at the best of times mules are no animals to charge upon or fight with as their stubborness precludes the possibility of maneuvering them to advantage. In addition to this the fight took place just as the morning dawned. The Americans had been riding the whole night in a cold rain, and most of them were so numbed that they could with difficulty grasp their sabres, in addition to which they were each lumbered up with an overcoat.

On the other hand the Californians had lain the whole night under shelter and by good fires, had each man of them a first rate horse, were forewarned of the approach of the Dragoons and chose their own ground to meet them. These circumstances, independent of their superiority of number, gave them immense advantages, and

3. General Stephen W. Kearny who, after having taken New Mexico in the summer of 1846, crossed Arizona toward San Diego accompanied by, as Downey says, approximately 100 men.

4. This was the battle of San Pascual fought December 6, 1846. For a thorough account of the battle and the rescue of Kearny's depleted forces see Arthur Woodward, *Lances at San Pascual* (San Francisco, 1948), and Bancroft, *History of California*, v, pp. 336–356.

5. The relief expedition was under the command of Lieutenant A. V. F. Gray. For details see Smith, *War With Mexico*, I, pp. 342 and 535.

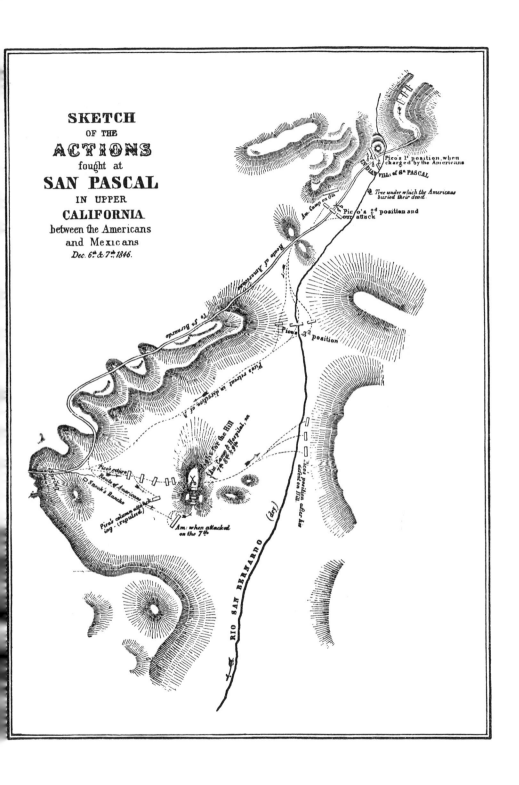

SKETCH
OF THE
ACTIONS
fought at
SAN PASCAL
IN UPPER
CALIFORNIA
between the Americans
and Mexicans
Dec. 6th & 7th 1846.

Pico's 1st position when
charged by the Americans

VILL. of Sa PASCAL

Tree under which the Americans
buried their dead.

Am. Camp on Hill

Pico's 2d position and
our attack

Road of Americans

Road of Bernardo

Pico's 3d position

Pico's retreat in disorder

Am. pick for the Hill
Am. Camp & Hospital, m
7th 8th & 9th

Am. position after he
acted on Hill.

Pico's retreat

Snook's Rancho

Route of Americans

Pico's column attacking (regular)

Am. when attacked
on the 7th

RIO SAN BERNARDO (dry)

the honor to be given to the Dragoons for remaining Masters of the Field and bringing off their Dead and wounded is greatly enhanced thereby.

By the time this sore news was digested, we had opened the point and saw the Town, *Congress* and Block House fair before us. As we drew near the Land the breeze gradually freshened, and by 5 P.M. [Dec. 10] we were at anchor in the Harbor of San Diego. Preparations were at once made to moor ship, but in the midst of all came a "Belay all" and the word was passed to get our suppers as quick as possible. What could this mean? It leaked out at last. "Fighting Bob" had sent down an order for our Old Man to land and despatch "forthwith" to town 150 men, with a due complement of Officers. Also to come himself, and prepare to remain in and assume the Command and Governorship of said Town.

You may rest assured that supper was but a short meal, and in a very few minutes the crew were again on Deck, when the appearance of matters looked very warlike. Muskets, carbines, Pistols, Pikes and ammunition were strewed all over the Quarter Deck. In a short time the Marines appeared full accoutered for Landing, and the Autocrat began selecting out his men to form the different Companies according to the species of arms he could muster. There were 25 or 26 Musketeers and the Balance were armed with Carbines, Pistols and Pikes, while each man carried a Cutlass. Every Officer fore and aft save the Gunner and 1st Luff was to go, and when the part who were to stay were paraded on deck, they could hardly be seen so small was the number.[6]

It was dusk before everything was in readiness for the debarkation and before all were ashore, it was dark enough. When however the last boat load were landed, we were ordered into line. The Marines on the Right, the Musketeers next and the Carbineers bringing up the rear. When we had got into Line, straight or not straight, 'twas too dark to see, the Soldier Officer who was ahead started off his troops, our 2nd Luff [B. F. B. Hunter] who had command of the Jacks sang out forward, old Pipes blew away upon his call and off we started on a dog trot.

6. Fortunately for his future readers, Downey was among those sent ashore from the *Portsmouth*. He must have been pleased to learn that Lieutenant Missroon was to remain on board, while B. F. B. Hunter, one of the few officers Downey liked, was sent ashore.

Of all the roads that were ever travelled by mortal man on a dark night, this was I believe one of the worst; it was for near a mile along the beach and rocks and pieces of rocks and stones of all sizes lay in every direction, and to mend the matter every few steps you would find a gully some 18 or 20 inches deep into which you would plump your foot, and 10 to one but you would fetch up on your nose. Now rooting up any kind of ground, be it ever so soft, in this manner is not very agreeable, but this soil, composed as it was of sand small pebbles and fragments of shells, was sudden death to a fellow's face.

It seemed however to make no odds to the chaps ahead how rough the road was; on they went at a Charge Step and the poor devils in the rear were obliged to keep up, or endure a severe cursing from Pipes, who was in the rear, driving up stragglers. Now and then he would Pipe "Belay," when we would come to a sudden halt, and wait for some unlucky wight whose legs were not long enough to keep up. When all was right, he would Blow "go ahead," and off we would start at the same Break Neck Pace. The distance to the town was 5 miles, and in about 50 minutes from the time we started we were brought up all standing by the Challenge of a sentry, who was posted on the road close to the outskirts. The answer being "Friends— Portsmouths" the Sentry hailed the Corporal and the Corporal passed us in. As we marched past the Barracks occupied by the *Congress* Musketeers, we found that late as was the hour, they were on parade. Something was evidently in the wind.

We marched at once to the Quarters of the Commodore [Stockton] and Commander in Chief, where having been reported to him, the Marines and Musketeers were ordered at once to the Commisary to procure marching rations, as they were to march in an hour, "en route" to relieve the Command of Genl Kearney.[7] Poor fellows, they marched the live long night, at a quick step and when morning dawned they were forced to climb a steep Hill, and there remain the whole day flat on their bellies, not being allowed even to rise to a

7. Downey describes the rescue party's trip in some detail, and at times gives the impression that he was on the expedition. But since he refers to the troops more often as "they" than as "we," it is probable that he is reporting a firsthand account told to him by a member of the relief expedition. Yet in his later account (1853) Downey leads his readers to assume that he was on the expedition. Rogers, *Filings from an Old Saw*, pp. 86–88; Woodward, *Lances at San Pascual*, pp. 43–45. For a firsthand account see "Duvall's Log of the *Savannah*," in the California Historical Society *Quarterly*, III (July, 1924), pp. 123–125.

sitting position for fear that the Enemy might see them, and suspecting the approach of relief, run away and give no chance for a fight.

That night as soon as it was dark, they marched again, and about 2 A.M. saw the signal fires of the Camp. It was well understood by both Officers and Men that the Dragoons were entirely surrounded, and consequently we expected to have to fight our way through the Enemie's camp to them. Thus when the Camp Fires were first discovered, each man braced himself for the conflict, and prepared as best he could for a desperate affair. Silently they marched on till within a mile of the Fires when suddenly they were hailed in Spanish "Qui viene?"—no answer—still they proceeded, again the same cry "Qui viene?" to this no attention was paid, the troops pressing forward at double quick time. Every musket was ready for the charge and every cartridge Box adjusted and opened. The person who had challenged was evidently a Spanish Piquet, and as he hailed no more, most probably rode off to give information of our approach. Presently we heard in a stentorian voice (which we had cause afterward long to remember) the cheering challenge . . . "Who comes there?"— "Friends!" was the answer and almost before we were aware we were in the Camp of the Dragoons. Greetings were exchanged on each side, and stories of misfortunes past related, and then all snatched such little sleep as they could preparatory to marching on our return at day light.

The situation of the Dragoons was miserable indeed, they were out of every thing, and had even killed their half starved mules and eaten them. They had waited for the relief until the Old Genl. lost patience, and that night had burned all the Baggage they could not pack and were determined to start on the following morning at all hazards. They had several wounded, too much so as to be unable to move. The Genl. and Lt. Gillespie had both been wounded with lances in the side, their transportation, rations, forage, all, all was gone but the indomitable courage of a Yankee. They could but die and they were determined to cut their way through or perish in the attempt.

At 8 that morning the assembly sounded, and we started on our return, escorting those poor fellows, who had already made a journey of some 2100 miles, and now had but just begun their difficulties. At night we camped at a Rancho belonging to one [Jose Maria Alvarado] who was said to be friendly, but 'twas all the same to the

174

Drags, who fell foul of his chickens and Pigs and slayed them without any mercy. This night they lived, and the next morning they were a different looking race of men.

On the afternoon of the second day we arrived in San Diego, and found our Men in Quarters. The party who had remained behind had made themselves quite at home, and had created a sufficient number of Sergeants and Corporals, and every thing wore the air of Regular Barracks. Roll Call at Revillee and a drill at 9 A.M. that would last till dinner time, was the mornings amusement. Then every half hour there was a call for a detail to catch and kill the bullocks. Provisions were scarce too, and our allowance now consisted of One Pint of Wheat (which we could grind ourselves) one Gill of Whiskey, one half allowance of Tea and sugar, and Beef "ad libetum" for 24 hours.

While however we detail transactions on shore we must not let the Ship be forgotten, and one incident transpired that deserved to be extolled high on the book of fame as a lasting testimony of the zeal which was exercised by our Autocrat for the benefit of the service. We had landed on the evening of Wednesday, at 2 Bells in the afternoon. According to custom our grub for the suceeding day, consisting of Beef, Flour and Apples had been served out. Of course the cooks of the messes, as in duty bound, had converted their flour into Duff, and deposited the same in the steep tub under the Ships Cooks charge. Now it would not do to let it lay longer than one day or it would become sour, so he boiled the Beef and Duffs and as there were but few men on board, of course there was a surplus on hand. Well the men who had remained on board the *Congress* were sent on board to moor our Ship, sand down Royal and Top Gallant Yards, and make all snug for a long tarry. As these poor fellows had been on short allowance for some time, such of our boys as were on board, had stuffed themselves up with the idea that they could give their Ship or Squadron Mates a grand blow out on the Duff.

This plan however did not meet the approbation of the Autocrat, and accordingly, after keeping the Congressmen at work till with 15 minutes of 8 Bells M. he then packed them off bag and baggage and ordered the Purser's Steward to take charge of the Surplus Duff and serve it out cold to the men, at the rate of 4 ounces per diem, in lieu of Bread. Now any one who knows what sort of materials a Duff is composed of can judge what sort of stuff it is when it becomes cold, and worse than all, when the allowance for 140 men is kept until it shall be devoured by 20 men at the rate of 4 ounces per day. Oh it must have been rare stuff by that time. At the same time, he stopped all rations of Beef and Pork and getting out the seine, bade them go and catch fish, which were served out to them in lieu of what the Government allowed them, and the order of the day was "if you dont catch fish to eat, you shall have nothing." Under such laws our situation in Town was infinitely preferable to theirs.

Meanwhile the preparations for the campaign were progressing very rapidly; all the mechanics that could be mustered were busily employed making waggons, carts, tents, shoes and all other necessaries for the men. Parties were daily sent out, to procure by hook or crook, Horses, Mules, Oxen, Bullocks, Sheep and Goats. All the Inhabitants who were in the town were strictly confined to the limits and furnished by the Government with rations for their subsistence at the same ration as the Men. "Fighting Bob" [Stockton] was a gassy old Cove, and would have "his bullies" as he termed them out every day, drilling, charging, forming hollow squares, and putting themselves in the best possible discipline. He would collect a crowd around him, and commence a harrangue, and chalk out to them the exact route he was going to pursue, the maneuvers he meant to execute, and the sure way in which the Californians were to be whipped. As our old Man was Governor of San Diego, it was for some time the current rumor that all the Portsmouth's were to stay to protect this place, while the Commodore and his own men, with the volunteers, were to have all the Honor of re-taking the Puebla de Los Angeles.

This arrangement caused much dissatisfaction, and no small share of growling and grumbling, on the part of our Stud's who were all eager to have a Brush with the Enemy. This matter was however soon put at rest by an order to detail all the party of Musketeers, and 25 Carbineers, to remove to a house in the lower part of the Town, and put themselves under special drill for Active Service. As there [were] 250 men out of whom these 50 were to be selected, it was a matter of impossibility to satisfy all; every one wished to go, and the poor devil who made out the detail was run nearly out of his wits by the crowd that pressed round him and stunned him with their noise. On all sides the cry was "put me down, dont forget my name" and at last in utter despair, he gave up the attempt to select and took them just as they came in order upon the Roll. When the Men were

Mustered, and those who were detailed ordered to form in separate company as their names were called, many awful long faces were seen, and dire were the curses heaped upon the head of the unlucky Scribe for not allowing all to go. But long faces and curses were of no use and the Detailed Command forthwith packed up bag and baggage and removed to their new quarters.

Quarters did I say? Such was the name given it, but such a place; the inventive genius of Cruikshank could never have imagined such a Hoghole to stow men in. It was an old, tumble down adobe house, with lots of holes where doors and windows ought to have been, but none were there. The dirt floor was covered to the depth of some 8 or 10 inches with all sorts of dirt and filth, the roof looked as if it were about to fall every moment, and to crown all, immediately in the rear, was a large Karall, where each night were penned up some scores of Bullocks, Calves, Horses and Mules, who of course promoted sleep by the conglomeration of musical sounds they produced from their united efforts at Concertism.

This last evil however was in the end productive of some comfort, and in plain contradiction of the Old Motto "that no good can come out of an Evil" this one was converted into a Public Good. Oh Thou Back Door, could'st thou only talk, and relate what thou has seen— how many poor unoffending calves have been ruthlessly caught, their innocent throats cut from ear to ear, and before they had yet done bleating, been dragged by the horns through thy opening, and all heedless of the sleeping forms crowded upon the dirt of the principal Barrack Room, transported "holus bolus" over them and conveyed to the kitchen, where its hide was quickly stripped from him, and he stuck up in various forms round a large fire, cooking for the palates of sundry of the wild Sailors composing Company "B."

Night after night were these transactions carried on, and astounding were the quantities of meat devoured by these worthies. Oh Sal P – – – [Samuel Parker?] dost thou remember that eventful night, when thou didst enter the aforesaid Karall on "murder vile intent" and didst in fault of finding a smaller one, fist on to a yearling and seizing him by his little horns, throw him to the ground, and apply that knife to his throat—how when he was stilled thee and thy aids did drag him through the Barracks, knocking in thy rapid progress his heels upon the bald pate of Sergeant J., [Charles Jones?] the Whistler, and how he the Whistler did raise upon his Elbow, and shower curses deep and bitter upon thee, and thy tribe? How thou didst scare him into a perfect silence, by the threat of ramming the whole carcass down his throat if he did not shut up? How that he, doubting his capacity of swallowing said carcass whole, did imagine that in case it was attempted he might be smothered or choked, and how that he did take the wiser part of valor, and closing his mouth resign himself to the arms of Morpheus, and leave the field clear for thee to operate in? How thou did drag the animal into the Cook House, and proceed to dress him? How that a stray Indian did peer into the window and watch thy proceeding with wondering eyes? How Billy W – – – [either William Wilson or William Walker] did seize almost a whole tree and chase said Indian away with awful threats and imprecations, how then for fear of discovery thou and thy companions did muggle on to the said carcass, and forthwith drag him away, across the green to the other barracks, and leave him, for the sleeping denizens of that house to answer for? Dost thou remember these things, and remember too the many, many nights thou hast visited the sheep pen and in the dark, sought about for the young and tender lambs, to be slaughtered to minister to thy inner man? Dost thou I say remember all these things, and the ghost of the murdered animals rise not up in thy minds eye, and upbraid thee? If not, thy conscience is very hard, that is all I have got to say.

And Sergeant Slim [George Miller?], too, he deserves a passing notice here. Here it was that his aspiring mind elevated him above the common herd, and he became a Sergeant; not in name alone, but a "bona fide" Skin and Bone Sergeant. He had his separate command, and to him were referred many Officials who enquired of the Adjudant as to the course to be pursued to accomplish certain ends. He was in constant correspondence with the Officials from High to Low, and even the Commodore and General themselves conferred with him upon weighty matters. Nor did this sudden rise in Rank tend to make him proud and overbearing, on the contrary he bore his blushing honors with a meekness that conferred an additional lusture upon his already glistening fame. He was condescending and kind to those beneath him, while his affability and cheerfulness and prompt manner of expressing his opinions and proffering his aid and advice when called upon by the dignitaries won for him golden opinions from all. He was one of the most valuable members of society who had ever promenaded the streets of this or any other Garrisoned Town, and to his exertions and untiring zeal are attributed in a great degree the general good health that prevailed here.

And what you will ask was his position? What high rank and station did he hold? I will enlighten you upon this point. He was—now prepare for a startling announcement—he was the Police Sergeant. He was Captain of the Shovel and Hand Cart Gang, and his duties were multifarious. He was to oversee the drawing of the Grub, to clean up all the dirt and filth about the environs, to bring from the Beach all the Fish that were left there from the Ships for our use, and deliver them in equal portions to the Hungry men, from the Commodore down. Late and early the Sergeant might be seen hurrying hither and thither, sometimes with a spade, sometimes with a Bag, and anon with a string of fish in his hand; again he would go scouring off all over town with his party of indefatigables, with the hand cart in tow, in hot chase of some pile of dirt or filth that threatened by a long stay to create a nuisance unbearable. His stock of patience, and a large one it was too, was sometimes nearly run off the reel, and yet he was always to outward appearance in good humor, and had a witty answer ready for any question that might be asked of him.

Yet with all this outward show, the Sergeant was not entirely content, "his soul burned in arms and was eager for the fray" and he did not fail continually to remind him, who had the detailing of men required to fill vacancies, of his wish to lay down his life, if necessary, in his country's cause. He was ready, he said, to sacrifice anything to go, ready to lay down the high command he now retained and descend to the ranks, shoulder his musket, and become a full private in the rear rank, with no prospect of in the event becoming even a Corporal, if such sacrifice was necessary to enable him to follow to the field the Warlike Commodore. It was of no use to put him off with common excuses, for he would not heed them. Tell him his shoes were worn out and no others could be procured and his answer would be, "but I have got the pair of feet and as I have been travelling on them some 25 years, I guess they'll last me to the Pueblo and back."

Tell him Grub was scarce and would be more so on the march, and he would reply "well I am thin and don't require much, and you see 'twill be a good plan to have some small eaters along, as they will show a good pattern to the rest."

Tell him the town of San Diego would go to ruin and all the so-journers therein fall victims to some foul disease if the Police Sergeant was to desert his post, and he would quote "let the dead bury the dead, but I am off to Pueblo."

Tell him the Governor could not dispense with the services of so efficient a man, and would not listen to the idea of his going, and he would swear to do him a private injury, by leaving a large pile of dirt before his door, so that he would fall over it the first time he came out, or else carry stinking fish to his Cook, for him to masticate, and thus provoke him to reduce him for neglect of duty.

Reasoning and argument were of no avail; go he must, and of course, he did, and throwing aside as useless trash the high stature he occupied, and the encomium that men daily heaped upon him, he shouldered his musket and strutted forth, as ferocious as any other Soldier, determined to do or die.

And a curious looking Soldier-Sailor he was too. He was so thin you would have to take two good looks to see him in the ranks, and even then 'twas hard to distinguish him from the musket, and when in the course of making evolutions he would (and pretty often too) miss his place and get astray in the crowd, he was never missed, but would twist and worm himself about, dodging through places seemingly not large enough for a needle to go without inconvenience, never treading on anybody's toes, or if he did, he was so light no one felt it, and at last regaining his position and coming into line, with head erect and look which seemed to say "here I am, all right and tight, you needn't think to fool me, with your marching and counter-marching. I'm up to snuff."

The Dragoons had, after a few days rest, recruited and were now ready for the march; everything was in a great state of forwardness. The quantity of Horses, Mules and Cattle required for the expedition were collected together, the cannon were all mounted and the teams for their transportation assigned to them, and nothing now remained to be done but to issue the necessary rations, pack the carts, issue and read to the army the General Orders, and we were off.

At this juncture the *Cyane* arrived, and brought a mail from home that had come out in the *Dale*, but as she was some 6 or 7 months out, there was nothing new by her.[8] It was near the end of December and already Rumor was busy fixing the day for marching, but still

8. The *Cyane* arrived on December 27, 1846. "Log of the *Portsmouth*."

the expected order came not, the days were consumed by drills in squads and companies in the morning, exercising the artillery, and firing at targets. Each afternoon the whole command was paraded and under direction of Genl. Kearney, who had so far recovered from the effect of his wound as to return to active duty, were exercised in the field movements. They were instructed in the mysteries of having no eyes but for the Commander, and no ears to hear aught else but the commands that emanated from him and his subordinates.

They were taught to march and countermarch, to "file right into line," to wheel by platoon and battalion, and to form the grand move of the whole campaign, a hollow square to receive a charge of cavalry. As each successive move was progressing towards perfection, the Old Veteran would over and over again express his admiration at the manner in which the Jacks, as he styled them, performed the parts allotted to them, and promised them complete success if they would remain firm on the field, and not allow their enthusiasm to overcome their reason, and so far carry them away as to induce them to break their ranks. They were also drilled to the charge, and as the word was given such another race and such a hurrah, as accompanied the movements would have scared the Californians if nothing else.

The whole of the marching command was mustered on the 26th, all the sick, lame, lazy, and those who thought they could not stand the fatigue were picked out, and their places speedily filled up with Volunteers from our Ship who were distributed about among all the companies so freely that at last we had a fair representation among those brave fellows who were to undertake this novel expedition.

On Sunday the 27th Dec the General Order was read, and the several Companies assigned their respective baggage waggons and ordered to draw provisions for 7 days at the rate of one half a ration per day. This was little enough, but was by far better than they had been in the habit of receiving, and was received as a good omen. They were also ordered to muster, armed and equipped with their muskets, knapsacks, and Haversacks in full marching order, in the Public Square on the morning of the 28th at 9 A.M. preparatory to taking up a line of March to the Puebla de Los Angelos. The certainty of going raised the desponding hopes of all, and the reading of the Orders were received with 3 times 3, by all the lucky ones who were to march, and by awful long faces, by those who were deprived of this privilege. Exchanges were however constantly taking place, even to the very last moment, and many who had cursed their hard fortune on the morning of the 27th wore quite a new face in the course of the day and night, and trudged forth with light hearts to join the several companies to which they were ordered to fill vacancies.[9]

The Artillery Company consisted of 100 men who had 5 pieces of cannon, mounted for Light Field Service, varying from 9 to 6 pounders. They were fitted and complete, and were well drilled and armed with pikes and pistols. This body was under command of Lieut T – – – n, better known among the Jacks as "Hobble the Mule."[10] The Marines of Both Ships then in Harbor and a detatchment from the *Savannah,* numbering about 100 muskets, were a firm and efficient body of men. They were under the immediate command of Lieut L – – – n of the Marine Corps, who was also Acting Adjudant.[11]

The Dragoons, numbering 57, were armed with Carbines and as they were compelled from the want of Horses to act on foot, the long sabre was discarded and boarding Pikes substituted in their place, and each one had in addition his Pistols in his Belt. They were a fine Body of Men and burned to get a chance to revenge the death of their comrades. They were commanded by Capt [Henry S.] Turner of the Dragoons, 1st Lieut [John W.] Davidson, and attached to this Corps was Capt [William H.] Emory of the Engineers, who acted as Aid to the Commander, and selected and formed the Camping Grounds.[12]

Then came the Volunteers, or $25 men, among whom were some 8 or 10 of the Savannahs, armed with Colts Repeating Rifles. These

9. H. H. Bancroft discusses the personnel and details of the expedition in such great profusion that they need not be repeated here. See his *History of California,* v, pp. 385 ff. Besides Downey's, two other eyewitness accounts of the expedition may be consulted: William H. Emory, *Notes of a Military Reconnaissance from Fort Leavenworth . . . to San Diego, California,* 30th Cong. 1st Sess. H. Exec. Doc. 44 (Washington, 1848), now more conveniently extracted in Ross Calvin, editor, *Lieutenant Emory Reports* (Albuquerque, 1951); John S. Griffin, *A Doctor Comes to California. The Diary of John S. Griffin, Assistant Surgeon with Kearny's Dragoons, 1846–1847* (San Francisco, 1943).

10. Lieutenant Richard L. Tilghman USN.

11. Lieutenant John W. Livingston USN. *Gen. Nav. Reg.* (1882), p. 437.

12. See Bancroft, *History of California,* v, pp. 385–86 for a full listing of the officers and their rank.

men were mounted and were intended to act as skirmishers and purveyors for the Main Body. They were part of the Corps which composed the Command of Lieut Gillespie.[13]

Another small Body of some 10 or 15 volunteers were called the Life Guards, though for what reason I could never discover, who rode ahead and acted as spies. This band was commanded by the celebrated Kit Carson, memorable for his adventures in the mountains with Col Freemont. There was also a company of Californian volunteers, under command of Don Santiago E. Arguello, who acted as Vaquerros on the march and rendered efficient service on the field; they were good marksmen, noble horsemen, and above all the rest, true blue to the cause they had espoused.[14]

All the balance of the Command, consisting of near 300 men, were Blue Jackets, and were representatives of all the Ships in the Harbor, *viz. Congress, Portsmouth,* and *Cyane,* and a detachment of 25 or 30 from the *Savannah,* under command of "that long ghost of misery" Lt R – – –n [Rowan], whose brave and manly deeds will *hereafter* be noticed. For the present suffice it to say that himself and one other Naval Officer attached to the *Cyane* were the only exceptions to the title of Gentlemen who marched with the Command. This large body of men were divided into 4 companies of Musketeers, belonging one to the *Congress,* under command of Actg Lt G – – – t, one to the *Portsmouth,* under our own well liked B.F.B.H., one to the *Cyane,* under command of Actg Lieut H – – – s, and the last as before mentioned to the *Savannah.*[15]

There were also Two Companies of Carbineers, who belonged part of each to the *Congress,* and part to the *Portsmouth.* One of these was under the command of Passed Mid J. M. D – – –n and the other under that of Mr. J. P – – –d,[16] the Sailmaker of the *Congress,* who had been an Officer in a Volunteer Company in the States for some years and being "au fait" in the Drill had rendered essential

13. Gillespie had been driven out of Los Angeles, defeated at San Pedro, and wounded at San Pascual, but he had now recovered enough to command the volunteers who constituted the 4th Battalion.

14. Downey is wrong in separating these men from Gillespie's command, of which they were a part. Santiago E. Arguello, a landowner at San Juan Capistrano and a judge at San Diego, had decided to aid the American cause. He served as a captain in Gillespie's Battalion. Bancroft, *History of California,* II, p. 702; v, p. 386.

15. Lieutenants Gough W. Grant, B. F. B. Hunter, and Edward Higgins, all USN.

16. Passed Midshipman James M. Duncan, USN, and John Peed, USN.

service in imparting his knowledge to the men under his command, which had the name of being the best drilled and disciplined company of Jacks in the Battalion.

There was also a small corps of Sappers and Miners, composed of the mechanics of the *Congress,* under command of the celebrated Mr. S – – –k, who found lots of work in repairing the carts, which often gave out on the tramp.[17] Last on the list comes some 35 or 40 Pike and Pistol Men belonging to the *Cyane,* who joined the morning of the march and of course had but little of discipline; they were under the command of Passed Mid S – – n, or, as he was better known, by the cognomen of "Center of Gravity."[18]

The Officer in General Command of the Blue Jackets, or as he would be styled in Military Parlance, the Col Commanding this Battalion, was Lt. S. C. R – – n [Rowan], the 1st Lieut of the *Cyane.*[19] Lt. Geo M – – – r [Minor] of the *Savannah,* had charge of the Waggons, Carts, Pack Mules, Bullocks, Sheep and all the other live stock attached to the command, and truly he did lead a miserable life in his attempts to "hurry up them Cattle."

Purser S – – – n [William Speiden] of the *Congress* was on the Staff, with the title of Actg. Quarter Master General, while his train consisted of one Assistant Quarter Master (whom the Jacks christened as "Bullocks Liver" from the fact that he was eternally on the run, with his old straw hat cocked up, and his everlasting Pea Jacket streaming behind him, demanding of the Butchers all the Hearts and Livers, for the sole use of the Commodore, and a vivacious appetite Fighting Bob must have had if he devoured them all) one Commisary, a fine good natured old Fellow named Fisher, and some three or four hangers on to the party, who officiated for the sake of the wee things they could pick up. We had also a full complement of those indespensible Gentlemen in War Time, the Medical and Surgical Corps, and this, together with a sprinkling of Midshipmen who acted as Lieutenants of the different Companies, and some Lieuts. as aids to the Commander in Chief and the General, comprised the whole of the Grand Army of the Pueblo.

A few days previous to the march, an idea popped into the brain

17. John Southwick, USN.

18. Passed Midshipman J. F. Stenson, USN.

19. Lieutenant Stephen C. Rowan, USN who was not attached to the *Cyane,* but to the *Congress. Gen. Nav. Reg.* (1882), p. 620.

of the Commodore that he would mount his Marines, thus forming a Corps of Horse Marines, a body which has often been talked about but never definitely seen. Whenever a whim of this or any other kind seized him, he was sure to make the experiment, and accordingly, the Volunteers were ordered to bring their Horses, saddles, and other Equipment into the Square, and the Marines were ordered out and each man had an animal assigned him. Now, as the Officer Commanding the Marines did not relish the plan at all, he paid but little attention to the distribution, and the volunteers cared not who got the Horses, since they were bound to lose them. In consequence the sharing out, was a one sided affair altogether. Long Marines got Short Horses, and Short Marines, Long Horses; those who were good Riders got gentle Horses and those who perhaps had never mounted a Horse, got the wildest of the Lot. All by accident of course. Well every man got his Horse at last, and having equipped himself with the enormous Spurs worn in this Country, with Rowels an inch or more in length, grasped his musket, and awaited the word of command of mount.

The crowd was waiting with gaping mouths to see how the Horse Marines would work. "Mount" was the word and they did mount, and no sooner were they mounted, than a number were dismounted again. Then commenced a scene which soon convulsed the bystanders with Laughter, and convinced the Old Commander that his scheme would not work. I have said a number were dismounted. I might have said a great number, but shall not, nor shall I say they were not at all particular how they dismounted, nor shall I say that some came over the head, and some over the stern of the Horses, some on the right, and more on the wrong side, nor how many legs were seen at once in the air, as their owners were describing involuntary sommersets, nor how muskets flew in all directions nor how some of the Horses ran away with their Riders and more without their Riders, how Marines, Muskets, caps and Horse Equippage was strewed in promiscuous heaps from one end of town to the other. Oh! no I shall say nothing about all this but I shall only say this scheme did not work.

Something however delayed the march on the 28th, but on the 29th, bright and early, every body was in motion and by the hour of 9 A.M. the whole Battalion were formed in line of march in the square, every man with a light heart and a tolerable heavy knapsack, where they were reviewed by the Commodore and General and pronounced in complete order. The Baggage, Provision and Ammunition Carts were got into their proper places, the Vaquerros were riding in all directions, shouting and hallooing at the top of their voices to keep the stray cattle in order, servants were running to and fro among the carts, carrying sundry mysterious bundles to deposit therein. Shaking of hands and wishes of success were passing between those who were to go and those who were to stay, the staff and General Officers were all mounted and their Horses were kicking up the very devil in the square, all was noise and hubbub outside the line, when out pops the Commodore and General, side by side; they take their station in the Center of the Square; the Band struck up a Quick Step, and with a Cheer that made the heavens ring again, the command obeyed that well known and so much revered voice as it gave the order to Forward, March.

Cheer after cheer ascended from that crowd of firm hearts, as each company defiled before the two Commanders, and each one was answered by a corresponding one on the part of the spectators, and as the last of the Battalion passed them, the General and the Commodore, with the Staff, wheeled and with a Doff of the Cap and wave of the hand responded to the good wishes of those who looked on, and then dashed off, to join their comrades.

It was a splendid and heart warming sight to see these brave men, most of whom had in a manner unsexed themselves, and become what a Sailor hates most, Soldiers, upon Emergency, but it was a proof of what Yankees can do in a pinch. Let us too give a just meed of honor to him who had the head to contrive and the tact to carry through such a plan. No man less acquainted with all the minutie of a Sailor's character could ever have done it, and no man could have ever succeeded who had not, as he had, cemented closely the tie of trust and friendship, so necessary to all well conducted plans between officer and men. This he has done by a series of conducts to those under his command which has endeared him to them, and the name of "Fighting Bob" is never mentioned in our Squadron but as that of a Brave Officer, and the Sailor's Friend.

The March—
The Battles—
Los Angeles Won

[In these last sketches Downey captures the whole flavor and atmosphere of the overland march from San Diego to Los Angeles. The almost hour-by-hour account of the trek, the difficulties of supply, the sandstorm, and the battles themselves need little clarification. This was another of those peculiar, even amusing, campaigns, like Doniphan's march, that defied the proper rules of war. Here was a land expedition in which the majority of the soldiers were sailors! It was fought with a minimum of the regular supplies of war and a great deal of ingenuity. Sail cloth was made into shoes; wheels for guns were stolen from carts; a shortage of draft animals was overcome simply by taking any animals found along the way. It was an army of infantry against expert horsemen—an army rambunctious, hungry, often drunk, but possessing all the needed courage. And when they finally fought the battles of San Gabriel and La Mesa, they provided great fun and enough glory for everyone. Downey gives us a delightful picture of the enlisted man's view of the whole campaign. He is a sort of "Private Hargrove" in the Mexican War, and what he has to say is a useful supplement to those more sober other eyewitness accounts by Lieutenant Emory of the Topographical Engineers, and Army Surgeon John S. Griffin.[1]]

THIS CHAPTER will be the most difficult of any for me to compile, for it is fraught with so deep interest in itself, that there will be no need of any embellishment, but dismounting from my horse of Fancy, I shall plod my weary way along on foot, with my musket on my shoulder and knapsack on my back, through a march of 160 miles, which consumed the better part of 13 days, and when coming in foot sore and tired after each days march, tell a sound unvarnished tale of the nightly occurrences of the camp, and if you have the patience to follow me, place you in perfect safety, despite the attempts of the Californians, securely in the Pueblo de Los Angeles, where you can pause and take a look at the Laurels won by our Sailor General and his better half the Old Soldier himself, and placed upon the Brows of the Dragoons, Marines and Tars of the Pacific Squadron, for let me tell you, the Dragoons claim to belong

1. See above, p. 182, n. 9.

to our squadron also, having thoroughly incorporated themselves with us among our trials, sufferings, hard fighting and privations.

On, on we marched, the whole live long day, halting now and then to right some cart that would capsize, or recover some unruly bullock that would despite of all efforts, stray away from the crowd, but our progress was but slow owing to the obstinacy of the Teams, who had not as yet got used to the moves, and were extremely averse to moving any way but that which suited them. To crown the whole, the evening wound up with a drizzling rain, which made the ground slippery and unsafe to walk upon, and as our route was for the most part up and down hill, with but little level road to travel on, it required a tolerable smart Sailor Man to keep right end uppermost, with the unusual load they bore upon their backs. Many and many a poor fellow measured his length in the mud, but 'twas in vain to look for sympathy or condolence, the best plan was to jump up and laugh the matter off, and stand by to join in the roar which was sure to greet the next stumbler.

It was after sunset before we reached the Camp Ground, and long after dark before we were fairly settled, and had Camp Fires going, and began to Cook our suppers. Then the Bullock were to be killed, dressed and served out for the next day. Parties were at once detailed from each company to assist at this operation at once so interesting and so much for the Public Good. The Cattle were shot down and each squad, seizing their own Bullock, went hard down on skinning &c. Here and there and every where, was "Old Bullocks Liver," flying about with a Lantern in his fist, and bawling at the top of his voice, that all the Livers, Tongues and Hearts must be turned over, without fraud, embezzlement or concealment, into the Commisary Dept. for the sole and especial benefit of the Commodore and General.

Now every body was aware that this was an order of his own, and that the Livers were to be saved for the benefit of the Quarter Masters own mess and to tickle his own palate, and the consequence was he got but few Livers from that crowd. Once or twice he got rather unruly and too near a crowd who had appropriated the aforesaid articles for their own use, and at such times a douse of his lantern and a slap across the face in the dark with the Liver, Lights and all was administered to him as a gentle hint to make himself scarce. Nor was he slow in taking the hint, for he would gather himself up, and securing his lantern, skulk off without another word in search of some other squad where he might try his luck.

Ill luck however never daunted him. He kept up the same cry the whole tramp, although on a general average he got more cusses then Livers for his pains. One wag to whom he had made his way, acquiesed with his demand with all seeming alacrity, yet while in the act of delivering the lot to him, managed to cut off the Heart and Liver, and off he trotted with the Light and Tongue in his hand, nor did he discover the fraud until he had gone some 50 yards, when dashing it down, he returned in hot chase, of the swindler, enquiring of every one he met, where he was.

The first man he met was Sergeant Slim, who upon his asking the question, gravely informed him that he had seen the Culprit but a few moments before, crawling into the Commodore's Tin Oven and the Cook was covering him over with a large spoon, and, said Slim, "if you go quick you will catch him." He enquired of many others, but the only answers he got were in this wise. One had seen him on top of the next hill with a lantern looking for blackberries, or another had just left him down in the hollow looking for a stone to sharpen the General's tooth pick on, or a third had just heard the orderly call him to go and chew corn for the Commodore's Pack Mule who was sick; at last despairing of finding him he gave up the Chase, and retired to his tent. The meat and bread was served out, and the next look was for a place to sleep.

There was not much choice of ground for 'twas all wet alike, consequently but little growling took place on that score, and soon the camp ground was silent, save with the noise of the Cattle and the deep tones of the sentry, challenging his relief, thus passed our first night on the march to Los Angeles.

At early dawn on the following day the bugles sounded the revilee and "rouse and bitt" was the word, "stir your selves" was the order of the day, and breakfast and something to carry in the haversack for the remainder of the day was cooked with all possible celerity, and in an hour the assembly called all Hands into line and again we plodded our weary way, beguiling the time till 10 or 11 o'clock by sundry yarns and witticisms, when getting sulky and tired, conversation was brought to a stand and every man strove to get on the best way he could without any regard to his neighbor.

Previous to the start the Guard was detailed and mounted, the

Old Guard relieved, and the new one marched in the rear, bringing up all stragglers and delaying with broken down carts until they could be repaired, often arriving in Camp an hour or so after the balance of the command, then having to stand "Sentry Go" all night. This was the worst part of the whole, yet there was little or no growling upon this head, as every man made up his mind to do and suffer all quietly for the Public Good. We progressed much better this day than the day before and had the good fortune to fall in with a drove of Sheep, belonging to the Lord only knows who, yet we captured them and drove them off as prisoners of war. Poor Things, if they had sense enough to rejoice at having fallen into Christian Hands, their joy was but short lived for upon camping that night the slaughter that was made by lawless hands among their ranks was awful to relate.

Scarcely were the Picquets posted and the fires light [sic], when some wag, not having the fear of the Law Military or Civil before his eyes, having broached the subject of having a Sheep for supper, was immediately joined by 3 or 4 messmates, and they in turn communicating the plan to others it soon flew like wild fire all over the camp and before it was fairly dark, every body who could raise a knife was into the mess. Down they came by scores upon the poor defenceless sheep and commenced a regular attack upon them. The assailants were ruthless, a longing to satisfy the inner man goaded them on, and in their wild fury neither age nor sex were spared, all, all fell in that horrid massacre. Rams, Lambs and Ewes were soon strewed all over the plain, some with Heads and throats cut, and many more with no Heads at all. Marines, Dragoons and Blue Jackets joined in this game and even the Indians who acted as Cattle Drivers came in for their share and snatched up the skins, yet warm from the reeking bodies of the slain, converted them into mantles for their comfort and convenience.

There was not a single Camp Fire that had not at least 3 or 4 and some 5 or 6 carcasses of whole sheep ranged round it and undergoing the process of baking. Not a mess that did not have a grand blow out of mutton for supper, and many and many was the tid bit that was reserved and backed many a weary mile the next day and roasted for supper the ensuing night. There were no exceptions to the partakers in this wholesale murder, and there lives not a man who was on this eventful march, that can with a clear conscience, plead not guilty to the charge of having at least once in his life been seen "with a sheep on his back."

For a time "Old Liver" tried his best to stay the current, but he soon gave up the attempt, and ran to the General with the report but to his dismay the only satisfaction he got was, "Oh let em go, let em go, they will stop when they are all killed and will march much better tomorrow for having a full stomach tonight." God Bless the Old Soldier, he always believed in giving us a full belly when it could be done, especially at the expense of the enemy.

There were some rare mistakes made too on this eventful night. There were among the flock, unnoticed by the assailants, a lot of Goats and, ever and anon some great *Two Horned William* of this species would be seized upon but before the knife could be applied to his throat, would make his sex and species known by the peculiar bleat and smell attatched to reverend *Gents of this Kind* and ten to one but on being released he would as if in sheer spite pitch his tough head, but into the bread bag of his assailant, and knocking the wind out of and flooring him, jump over his fallen enemy with a Bleat of Triumph at having thus freed himself. I saw more than one poor fellow limping along, cussing all the Billy Goats in the world in General and all those in this particular part of California in particular.

The dawn of morning saw but few of that large flock of Sheep in existence and they though seemingly lost in wonder at the sudden disappearance of their companions had still sense enough to decline accompanying us on another day's march, for fear perhaps that they themselves might fall victims on ensuing night.

The next day's march was but a repetition of that of the day before, as every day was much the same. This night we camped near Mule Hill, for such was the name given to the Hill where we found Genl Kearney and his men when as before related we came to their relief. This name was adopted by the Sailors from the fact that the Dragoons had here killed and eaten some mules, in dearth of any other of the meat kind.

Upon examining the ground we found that the Californians or Indians had dug up the bodies of the killed and stripping them of their clothes, left them laying on the ground, a prey for the "cayotes" or prairie wolves, crowds of whom are to be met at every foot of the way. We buried them again, and the next morning started our march and at between 3 and 4 P.M. on the 5th day arrived at the Mission of St. Louis Rey [San Luis Rey], one of those ancient and massive structures found all over Mexico and California, at once wonderful and pleasing to the weary traveller.[2] This Building is an immense structure of Adobe rising to the hight of one very lofty story, in the main Body, and enclosing a court yard of an acre or more. The rooms are large and airy, and a splendid collonade runs the whole length of the front of the building. The rooms in the interior all open into the square and in this square we were all quartered.

Directly in front of the Main Building is one which was from its appearance and the arm racks, stock &c contained in it evidently built for a Guard House, and to the right of this is a splendid garden, and two magnificent fountains of pure and limpid water. I say magnificent for I saw them afterwards when they were restored to good order by the Mormons under Col Cook of the U.S. Army, but at the time of the visit of the Battalion the gardens and fountains were overgrown and choaked with weeds, tall grass and mud.[3] Bad as they were however they could not stop the running water, and a cool refreshing bath we all had here.

Here were lots of workshops of all descriptions, denoting strongly the progress of civilization among the Indians. There were also some splendid vineyards close by the Mission, and more grateful than all to us, there was found after inspection a quantity of good old wine, which was served out to us, at the rate of a pint to each man in the evening and the same quantity on the next morning.

On the extreme left of the Structure was the Church, standing in the Grave Yard, and connected with this Church is a yarn which casts a deep stain upon our little army. Some lawless fellows, who certainly deserve not the name of men, or a class in society of those who pretend to be civilized, having by some means got into the interior

2. The largest of the Spanish missions in California, built in 1798 on the Camino Real some miles north of San Diego.

3. Colonel Philip St. George Cooke was given command of a Mormon battalion of soldiers by Kearny. After an incredible march across desert and mountain, they arrived in San Diego on January 29, 1847. Cooke was then made occupation commandant for the Middle District of California. He and his Mormon troops improved the mission and its grounds, since it was the location of his headquarters. See his *Conquest of New Mexico and California* (New York, 1878).

of the Church, stole from thence a lot of the gold and silver utensials used in the celebration of the Rites of this sect and feloniously carried them off and sold them at the Pueblo.

They were one degree lower removed than the common run of thieves for there is an adage that there is honor even among this class of Gentry but here there was none, for they even descended so far as to steal one anothers plunder after it had been buried for the night. This sacriligious act was not countenanced by any of the men but themselves, and had the facts that afterward came to light have transpired in time they would have been delivered up with the execration of their Squadron mates on their heads, but twas kept a secret till long after our return and the dispersion of the squadron, consequently an exposure was of no use.

We arrived here on Saturday and expected to remain here during the Sabbath following, but a courier came in with some news which decided our commander upon marching on the morning of Sunday, and accordingly we took up the line of march that day from the most comfortable quarters we had as yet enjoyed in California, after leaving as mementoes the names and effigies of our separate Ships, done in Charcoal upon the Whitewashed walls of each separate Companies rooms.

Before I leave this place I must mention one incident that occurred that gave us a good taste of *Our Old Soldier* [Kearny] and of his ideas of proceeding with men whether Soldiers or Sailors. Upon this turned too the crisis of our fate and from the issue we were to judge whether we were hereafter during the campaign to be considered as Soldiers and governed by Martial Army Rules or as Sailors and be treated according to the rules of the Navy.

Some of the Cyane's had done something which displeased the Officer in Command of that Company, and he accordingly gave an order to a Buffers Mate who was in his gang to set to work and make a set of "Cats," intending therewith to punish the offenders of this time and have them ready for future service among the Jacks of the Battalion. This Officer was a Cold Blooded Fellow and ranked with Lt R – – – h [Renshaw] in devices of imposition and acts of meanness.

Now by some hook or crook the Old General had got hold of the story of said manufacture, and to show the manner of his approval he coolly walked into the room, and taking up the articles in question, asked in his easy manner what they were and what they were for?

"Them," said Lt H – – – s [Edward Higgins], "why General, them are cats and are for the punishment of Sailors when they are unruly."[4]

"What," said the General, "do you mean to say you intend to whip any of the Jacks with such things as these?"

"Oh yes," says H – – – s, cringing and bowing all the time, "you see I find it impossible to keep my men in order without them. My Jacks as you call them are a very wild set."

"Well, well" says the General, deliberately taking out his knife and cutting the "cats" to pieces, "if you find it impossible to curb your Jacks, without resort to these things, allow me to tell you, that you shall punish none of *My* Jacks with any such articles, and allow me to inform you at the same time young man, that every Jack in this Battalion, is heart and soul mine." When having finished cutting off the Tails, he deliberately threw the handle into the fire, and turning on his heel, left the young officer, with something very like a flea in his ear.[5]

Nor was the *Old Soldier* alone in his deprecation of this way of promoting discipline, but when the matter came to the ears of "Fighting Bob" it was but a short time before his voice was heard in tones of thunder, reverberating through the whole Garrison, demanding to know who had dared to attempt such a course of proceeding without consulting him, and the young officers that day received a lesson that taught them that they were not pre-eminent where they stood, and that there was some higher powers to be consulted when punishments were going on, than their own immaculate wills.[6]

This matter made all hands much happier, for they had now found out beyond all question that there were at least Two along, and big bugs too, to whom they could appeal in case of need, and

4. Edward Higgins, USN. *Gen. Nav. Reg.* (1882), p. 345; Bancroft, *History of California*, v, p. 386.

5. In his later version Downey has Kearny speak this warning before a muster of all the officers. Rogers, *Filings from an Old Saw*, pp. 95–96.

6. The Lieutenant would have gotten small sympathy from Commodore Stockton who was instrumental in banishing the practice of whipping from the regulations of the United States Navy. See "Stockton" in the *DAB*.

who would see Justice done them. What wonder then that the Tars of the Pacific Squadron look up to Genl Kearney and Commodore Stockton, as children would to a Father, and find words more than useless when they try to express their thanks to them. Nor were these sentiments confined to this Squadron alone, for all Soldiers who have ever served under Genl K speak the same of him, and reader, who ever you are, if ever you fall in with him you will find him, take my word for it, the same slow and easy, fatherly old man we now describe to you. Commodore S. is well known to all Sailor Men and you have only to be under his command once to learn to feel towards him the same sentiments the Pueblo Soldiers cherish.

To return to the march, we plodded on in the same old routine, encamping at night and resuming the march in the morning, meeting with nothing extraordinary until Monday the 4th Inst., when we came in sight of the Mission of San Juan [de Capistrano]. Here we collected a goodly quantity of Californians and Indians, who however seemed to take but little notice of us further than a vacant stare at the show. Fond of pomp and display, the Commodore ordered up the Band and we marched past in all the pride of Military Display, the air meanwhile resounding with the Soul Stirring Quick Step of a "Life on the Ocean Wave."

The long train slowly wound its weary way along and the gazers never stirred until the last of the stragglers had disappeared from sight and then most probably returned to that height of Californian Comfort, a paper cigar and a dish of "Frijoles," and never troubled themselves further with the march of an enemy through their country.

When we camped this night we caught the first sight of the Hostiles. There were some 2 or 3 came in, mounted on fine Horses, bearing a Flag of Truce, and a letter from Genl Flores offering if we would return, on his part not to molest us, but saying if we did persevere in our march, that he would meet us on the Plains of San Gabriel and woe betide the poor Sailors then, for they could cut us into peace meals.[7]

This was a heavy brag, but it disconcerted nobody here, for Fighting Bob sent him as good a reply as was his offer and in few words

7. José Maria Flores, who acted as governor and commanding general of the Californians from October, 1846 to January, 1847. Flores eventually removed to Mexico rather than live under American rule. Bancroft, *History of California*, III, p. 741.

too. "Tell Genl Flores," said he, "he has broken his parole of honor and I will not correspond with him, in any manner but verbally—and tell him too that we shall march on to the Pucblo, that we shall occupy it on the 10th of the month, that we hope to see him at San Gabriel and that if I catch him, I will hang him on sight, as an example to all Traitors. Now you can go." This was all the satisfaction they got from us and off they started, bearing this unwelcome message, while we, nothing frustrated by this bragadocia, prepared to spend a pleasant night upon our camp Ground.

The next night we camped upon a hill where there was lots of wood and water, and here some scores of unfortunate chickens fell victims to the hungry propensities of the Jacks.

The next night was the 6th of Jan 1847 and the memory of that eventful night will never be erased from the minds of any of the poor devils that roosted in that Sandy Plain. Talk of Mansanilla, we had thought that was horror piled on horrors, but 'twas laid in the background entirely when put alongside of this night.

We had this day a pretty severe march, and at the close of it we came upon a fine level plain from which there had evidently been made a large quantity of adobes at some no distant period. It was extremely hot in the middle of the day, and not a breath of air was stirring at the time the halt was called to form Camp. It was a fine looking place and we fondly hoped we were to have a good nights rest, but how we were disappointed, the sequel will show.

Scarcely was the ground laid out and the camp formed when the wind breezed up, and steadily increasing, in the course of one half hour blew a perfect gale, and our Camp Ground, fore and aft, crosswise and cornerwise, was completely clouded and choked up with columns and moving masses of dust and fine sand.[8] Look to windward you could not, for the least attempt at such a rash proceeding was sure to fill the Eyes, nose and mouth of the rash adventurer, with the Dust, to give him a half hours good work, with both hands to dig it out again. Men turned to one another to give orders and before the words were half uttered, they would be carried down your throat

8. Downey's later version is not so graphic and John Griffin only mentioned the storm in his diary. "We had a very disagreeable night of it. The wind blew a perfect gale all night and kept it up until ten o'clock today. The dust was most distressing for weak eyes." Rogers, *Filings from an Old Saw*, pp. 96–97; George W. Ames, Jr., editor, "A Doctor Comes to California, The Diary of John S. Griffin, 1846–47," in California Historical Society *Quarterly*, xxi–xxii (1942–43), p. 349.

by a mass of dust, and immediate chocking or strangulation was your doom if you persisted in the attempt.

The Camp was pitched however and here we had to lie. Tents were erected and fires lighted, but what was the use, a man might go and get his pot full of water, but before he could by any means coax it to boil, it would be thickened to the consistency of mush by the cursed dust.

Bullocks were shot down, but no one would skin them and for one night even "Old Liver" did not go his accustomed rounds, for twas of no avail, before you could have gotten the half of a Jacket off, the carcass would be smothered in sand and rendered unfit for eating.

To crown the whole, the Tents blew down, many of them with the occupants crowded in them, yet such was the misery of this night that they preferred remaining in them, to the imminent danger of suffocation, to hazarding the attempt of facing that cloud of dust they knew to be their destiny outside. Growling, grumbling and cursing was the order of the day. Many a poor fellow in pure desperation, would wind his blanket in many folds around his head, and cast himself upon the ground in mute despair and lay there until his body was nearly covered, but 'twas of no use, the fine dust and sand would penetrate even through the covering and he would rise, choking and smothering, with eyes and nose full, and begin the world over again by a good cleaning out.

There was a deep trench or gully in this plain and here lots of men had taken up their sleeping places and found a sort of shelter here, but even there you were roused up every moment or two by some half blind and half smothered poor devil, who would stumble over you in the vain attempt to find a shelter for himself. Growling was of no earthly use, for it did not mend the matter one whit, but then it eased a fellow's mind a little, and I verily believe that all the Growling done by the Sheet Anchor Men and Quarter Gunners of a squadron of 15 sail of the Line in a 3 years cruise might be crowded into as small a space as one night, and then would fall far short of what was done this night of sandy memory.

The Commodore's tent blew down among the rest, and he and his suite had to take a Cast for it, first having it securely propped up to Leeward to secure it from a Like mishap. There was one comfort however, for misery has some comfort when it has lots of company, and that was that there was no distinction of persons, no favors shown in this disbursement of dust. Officers and men all shared alike and every one dished an equal ration of Misery.

To mend the matter also, when at last the camp had become still, partly because no one wished to stir and partly because all those who might have wished to have done so were perfectly blinded, when those who had the least sign of shelter had got into a sort of drowse, Bang, Bang, went the Alarm Guns and to Arms, to Arms resounded through the camp.

All was hurry skurry, such a hunting for muskets and carbines, such feeling for pikes and pistols was never seen before. At last we got into some sort of a line, with our backs to the windward, for twas impossible to face it, and with shouldered arms awaited the attack, and had the Enemy known our situation and rode down upon us from the Windward they might have cut the whole command to pieces as easily as have formed the thoughts, for when we were ordered to "right about face" every musket was down and every hand up to the eyes, digging for dear life for day light or at least for starlight and thus we were forced to stand. If we stopped digging to grasp our arms, we were paralyzed by the dust, if we dropped our arms to dig we were of course useless. Oh the horrors of that night. Luckily for us, twas a false alarm, and though we had two alarms the same night and both times went through the same maneuvers, no enemy came upon us.

Daylight came, but brought no relief, except such as was afforded by excessive Laughter, every man upon looking in his neighbors face would burst into roars of that, and would in his turn laugh and be laughed at by the next who came along. Washing or attempting such an absurdity was of no use, as it only showed more plainly the dirt which was encrusted on the face, and the streaks formed by the streams of water trickling down the countenance only rendered more deplorable the phiz of any wight who undertook it.

Some of the most desperate went to the carcasses of the Bullocks who were shot down the night before, and cut out some chunks of meat, without any attempt at skinning, but merely plugging it as you would a melon, but even these attempts to procure a breakfast were abortive, as there were no possible means of keeping it free from sand long enough to cook it or even get it to your mouth raw.

A fight could be picked up here at a moments notice and Sergeant Jo the Whistler [Jones] got a slap in the Chops, merely because he looked crossways at a brother Sergeant and gave a little lip; said Slap causing his sombrero to jump off his head and cut various awful contortions in the air before it struck the groun, and setting his muster roll spinning at such an awful rate that I much doubt if it has stopped going yet.

As soon as it was day, all hands were on the "qui vive" to get out of this hell. Tents were struck and baggage packed in double quick time and off we started, nor paused to look back until we had placed 10 good long miles between us and the Plain, and hardly then dared look, for fear of a return of the Awful Plague of the 6 Jan 1847. The first water we came to we halted and had a general wash and took time for a bite of whatever we had in our haversacks, after which we marched on much refreshed, wondering if there were many such comfortable places in California.

Towards the close of this the 10th day of our march, we arrived near a Rancho, some few miles distant from the Banks of the Rio San Gabriel, where our vaunting opponent had promised to meet us, and sure enough, as we rose a small hill, we saw full before us on another and somewhat higher eminence a party of from 25 to 30 Horsemen, armed "cap a pie" while their lances, bright as silver and decorated with red flags, glistened and flashed in the last rays of the setting sun.

He had kept his word, there they were "bona fide" flesh and blood, and that hill no doubt concealed the rest of his force, who were laying there, in the full enjoyment of all the luxuries California could produce and perfectly recovered from the fatigue of marching from Los Angeles, a distance of some 10 or 12 miles. They had without a doubt been occupying this position some days, had selected their own ground, had perhaps formed an entrenched camp, which they would defend with the last drop of their blood, while we had to offer against these advantages a motley crowd, the greater portion of whom were literally out of their element and had not passed over so much ground on foot before for many, many years, shoeless and many of them shirtless, on a short allowance of every thing but Beef.

Yet still we had our advantages; we were actuated and led on by a craving desire to win back our lost honor, to plant the Stripes and Stars once more in the square of Los Angeles, to show these haughty dons that sailor men were invincible by any thing near equal numbers, we were headed by Chiefs in whome we had learned to place the most implicit confidence, who we were sure would lead us on to victory and above all, we were one and all animated by that indomitable spirit of courage and perseverance that has ever been and ever will be found in the Breast of Yankees, from the first movement of the War of 1776 down to the present.

We were all aware they would not attack us this night, but on the morrow we were more than sure that we should have a crack at them. We knew that the chances of war were such that more or less of our gallant band would, ere another 24 hours rolled over their heads, lie cold and motionless on the field of action or what was worse in the prospective, would be suffering and groaning with perhaps the loss of a leg or arm, and writhing under the hands of the Surgeon. All this we knew, and yet the knowledge did not tend to dissipate the good humor and hiliarity which pervaded our Camp from first to last.

If it was to be our last night we were at least determined it should be a jolly one, and as Grub in the meat line was plenty, we went to work with a right good will and soon our Camping Ground presented the picture of one immense Cook Shop, where in all directions might be seen joints and slabs of Bullock, Sheep and Goats in every possible position the imagination could picture, undergoing every sort of cooking that ever entered the mind of the most perfect mountain gourmand or rather let me say that our limited means would allow. Nor was this disposition to make the most of the present confined to the men alone; the Officers caught the infection and mirth and amusement was the order of the day, or rather that part of the day left and the night.

As soon as we came in sight of the party of Horsemen before mentioned, a Company of the mounted volunteers were detatched and ordered to reconoitre and see how strong their force was and feel for their intentions. No sooner said, than put into execution. Off they scoured across the narrow plain that divided us, and in a few short moments were at the foot of the Hill on which the Enemy were. They began slowly and cautiously to ascend, the Horsemen meanwhile watching them with wary eye, but before they could come within Rifle Shot, presto, they all turned tail and scampered off, the serapes and Red Flags fluttering behind them, and disappeared, leaving the Hill in charge of our party.

They were no doubt a party who had been posted in the advance to note our numbers and strength, but as the main body had been ordered to halt at the foot of the last hill they were somewhat in error, and saw only our advanced guard and skirmishers. After they had betaken themselves off to parts unknown, the main body were again put in motion, and in a short time we were snugly encamped on the same spot that had been occupied by them, on our arrival in sight.

Now there was one peculiarity about the Commodore which should have found a place in our Journal at San Diego, but as it slipped our observation there, and as "better late than never" is a good motto, we will put it down here. He was passionately fond of dancing, not so much for the active chance of the heel and toe performance then offered to himself, but for the opportunity it afforded of gathering around him a fine large party and thus promoting the happiness of a great many at a small outlay of money.

Now in this particular, he coincided perfectly with the idea of the California Ladies, who are so much devoted to this sort of amusement, that they will make a meal of it, even when there is no mush in the cupboard. This foible was nuts to them, and true to his profession he never failed when the fair sex could be collected together to have a hop on the picnic principle, and our young Officers were all glad to join in the sport, and it made no manner of difference about full dress; they went as they were, and the Ladies took them as they were "for better or for worse" and I rather fear some of them were found to be worse than they were taken for. In one thing however, the Officers were all uniform, they one and all wore Common Blue Flannel Shirts, rigged into a sort of short coat, decorated with pockets and buttons and a large Leather Belt to which they apended [sic] a pair of Pistols and a sword.

In pursuance of his plan of amusement, the Commodore had the band over to the Rancho and the California Ladies were soon whistling around in the giddy mazes of the waltz, with their taper waists encircled by arms, which on the day following, would beyond a doubt be dealing death blows upon perhaps friends and relations. But it made no odds to the Ladies, there was the music and there was a chance for Dancing, and at it they went, as if this was the last night in the world and their eternal salvation depended upon the manner in which they should acquit themselves this night. But every thing must have an end and of course this Dance could not be exempt from the common lot of mortality, and by the hour of 12 midnight, all was as quiet as the grave in our Camp.

Friday morning Jan 8 broke bright and clear and at early dawn the soul stirring notes of the bugle called us to duty. The usual routine of Camp Duty was performed, breakfasts were cooked and dinner stowed in haversacks, plenty of time was allowed and by 8 A.M. we were again all ready for a forward movement. When we had got into Line, the Old Soldier addressed us, and bade us recollect that this day we were to cross the Rio San Gabriel, where Flores had promised to meet us, and from the signs of the night before, he believed he was about to keep his word, "but I want you all to understand distinctly," said the Old Fellow, "that we have got to cross that river and more than that, we have got to whip the Enemy, and plant our Colors in the Pueblo."

"We can do it," said he, "and we will do it, if you Jacks will only put the curb rein on your impetuosity for a short time and obey implicitly the orders that are given you; I have got the sole charge of you Jacks, the Commodore has given it to me, and if I dont put you on the Track that will run you straight to the arms of victory, call me no Soldier, that's all. Keep perfectly cool until you are ordered to act, and when you get that order go it with a perfect rush."

"I want you all to remember too, what day it is. This is the glorious 8th of January, memorable in our Country's History, and now let every man of you think of this day and strive so to conduct himself that the anniversary shall never be disgraced and that the 8th of Jan, 1847, may be placed in the calendar of fame, alongside of the 8th of Jan 1815, and still later the 8th and 9th of May 1846."[9]

As he concluded his address, a cheer ran from one end of the line to the other, and such a cheer, twas the spontaneous effusions of Gallant Hearts sent up to honor a man whom all had been taught to revere and love. At the close of this short address the word of command was given and Battalion moved forward. Every eye was fixed in the advance and every ear on the alert to catch the first sign of the Enemy. On, on we plodded the whole forenoon and as yet no one had shown themselves, and we had almost begun to think that

9. Kearny referred to Andrew Jackson's victory over the British at New Orleans on January 8, 1815, and to General Zachary Taylor's victories over the Mexicans at Palo Alto (May 8, 1846) and Resaca de la Palma (May 9, 1846).

they had forfeited their word and did not intend to dispute the passage of the River with us.

At length we came to the Plain bordering the river [the San Gabriel], which is here about 2 miles wide, and runs on a gradual descent down to the River on one side, while on the other it rises to a small bank, then a plain some 2 or 3000 yards wide, and then rises another hill or embankment. The River of itself is some 30 or 40 yards in width and is in no place deeper than a man's hips but the bottom is formed of quicksand and is rather difficult to ford.

When we first came on to this plain, a halt was called and we took our dinner, but before we had fairly finished, the Enemy were seen in considerable numbers in advance of us on the side of the river next to us. They were however merely reconoitering and soon crossed over and were lost to view on the other side.

When the time of halt had elapsed we again formed in line of march and prepared to cross the river in face of the enemy, who we now knew were there in force. Small parties could be seen from time to time, dodging and flying about among the hills. Soon they were re-inforced by others and again others, until the force in sight, seemed to swell in numbers to at least some 6 or 700 men, all mounted, with their lances and sabres glittering in the sun.

The time for action had now arrived. We were formed in two columns marching by flank, while the Dragoons in front and the rear guard in the rear marching by company, formed a perfect square in the center of which were our Waggons, Carts, Cattle and Mules. The spy Company of Volunteers were skirmishing out on the flanks, but as we drew nearer the river they dismounted and operated on foot. The Old General passed along the Line and as he passed gave words of advice and encouragement to Officers and Men. No answer was heard, no cheer greeted him, but the looks that flashed from an hundred eyes, told more plainly than words what was the inward resolve of all.

It was indeed even to the experienced eye of the veteran, a dangerous attempt we were about to make, the enemy had every advantage of us, and if they had defended the ground they had selected with anything like the determination of brave men we would either have never crossed the river at all, or our crossing would have been attended with heavy loss. Had the case been reversed and we placed in their position, they would never have placed their feet upon the east side of the San Gabriel, if they had striven until the last man fell a corpse upon the Bank.

As it was, we steadily pursued our march toward the river and as yet they offered no opposition, and we were in the dark as to whether they had any artillery to operate against us. Three pieces of our Artillery were in the advance, directly in the rear of the Dragoons, and the other two were in the rear for the protection of the rear Guard and Baggage. When we were about one half across the plain, the first shot on their part was fired and set all doubt at rest as to their intentions, at the same time disclosing their position, and well was it chosen too. They had planted their artillery on the second bank and directly in range of the fording place, and two large trees which stood on the lower bank became to them a sure mark at which to discharge the missiles of death, in the Shape of Round and Grape, full upon our little band. There was no other means of approach to the ford but in this range, and it was do or die now.

The first Shot however fell so far short of our ranks that it caused a laugh of derision from all in front, and the remark was passed from one to another, if they can do no better than that, they had better be off at once. The second was no better aimed, for the piece was elevated so high that the Shot flew clear over our heads and landed a long way in the stern of the rear Guard. Again the laugh and jest ran round at the expense of the Enemy, but as we were each moment drawing nearer and nearer it was soon absorbed in one breathless feeling of intense interest for now the Grape began to fly thick and fast and each moment may be our last.

The Dragoons have crossed the River headed by the Gallant Commodore, where are the artillery, why do they hesitate, why do they pause on the near bank of the River? An order has been given for them to unlimber and throw a few shot at the Enemy from this spot. "Fighting Bob's" dander is up, he dashes again into the River, recrosses and shouts at the top of his voice, "Not here, not here Limber up again, forward, we must, we will cross the River with these Guns." Nothing can stay him, down into the River go the Mules, the Guns are heavy, the quicksand is hard to drag them through, the mules pause, one moment, and they are lost, off he comes from his horse, seizes the drag rope, "Now men, now pull for your lives, your commodore is here, dont desert him, dont for the love of God lose

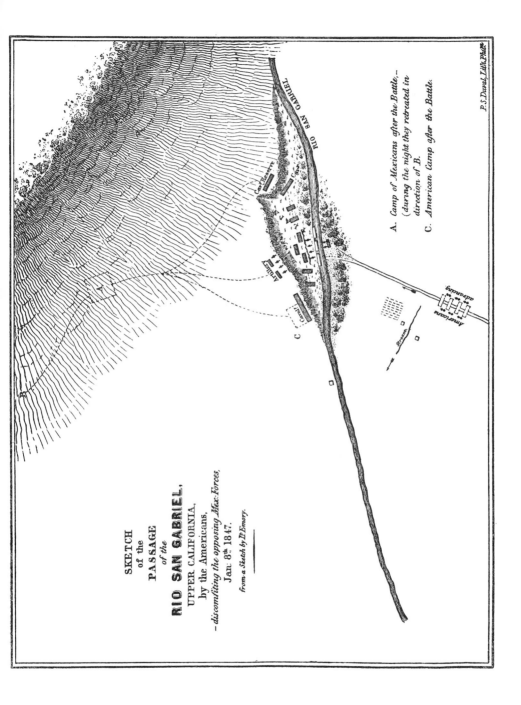

SKETCH
of the
PASSAGE
of the
RIO SAN GABRIEL,
UPPER CALIFORNIA,
by the Americans,
– discomfiting the opposing Mex. Forces,
Jan: 8th 1847.

from a Sketch by P. Emory.

A. Camp of Mexicans after the Battle. –
(during the night they retreated in
direction of B.
C. American Camp after the Battle.

RIO SAN GABRIEL

Cav. Reserve

Artill.y

Mex. Cav.

American Crossing

Stream

P.S. Duval, Lith. Phila.

205

these guns," his words are fire to them, they seize hold, each man with a will, they move, they start and with a cheer over they go, while the water is ploughed in all directions by repeated discharges of grape, which flew like hail round them.[10]

The Guns once crossed, the Commodore took charge of them himself and soon 'twas seen that fame had not overrated his powers with a Big Gun. He was as sure of his mark as if he had held a Rifle in his hand, and in less than three discharges, a loud cheer from the Artillery men and Dragoons announced that he had capsized one of their Guns and rendered it "hors de combat" for that day.

While this was going on, the main body with the old Soldier at their head were steadily advancing; now they enter the water, the Old Fellow on his Mule, leading the way, and loud above the din of battle can be heard his voice, "steady my Lads, steady. Keep perfectly cool there you Jacks, dont hurry yourselves, I'll find some work for you presently." In the middle of the stream his mule stopped stock still, nor could he be persuaded to move another step; not at all disconcerted but proceeding as leisurely as though he were dismounting at his own door, the Old Soldier gathered his pistol in one hand, and with his riding whip in the other, he got off the Animal, and resigning him to his fate, kept on the same old pace and reached the bank at the head of the column.

We arrived on the Bank we deployed to the right and left and marching in single file, as soon as the last were across, covered ourselves from the fire of the Enemy's Artillery by laying down close under the Rise. We lay in this position for near a half hour and all this time the artillery were battering away at each other, and there in the midst of all, while Round and Grape were flying as thick as Hail about him, stood "Fighting Bob" here and there and every where with his telescope in his hand, sighting first this Gun and then that, and giving the order to fire at the proper moment, his face glowing with animation, and showing plainly by his every action that he was half wild with excitement.

We never raised from our hiding place but once when we were ordered to form to repel a charge of Cavalry. We rose to our feet and the sight was a Glorious one, down they came, in one long line, their Red Blankets, Black Hats and Bright Lances glittering in the sun,

10. See Downey's other account of the Battle of Rio San Gabriel in Rogers, *Filings from an Old Saw*, pp. 98 ff.

on, on they came and death seemed to stare us in the face, for what could stay the power of that tide of Horse and Human Flesh that was rearing toward us.

And still they came, the loud voice of the General resounds over the field "Steady my Jacks, reserve your fire, front rank, kneel to receive cavalry." Silently each front rank man drops upon his knee, and placing his musket or pike at an angle of 45 degrees elevation, with the butt firmly burried in the earth, enclosed that mass of men in a solic body of glittering steel, while his file leader in the rear cocks and makes ready his musket, and prepares to deal death upon the foe, while every face glowed with enthusiasm. There was no quail, no blanch, there, every man was resolved to maintain his position or be a corpse upon the ground where he stood.

For a single moment they stood, and then came the word "Fire" and at the word a sheet of fire flew along that line and the rattle of small arms added to the clangor of the day. Oh that volley was so deadly, so destructive that the cavalry paused in their mad career, and then turning, before another volley could be poured into them, regained the cover of the Hill.

Twice, thrice, did they attempt the same move, each time changing their place of attack, but twas all the same, in the front or flank, on the right or in the rear, there was the same wall of steel and the same steady eyes ranging along those fatal tubes dealing death among their ranks. At length the proper moment arrived, and the Old Soldier, raising himself to the full height of his muscular frame, gave the word, "Now Jacks, at them, Charge, Charge and take the hill!"

Like one man this mass arose from their hiding places and with a yell of fury dashed on to the Hill, with bayonets and Pikes at a charge, up, up they went this wild yet still orderly mass, plunging and rearing in their mad career, and at their head was "Fighting Bob" and the "Old Soldier" side by side the one mad with excitement the other cool as a Julap. The foe paused but a moment, one look was enough, they fled on all sides, dragging their artillery after them, and when we gained the Hill there were no foemen there.

Having now gained the Hill we will pause and blow awhile, and while the artillery are coming up, detail a few of the minute incidents of this days fight, for there are many and some of them laughable too, and after the danger is passed, if we did not pass the Joke and enjoy the laugh we would be no sailors. No matter who was killed, it was but a moment's work to say "poor fellow, well he is gone, he was a good shipmate and I hope he is better off," and then he was forgotten. No matter who was wounded, there were of course some words of sympathy for him and wishes that he might recover and then this sort of conversation was stashed; but get off on a yarn in which there was any sort of amusement or any thing to be laughed at, or any bit of satire upon an Inferior Officer and you could collect a crowd that would hang round you for hours and never tire of the theme. We had lots of wags along, and many who could manufacture a good yarn out of small pieces, and they did so, too, and whiled away many a weary hour afterward in relating their experience of the Pueblo War.

The first man who was struck by a shot belonged to our Ship. His name was Strauss, he was a kind hearted chap and a good shipmate and many eulogies were passed at that time on his name.[11] He belonged to the Artillery and was Fire and Match Man to the Gun, the Commodore had just sighted the piece and he was in the act of applying the match, when he was struck in the left shoulder by a round shot, which completely carried away all that side of his neck and killed him instantly. His death was a quick one for he never knew what hurt him. His body was quickly removed to one of the waggons and that night he was buried, at the foot of the Hill. Peace be with him, he died an honored death. His remains lie where he fell and strangers have raised a mound over his grave.

There was but one other death occurred this day and that was not from the shot of the enemy. Twas an accidental shot from one of our own men, and the victim was a youngster [Thomas Smith] belonging to the Cyane, a merry light hearted soul who was the life and glee of his mess. During the progress of the Charge up the hill, he in some manner got entangled with the undergrowth and as he turned to clear himself, the man next in his rear, who fool like had his musket on the charge, at full cock, touched the trigger and she exploded, lodging the whole charge in the abdomen of the boy, who fell and was conveyed to the rear. He lingered in great agony till near morning when he expired. He was cheerful to the last, and said he was ready to go, he had fallen in the execution of his duty and twas well that it was no better man. Poor Smith, your body lays in the

11. Frederick Straus, Ordinary Seaman. "Personnel of the *Portsmouth*."

208

same grave with Strauss, and your friends in your far off home, will look with anxious eyes for your return and may never hear of your sad fate.

These were the only deaths that occurred that day, but we had a number of wounded, all save one however but slightly. That exception was a man named Jacob Haight, who had once been a Dragoon but his term of service having expired, had come out with Genl Kearney, in the Quarter Masters Department as a Teamster, and had joined the Volunteers at San Diego and drove one of the Guns. He was struck in the breast with a small grape shot, which went completely through him, and though his recovery was hopeless yet he lingered on until the next night, when he too died.

These three comprised the whole of our loss on this day though how the grape and Round Shot, to say nothing of whole charges of Balls and Slugs from Blunderbusses, dodged around among our men and hit so few is a mystery.

In the early part of the Charge, before the order was given to fire, one of the Savannahs a great two fisted fellow, had singled out his man from among the crowd, and as the Californian was cutting up some very curious antics about, kept a wary eye upon him. He was evidently under sole charge of some spirit, at total variance with courage, or at least true courage, for his was the most glaring sample of foolhardiness I ever saw. He rode down alone, close to our line waving his lance and then laying that to rest took deliberate aim with his blunderbuss at the man before mentioned. The Jack, who had his eye upon him, raised his piece to reciprocate the compliment when Lt R – – – w, who at this moment caught a glimpse of him, sang out with an oath—"dont fire Cope, G – – d d – – n you dont fire!"[12]

"But Sir," said Cope without lowering his peice, "he is aiming at me and if I dont save him, he'll shoot me certain."

"I dont care a d – – n, dont fire, if you do by the Living God I will cut you down, where you stand—" and suiting the action to the word, he sprang forward and throwing his arms round the man, held him fast, and totally prevented his firing his piece, taking good care however to keep the man between himself and the Mexicans. Hardly had he done this when the Mexican fired and lodged the whole con-

12. Either B. or William B. Renshaw. The reasons for his actions cannot be explained. *Gen. Nav. Reg.* (1882), pp. 597–98; Bancroft, *History of California*, v, p. 386 n.

tents of his blunderbuss, amounting to some 10 or eleven balls in the arms and legs of the unfortunate man thus pinioned. The man turned, dropped his gun and exclaimed, "now Mr R – – – w you see your work, now I am shot and all by your doings." Mr R – – – w turned as pale as a sheet, and walked away, but twas not long before his cowardly soul forgot the shock and he was dodging about hallooing louder than before.

Sergeant Slim comes in for a notice here; he was in the rear guard this day and his carriage was portly as his thin carcass would allow, and his head as erect as if he had bean pole rammed through him, and could not bend. Fire flashed from his eyes at each discharge of the artillery, and he longed to get a chance to distinguish himself. At length his wish was gratified, a grand charge was made against the rear guard in the hope of cutting off the Waggons and Cattle. They were however disappointed here, being met as firmly as at any other point, and as they turned to retreat they fired one charge from their blunderbusses and Rifles.

The Sergeant was as busy as the devil, ramming down his charge, when a ball came, and cutting away the upper half of his ramrod, left him standing unarmed with the lower half still in his hand. "Well now," says Slim, "aint that wonderful, they've cut away my ramrod and not touched me, and it aint so much of a wonder neither. I am infernal thin, and they cant see me, although they can see the ramrod. Oh how lucky I am that I have not got much flesh on me. All I have got to do is just to turn sideways to them and they cant see me, so you see I can walk right into 'em and they wont know I am there."

There was some very curious sights too among officers, which savored but little for their bravery, and tended to lower them much in the eyes of the men.

As soon as we had gained the hill we began to look about for a camp ground, and while the enemy were yet in sight retreating, though out of reach of our small arms, a Camp was laid out, and some of the Sapper and Miner Corps came up to "Fighting Bob" and enquired where they should pitch his tent; he had hardly got over his excitement and was roaring at the top of his voice for the Band, who with instrument in hand were running up the Hill in obedience to his Call. "What?" said he to the man who addressed him. "Where will you have your Tent pitched Sir?" "Oh dont talk

Tent to me now, I'm chock full of fight, d – – n the Tent, where is that band?" "Here Sir," said the Capt of the Band as those Gentry puffing and blowing from their exertion in running up hill appeared. "Now here," said the Commodore, "stand you here, and give us "Hail Columbia" and in your best style too!"

The Band struck up and as the last rays of the setting sun gilded the tops of the distant mountains, the retreating enemy were regailed with the soul stirring strains of that National Anthem, to refresh their spirits, and comfort them in their march.

Our camp was formed and fires lighted, mirth and good humor reigned supreme, and though the night was cold and we were wet through, yet none wore long faces save a few of the volunteers, who had lost their horses, packs and all, and some of the Tars who had lost their pea jackets and Blankets through the obstinacy of a mule who lay down in the River and rolled his pack off. When Lt. Gillespie reported to the Commodore that his men had lost their horses, the Old Man good humoredly replied, "d – – n the Horses, Major, we have gained the day, hill and all."

We had an alarm or so during the night but no one came to molest us, and at early dawn we were again on foot and eager for the forward march. At the usual hour the assembly sounded and we fell in, the same order as the previous day, marching in a Square, enclosing the Baggage, Ammunition and Cattle in the Center.

We all wished for another crack at them and expected to have our wish gratified on the large plain that lay at the foot of the hill where we were encamped, which bore the name of the "Mesa" that being the name of another small river [the Los Angeles River] between us and the Puebla. We imagined they would think their force could operate more favorably on a plain, and perhaps they might induce us again to charge in line upon them, and being in so large a space, they would break us, and if they could once do that, they would have it all their own way. Nor were we wrong in our conjecture; we had not marched far, before we saw them, formed in line of Battle, apparently waiting our advance.[13]

The Old Soldier now gave us another word of caution—"now my Jacks," said he, "you see I did not promise you falsely yesterday. I told you we would do it, and we did—you behaved nobly then, do

13. For a map of the Battle of La Mesa, see p. 214; see also Smith, *War With Mexico*, I, p. 344. See also Rogers, *Filings from an Old Saw*, pp. 101 ff.

the same to day—let no man leave the station he holds in the line till I give the order; those fellows will make a charge on you, and then retreat thinking to draw you after them, but dont you let 'em fool you—stand firm when they charge and when they run, let them do all the racing themselves, give them a few such vollies as you did yesterday, and my word for it they wont come often."

The Old Commodore too put in his oar here. Said he, "I dont mean to say much about field fighting, for I am a poor hand at that, but just you keep them out of the Center of this Square and them chaps," pointing to his artillery, "will do their share at long talk. And another thing, too, I have found out that dodging Pompey is a good thing, dodging is my trade, and I am as good a dodger as any he in California, just keep your eyes on their Big Guns, and when you see the flash, fall down where you stand, and dont rise again till you hear the Ball whistle over your heads; I tried it yesterday and found it a good plan, but dont stop in dodging moves, keep going ahead and you will drive these Lance Gentlemen before you like chaff before the wind!"

We then resumed our march again and soon the artillery opened on us and true to the orders of the Commodore, every man fell at the flash; this move seemed to astonish the Enemy who cheered lustily, but changed their tune when they saw us rise and come forward in as good order as before. This game was played some time and always with good effect, and so secure was it, that though their artillery was served much better this day than the day before, we had not a single man in that whole square hurt that day.

On the other side though, the case was different. "Fighting Bob" was with his pets, and so well were they served and so deadly was his aim, that wherever two or three were seen together, there was sure to be a saddle or two emptied, so that at last they took the precaution to ride alone at any distance less than two miles. This dodging game gave room for many jests and witticisms and it has been said that many, among whom were even our own valiant soldier officers, were more than once caught in the fact of dodging at our own Guns —and wondering where the balls went to. One fellow in the rear who had fallen at the flash and remained prostrate rather longer than his Commander thought necessary, upon being asked what he was doing down there, exclaimed "Oh by the Lord we're all right here, it's our watch below now!"

As we continued to advance they prepared for a Grand Charge and getting into Line, put their Lances in rest, and down they came at the full speed of their horses, yelling and shouting like madmen, but they might as well have charged at the trees with the hope of moving them as against that mass. With the front rank at a charge to repel, and the rear ready to fire, we waited patiently till they came within good shot, and then volley after volley was poured into them from that part of the square on which they charged, causing them to reel in their saddles (for, being strapped on they could not fall off even if dead) and face to the right about and retire for another chance. Still no pause ensued in our onward progress, on, on we came in the same solid square as before.

They tried the front, they tried each wing and then the rear 'twas all the same, they could make no impression upon us. The same row of steel, the same array of death tubes, the same withering volleys awaited them at every attempt.

At last they resolved to make one last and desperate charge to surround and charge on all sides at once; the artillery was now drawn into the square, and we still marched on, keeping an eye upon their moves. They now extended their line until they had completely surrounded us, then one Gun gave the signal and on they came upon all sides. "Stand firm, my lads" said the General, and we were firm. As soon as they came within shot, the volleys were commenced and the rattling was so constant you could hardly have time to think, yet on they came, volley after volley was poured in and yet they did not pause, soon the contest would be hand to hand, the roaring was kept up and the Cavalry still advanced until within 50 yards of our line. They could come no further, it was beyond the power of man to face that shower of bullets and again, for the last time, they turned and fled to the shelter of a Ravine and left us a second time masters of the field.

Some two or three came in this evening to surrender themselves as prisoners of war, and on being asked why they did not come on, answered, 'twas of no use to charge on that "karall," for the devil himself could not have got in unless he had used his wings.

We continued our march and camped on the Pueblo side of the Mesa that night, in the full faith of occupying the town the next, notwithstanding the row they kicked up the whole night. They kept up the pow wow until 3 the next morning and then only knocked off

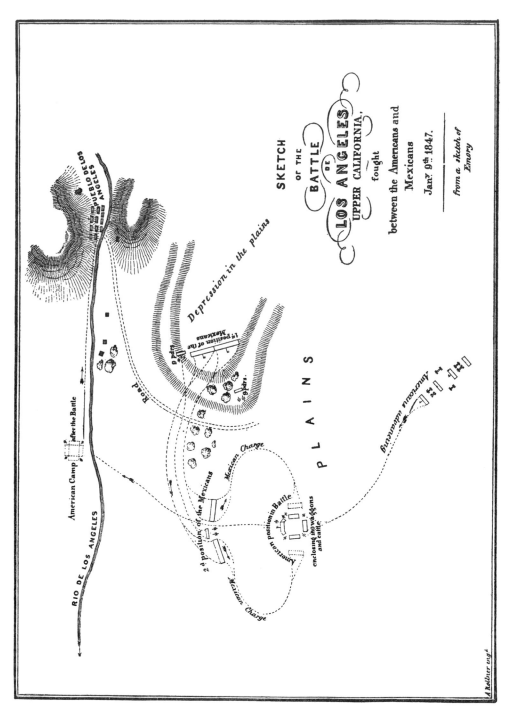

SKETCH
OF THE
BATTLE
DE
LOS ANGELES
UPPER CALIFORNIA,
fought
between the Americans and
Mexicans
Jan.ʸ 9ᵗʰ 1847.

from a sketch of
Emory

PUEBLO DE LOS
ANGELES

Depression in the plains

1ˢᵗ position of the
Mexicans

6 prs.

9 prs.

Road

American Camp after the Battle

RIO DE LOS ANGELES

Mexican Charge

2ᵈ position of the Mexicans

American position in Battle

enclosing into waggons
and cattle.

Mexican Charge

American advancing

P L A I N S

A.Keltner eng.ᵗ

214

as we were told because they were too drunk to make any more noise.

Before I close about the fights, I must give Kit Carson a parting glance, he was the coolest of all the cool ones that ever was in a fight. At the commencement of the first days action, he stripped himself to a red shirt and trowsers, and binding a hankerchief around his head, tied his horse to his arm, and then lighting his pipe he was off. Wherever the Mexicans were nearest there was Kit, with his eternal pipe stuck in his mouth, never removing it, but to fire his rifle, and every time he fired he brought his man. He would then resume his pipe and go on loading as coolly as if he were shooting ducks for amusement.

On the morning of the 10th of Jany we took up our line of march and formed what was now termed the "Karall" and trudged forward to the City of Los Angeles.[14] We expected to have another brush there, but there was no opposition. The town was deserted; as we entered the Encmy retired and save one or two drunken fellows that lagged behind and tantalized our fellows a little, we saw no more Belligerants. These chaps too got well peppered for their pains, for the Blood of the Tars could not be restrained and they gave them such a volley of Balls as sent the Horses scampering off, if it did nothing else.

Behold us then gentle Reader, with a Battalion of sea boys, safe in the City of Los Angeles, the Stars and Stripes waving over us, and our Band playing away for dear life the Quick Step of a "Life on the Ocean Wave" while every Tar shoulders his musket and steps out in as true dress as if he had been for 40 years a Soldier.

14. Downey is referring to a "hollow square" formation for which Stockton had a great fondness.

The Occupation—The Evacuation
Return to San Diego

As I HAVE SAID in my last, we were now in full possession of the Town, now to keep it was the grand question; we could not remain here long, as our services were required on board of our several Ships and the Body of Dragoons and volunteers were not in the opinion of those who had command sufficient to guard the Town.

We knew that Col Freemont and his party were on their route to co-operate in our attack, but where he was the Lord only knew, he had been some three months "en route" and as yet we had only heard of him but once, and then he was at Santa Barbara, some 300 miles from Los Angeles.

This was the trouble that was now on the mind of the Commander in Chief, but Jack had none of these fancies to disturb his brain, and finding himself in town, went to work to provide for his inner man, in the matter of eating and drinking, in the best manner that supplies, in said town would allow.

No sooner were their Quarters assigned there than parties were out, all over town, foraging, and woe betide the house that had no occupants for it was sure to be ransacked from clue to earing and every thing that was useful or ornamental carried off to the Barracks. Nor were they long finding what they sought for; first the grub matter was hunted up, and go where you would, you was sure to meet lots of Matelo's [*matelots*—sailors] wending their way to their various quarters, loaded to the bends with what they called Belly Timber.

There would be one bending under the weight of a sack of Beans, then another with a skin of Wheat, close to him would come the third with an enormous pumpkin on his head, while in the rear trotted a fourth, with both arms full of crockery and utensils for cooking. I met Sergeant Slim, wending his weary way up the hill with a most collossal one mounted upon his calabash, he was toiling and sweating, and from all appearance seemed about to give out with his load.

"Hello Sergeant," said I, "you seem to have your match there."

"Yes," gasped he, "this is rayther severe, something worse than licking the Mexicans, this way of providing for the belly is clear hell; if I had only got the chance, I would have made a prisoner the other day, and had him for a servant, you know, so he could have done all this toting for me."

"Yes," said I, "this going up hill is rather too much for you."

"Well do you know," said he, (setting down his pumpkin, which was something less than 3 feet high, and seating himself on top of it, and then after taking a chew of tobacco, crossing his legs and looking up in my face, in his peculiar knowing manner) "do you know, I have been considering on that same thing ever since I left the house, where I made this pumpkin a prisoner?"

"A Prisoner?" said I with surprise.

"Yes, a Prisoner and of War too, you needn't look so fierce about it neither, it is my Prisoner and as the Law says all private property found on or in a Prisoners possession shall be inspected, I dont mean that they shall catch me foul this time, for I am going to take out all his inwards and let them go scott free while I mean to eat all the Rhind myself."

"Well that is a novel idea," said I, "but what has that to do with getting it up Hill?"

"Wal I was just a goin to tell you when you stopped me, and looked so fierce when I said it was my prisoner. You see I've just been thinking as I came along, how I should go to work on this to rig a plan to get it up hill without carrying it, and I've hit it at last. Now if there was any mechanics here, and I could get a propeller made after the principle of "Fighting Bob" in the Princeton, and then scooping out the insides, I could crawl in and work the machine myself.[1] Now wouldn't that be a nice plan?"

"Tis," said I, "but that is impracticable."

"I know it is," said he, "and that's what makes me feel so melancholy. I really believe I shall have to tote it up and else I shall never be able to have supper of it tonight. By the Lord, Peak," said he, jumping up. "I've got another plan; now you see I'll cut a big hole in the Top and another in the bottom and it wont take such an awful large one neither for I am small in circumference you know, then I'll scrape all the guts out, and then I'll make two smaller ones for my arms, then I'll put it on like a shirt and ram my arms through the holes and my leggs coming out below will enable me to walk off, and

1. See above, p. 104, n. 2.

all I have got to do is to imagine it a Pea Jacket and then it will be no load at all."

No sooner said than done, at it he went, and in a few moments, he was off, full speed, with his head above the top and his legs below the bottom, laughing to split himself at his novel Idea.

But the eating part was not all that was found in the premises searched on the occasion, there was lots of Aquadiente about, and as Jack never lets that pass within a mile without at least smelling it, so on this occasion when he had got a smell, he must have a taste, and one taste was nothing for him, and of course all his Shipmates and Mess Mates must have their share, but as a Barrel was rather an unwilling thing to roll up a hill in broad daylight, consequently, they fisted on to all sorts of utensils to transport the precious beverage about town. Pitchers, wash bowls, bottles, pickle jars, soup tureens, and some unmentionable articles in the crockery line were soon hunted up and put in immediate requisition and one would imagine that tin, crockery and Glass ware stores were being removed from one part of the Town to another by the quantities that were thus perambulating around the streets.

Now this said Aquadiente is awful strong stuff, and soon began to show the mastery he had obtained. The Matelots began to show strong symptoms of inebriety, and though they strove to walk erect and with a Soldier like bearing, their head gear was too top heavy, they would roll from side to side, often times nearly gunwale too. They seemed to be trying as if for a wager how much ground they could walk over in going from one place to another. It was a head wind, no matter which talk they stood upon, or what direction they were going, and soon it took both sides of the street for them to travel in, and the middle was all their own.

Sergeant Jo the Whistler [Charles Jones?], was standing at a corner, holding on for dear life to a Lamp Post, and seeming in a profound consultation with himself, upon some subject of vast importance. He had his eye firmly fixed upon one particular stone that lay near him, and was addressing some very strong language to it when I came alongside of him.

"Well Jo," said I, "you seem to be cogitating deeply there, what is the matter can I help you?"

"Ye-yes," hiccupped he, "you are just the man I want to see. I've just been trying to find out what sort of a d – – n country we have got into any how, why dammit, the very ground seems to be against a fellow here, and the stones are as pugnacious as the devil himself and that stone in particular. Do you know I have come out from behind this post, three times, to start for the Quarters and just as sure as I let go, up jumps that cursed stone and hits me a dig in the face, and the first place I find myself is flat on my back—but the feller is honorable though, he wont hit me when I am down and ya see he cant hit me when I am behind this post—but just as sure as I try to get away from here, he gives me a plumper, right between the two eyes."

"Now, I dont know as I have done him any particular injury that he should serve me so, I might have hit my toe against him when we marched into town, but that was accident you know, and 'forget and forgive' is my motto, and so I have told him three or four times, but he dont seem to pay any attention to Scripture rules, or else he dont understand English. Now as I cant talk any other Lingo, I dont see as there is any chance of him and me coming to terms, and as I am sure he can lick me, I shall have to stand behind this wooden friend of mine all night and that would be agin orders you know. Now I wish you would 'Parley vous' a little Spanish to him, just tell him how things is, hint to him that I am a Sergeant, and have got lots of business at home to night and you can say that I'll come down and see him righted tomorrow, or some other day when I can get time, (though damned, added he in a low tone, if I dont give him wide berth if I get clear this time) and try and settle the past, do this good soul and I'll give you a thimble full when I serve out Grog tomorrow if there's any plush."

Laughing heartily at this whim of a drunken man, and yet being well aware there was no other means of getting him to go with me but humoring him, I pretended to hold a conversation with the stone in Spanish, and then turning to Jo, told him 'twas all settled and there was no further danger, persuaded him to take my arm and leave his friend the post. He was very careful however to place me between him and the stone and kept his eye upon him, until we passed and after a tedious time in lugging him along, I at length safely deposited him on a Blanket in the Barrack Room.

Sergeant Jo had lots of Company in the same fix as he was and stroll from Quarters to Quarters, and you would see drunken men on all sides, the Guard house was full, the very Guard was drunk.

Sergeants, Corporals and all, three or four new Guards were detailed but in a few moments after they reported themselves, they would be as Drunk as the Old Ones and at last the Officer of the Day gave up the attempt in sheer dismay and reported that there was not in the whole Garrison sober men enough to mount one relief of sentinels. In this case he was fain to content himself, with posting such as were the nearest sober and let chance do the rest.

Nor were the men alone in this spree, the Officers had all imbibed their juice and save only the Old General and the Commodore, who are always excepted when Officers in General are mentioned I do not think there were many who could have conveniently told at 12 that night, how many blue beans it took to make five.

Strange as it may seem however, when the alarm was given that night of the Enemy approaching, every man sprung to his arms, thus proving that drunk or sober, they were always on hand and were not to be caught napping by the Mexicans. If chance had have offered, they would have made that night a very strong, if not a very orderly fight, for between "aquadiente" and natural courage, they would have faced a Battery of 500 pieces of cannon, backed by 10,000 Cavalry and fought till the last man was cut down. Happily there was no need to test their courage this time, and during the next day measures were taken which made Liquor a little more scarce, though there was lots of it yet, floating about, and there were plenty of men who never drew a sober breath while we lay there, and had some left to carry on the return tramp.

But let Justice be done say I "though the heavens should fall," cases of severe or blind drunkeness were rare after that night and queer indeed were some of the plans worked to procure the juice on the Sly. One of these expedients was so good that I cannot pass it by. Among the rest of the Gallant Tars was a jolly Irishman, who belonged to the *Congress,* who went ashore from the *Ohio* when she was receiving Ship, and just before our Ship sailed one Sunday morning, to get his mustering trowsers, and forgot to come back; most anybody will recognize him.[2] Well he was a jolly fellow to be sure and awful fond of the "cratur," or anything which would make him feel as if he had imbibed some of that same.

He was in despair when the Taboo was put on and racked his

2. Downey identifies the jolly Irishman elsewhere as Tom Roach. Rogers, *Filings from an Old Saw,* p. 107.

brain to invent some plan to raise some stuff. He knew where there was a cask of good wine, but how to get it to the quarters was the difficulty—after a great deal of cogitating he hit it at last. He took some 3 or 4 trusty fellows into his confidence and equipping himself with musket and cross belts and arming his comrades with a supply of bottles, he proceeded to the house where the wine lay, and they at once set to work to fill their bottles and such other articles as they had with them.

While they were thus engaged the Greek stood watch at the door and soon the necessity of such a plan became apparent for in a few moments the long form of Lt R – – w [Renshaw] was seen stalking down the street. Giving his comrades the wink to hide in the corners, he walked out of the house and leaving the door wide open and the cask in full sight, he supported arms and promenaded up and down the side walk, as grave as a deacon.

When the Lt arrived opposite his post, he of course brought his Gun to the Carry and stood at "Attention." The Dig raised his quizzing glass to his eye and peeping in at the door asked what he was doing there? "On Post," says the Greek. "Over what?" says the Dig. "Over that cask of wine," says Pat. "Ah, that is mine," says the Lt. "So I was tould," says Pat. "Is it good?" "Devil the taste an I had of it, good or bad." "Let me see it," says the Lt. approaching near, and putting his foot on the door sill—now was the trying time—Pat was near being sold and his comrades began to shake in their shoes inside.

Pat was no ways daunted however, but stepping between the Officer and the door, he presented his bayonet at his breast, and said, "you cannot come in here." "Why not?" "Because tis me orders." "Do you know who I am?" "I didn't care if ye were the General himself, and I like him better nor any man in this wide world barrin Commodore Stockton, and its a tie between them two, you couldn't come in here unless the Sergeant of the Guard passed you. Stand back or by the Lord, I'll ram this bayonet through ye!" The Lt. looked in his eye and seeing he was determined, back out and went away muttering something about reporting.

As soon as he was out of sight, Pat stuck his head in the door and sung out, "by Jabers, but didn't I do that nate, make haste now ye divils ye, and pack up, for if he meets the Officer of the Guard, we're in for it any how."

They did make haste, having secured a bushel basket full of bottles and off started Pat and his comrades with a full Load they carrying the basket and he following with his musket at a Shoulder answering questions, by saying, they were two prisoners under his Charge who were carrying wine to the Barracks for the Officers. Luckily they met no one on the way who knew aught but this story was true, and that night they had a grand blow out, and to this day no one of the officers is any the wiser of this plan.

They played the same old game here they had done at San Diego with regard to rations, and only served out from the Commisary Department the allowance of Wheat, some few Beans, and fresh Meat. A Gill of Aquadiente was given each day and this comprised the sum and substance of what we were supposed to live on. But the Jacks knew a trick worth two of this. There was lots of Grub in town and when it is there and Jack is hard up, he is sure to have his share. No one had any cause for growling there for that matter, for such quantities of beans, pumpkins, wheat, garlic and even potatoes (though when the devil they raised the latter article I could never discover) as were toted up that hill was enough to have satisfied a whole army of Martyrs with Old John Rodgers himself at the head.

The next day after we arrived, there was a large body of horsemen discovered advancing on the northern road, and we were at once got under arms to receive them let them be who they might. It was raining as if Heaven and Earth was coming together and if the force seen in the distance were the Enemy, it was to say the least of it, a very uncomfortable day to fight. Upon their approach however they proved to be the command of Col Freemont who had just arrived from Monterey after a most fatiguing march of 400 miles, over mountains, valleys, and a decent sprinkling of rocks.[3]

Poor devils, their tramp had been a hard one and they had not arrived in time to share with us the honors won on the Plains of San Gabriel and the Mesa. They all being composed of hunters and backwoods men, we expected when we saw them that no matter how long they had been out, or how hard a time they had experienced, that they would look at least spruce and in some sort of order, and not be like Jacks a conglomeration of rags, tatters and motly dresses.

3. Frémont finally reached Los Angeles on January 14, 1847. For a contemporary account of his march as set down by one of his lieutenants, see Edwin Bryant, *What I Saw in California*, pp. 365 ff.

But what was our surprise, when they formed in the square to find they looked worse than ever we dared to. Such a tribe, I verily believe was never dreamed of before (unless it might have been by some Jew, who had an eye to old clothes) and to make the matter better and mend their appearance, it rained incessantly for the last 24 hours before they came in. This might have improved them a little by washing some of the outside of the dirt from their clothes, were it not counteracted by the fact that there were such quantities of grease and slush smeared over them that they turned water, and thus prevented the good effects that might have occurred from the drenching.

They too had a yarn of the Hostiles to spin, they had come out to where they were encamped and sent in a Flag of Truce and asked an Armistice to settle affairs. Col. Freemont who knew nothing of our approach or Battles, had granted it. The leaders of the Party, headed by Andreas Pico had come in under his safe conduct and then for the first time he learned that Flores who was known to be at the head of the revolutionists had with a small party fled to Sonora, after getting his countrymen into a scrape and leaving them to foot the Bill in the best manner they could.

Pico also said that the Californians were desirous of Peace, that they were willing to come under the American Government and would if allowed, resign their arms, and return peacably to their homes, and become for the future, quiet orderly citizens of the Republic.

All this time, however, he said nothing about Commodore S or Genl K being at the Puebla, well knowing, if he disclosed that fact, as also that the insurgents had been whipped but 2 days before and that this peace move was a force put with him, that Col Freemont would knock off all negociations and march at once to join his Superiors.

Pico dared not surrender himself to the Commodore for he had taken the answer sent to Flores, previous to the actions to include himself also and he was fearful that the Old Fellow might put his threat in execution and give him a swinging billet, between Heaven and Earth, with no convenient place to rest his feet upon.

In this conclusion however he was wrong, the Commodore never meant to include him, as he had broken no parole, he had remained neutral, the first time Los Angeles was occupied by U.S. Forces and it was well known to our Officers that he was forced to join the Insurgents by fear that if he did not, they would murder him, and destroy his property. He did not like to join the Americans and operate against the Flag, which he had been born and raised under and consequently his condition was a peculiar one.

At all events, he entered into Articles of Capitulation with Col. Freemont and surrendered his whole force up to him, who were allowed after depositing their arms, except such as were considered necessary for their protection against the Indians to depart for their homes, which they did in an incredibly short space of time and thus was Peace once more proclaimed in California. The whole of the Arms and Ammunition, Ordnance &c belonging to the Government were in possession of Col. Freemont and amounted to but little at that.[4]

After the articles were signed, the peace ratified, and a large majority of the Californians off, Col Freemont learned for the first time of the near vicinity of the Commander in Chief, of his two actions, and began to see the game Pico had played on him, but it was too late to retract now, so he up stakes and put out to report the whole matter to him and get his approval thereof. Now as Pico could have got precisely the same terms from our Party, there was no difficulty about the approval and in a few days the Revolutionary Col himself came into town and being a jolly soul was soon cheek by jowl with all our Officers.

Californians too began to pour into town and what with our Force, Col Freemonts men and the influx of Inhabitants folks began to get rather too thick here, and strong talk of a removal was heard.

We now renewed our acquaintance with the Volunteers whom we had enlisted in San Francisco, and pre-eminent and above all the rest stood "Oregon" [Savage] and "Grizzly" [Isaac Graham?]. These two seemed perfectly at home wherever they could get alongside of one of our Ships Company and never perfectly at home but then.

Sergeant Slim and Oregon were hardly ever seen apart and there were some strong suspicions that Oregon had broached a plan to the Sergeant to induce him to leave us clandestinely and join Giblets with him, in order that the Post Master at the Cross Roads who had

4. For an account of the Frémont-Pico agreement, see Nevins, _Frémont, Pathmarker of the West_ (N.Y., 1955) pp. 299–300; Bancroft, _History of California_, v, pp. 404–5.

so unceremoniously packed him off to California might by their united efforts meet punishment.

The Sergeant however had no great taste for land tracks, and compromised the matter by assuring his friend that he would use his powerful influence with the Department and have the matter set at rest at the next session of Congress or else there would be a reaction in the Cabinet and somebody would be turned out of office and no mistake. When they parted the Sergeant pressed his Friends hand and bade him be sure and drop him a few Lines when he got back to Oregon, just to let him know how things went on there, "and you may be sure," said Slim, "that I will return the compliment; for when I get home this time I mean to quit the Sea and retire in dignified disgust into private life. For to tell you the truth I am sick and tired of being a Public Man. The cares of Office and the zeal with which I work for the public interests are undermining my constitution and much as I love my country, I feel that I owe a duty still more binding to the family of young Slims, which I see shadowed in the future, and for their sakes I shall retire, get me a good wife and then go into the manufacturing business."

"If you just put on the outside of the letter this address, I shall be sure to get it, 'To Sergeant (for I shall still retain my military Title) John A. Slim, Slim Township, County of Keebusset, State of Maine, U.S.A. Put that on in big letters and it will come straight to our house and when I write to you as you will most probably be travelling a good deal and not have a chance to call at any Post Offices, I'll have the letter printed in the "Slimville Piney Woods Roarer" a fine Democratic Paper published in our town by a second cousin to the aunt of my wife that is to be; noble fellow that editor; has an enormous circulation for his paper and will do anything for me, as it is all in the family." Having arranged these matters Slim and his correspondent that was to be, parted on the most amicable terms.

There were laughable things enough turning up each day we lay here to fill a volume were they all recorded, but as I think I have given a pretty fair specimin I shall close the Aquadiente subject with one more yarn. The Hero of this wine-astrophe (excuse me for coining a word for it) was a rollicking mirth loving son of the Emerald Isle whose laugh, when he let himself out on that score, might be heard from one end of the Deck to the other.

Teddy was like the most of his countrymen, an enthusiastic examiner of the Juice of the Grape, whether it was known under the cognomen of Wine or Aquadiente and was most persevering in his attempts to hunt it up, no matter in what quarter of the Town it was stowed. He could carry off an enormous load of it too, and was so good humored and withal so witty when under its influence, that it was rare amusement to see him half corned.

He rarely if ever allowed Alcohol to obtain the mastery over him on board Ship, "for," said he "If I do that, and get into a fit of Laughing, I shall be very noisy and if the Autocrat then should get a sight of me in that frame of mind, he'd be sure to have me at the mast, and then he would kindly accomodate me with lodging at the "Sign of the Soldier" and I dont like them quarters, no how; not but that a chap can live quiet enough there, but then you know when you come to leave and settle up, that footing of the Bill at the hinder end of No 1 Gun and signing your receipt wid that pin wid the 9 points to it, is quite disagreeable. Oh no I thank you, I dont care much about patronizing that house."

But now the case was different, he could drink as much as he liked, could laugh as loud as he liked, go to bed as drunk as he pleased and get up as sober as suited his fancy and there were no bills to be settled after it was all done. This was just his play and as liquor was plenty and awful cheap, only requiring the going after, he kept his spirit room plenty full and his clay well moistened the whole time.

One day as he was out foraging, he came across (in a lone house) a pipe of wine standing on its head; his thirst being very urgent just at this time, he went to work and stove the head of said Pipe in, and after sundry pretty deep potations, he pronounced it good and trotted off to his Quarters, to raise some assistance in the shape of certain messmates, armed with Buckets, Pots, Bottles, Tubs &c to enable him to tranport his prize to where he might be able to imbibe more at his leisure.

He accordingly procured his re-inforcements and returned to the house, and mounting upon an empty keg he found there, began to bale out the liquid to his customers; he kept on at this sort of work until he had more than half emptied the pipe and had dispatched the last of his companions with a load to the Quarters, when reaching over for the last time, to procure one more drink for himself, the quantity he had already stowed under his jacket, the steam and smell of the interior of the cask and holding his head down for such a length of time all combined against him and in addition to all this, the Keg on which he stood took a motion to cant at the same time and over goes our Hero head and ears into the cask.

The pipe was so contracted in its circumference that he could not turn himself to get out and his most arduous struggles would not suffice to keep his head above water or rather wine more than a minute or two at a time, and thus between the wine on the outside and the wine he had inside, he was in a fair way of drowning and stepping out of this world without benefit of clergy.

As often as he managed to get his mouth above the surface he would bellow, Murder—Help—Help at the top of his voice but no help came. After a hard struggle he was almost worn out and resigning himself to his fate, murmured out—Oh Lord J – – s what a scrape I'm in now.—down he would go again, after a second up would come his mouth.—Well I suppose I've got to die—Tis a hard case too after running clear of Grape and Round shot to drown like a puppy. I wonder if the coroner will sit on my body—will he call this suicide—by the powers but its an involuntary one any how—Oh what an Idea, an Irishman preserved in wine—Murder—Help, well its no use, I cant hold out any longer—It's a very happy death at any rate, I'll just say my prayers and then let go—Now I lay me down—no I dont lay down for by Jabers I'm standing up on my head—and that aint the prayer neither—Let me see Oh! How doth the little busy bee—no that aint it—Get out of the way Old Dan Tucker—no nor that wont do—I've forgot all my prayers but I hope I'll get along somehow in tother world widout them. Here I go, Good bye, goo—he was just saying good bye for the last time, when long Bob, who had been laying pretty well corned in one corner of the room, fast asleep, but who had been roused by his shouts of murder, seized him by the legs and hauled him out, having laid Teddy on the floor, he looked first at him and then into the cask and at last opened on him.

"Wall now, I swan to man, you are what I call a touch of the entire swine, tail and all, you've gone and drunk a half a pipe of wine, and not content with that, you've got in all over and gone swimming in it. Dont you think you are a Corn? Why you are a regular tank and if you dont bust after this I'll give up. Come, come, Old Feller, I say get up and go home." But Ted was too far gone. The Liquor and his exertions had overcome him and he could not stir a limb, so Bob after taking a good pull at the halliards, took him on his shoulder and trudged off to the Barracks with him.

Such sort of incidents as these related sufficed to while away the hours of the day, and no incident of much importance transpired after the 3rd or 4th day of occupation save that once we were ordered to detail parties to go on the Hill and commence the foundations of a Star Fort, that was laid out by Capt [William H.] Warner and intended for the defence of the town.[5] This arrangement the Jacks kicked strongly against and they only had one day's work on it and a bit of a Row was kicked up one night at the Barracks, when Mr. Alchohol was in full bloom, which gave Lt R – – w [Renshaw] a hint of the kindly dispositions of the Sailor men toward him, and was near proving fatal to him too. He was accustomed to travel round town and pick up all stray sailors and consign them to the Guard House and report them daily, and his will was good enough to have given every man a dozen, fore and aft, but the Commodore stood our Friend, and put a stopper on all such doings.

This Gentleman, forgive me reader for calling him out of his name, this thing in the shape of a man, came up to the Barracks one night and began to kick up a considerable of a noise there and haul the men about, hoping no doubt to find some poor fellow whom he could accommodate with lodgings in the Guard House.

The men stood his abuse for some time patiently but after a while thinking he had gone too far they began to hoot and blackguard him in fine style. This so enraged him that he fairly foamed at the mouth and groped about in the dark in the vain attempt to get hold of somebody to vent his spite upon. The Dodging Plan was now resorted to and not being able to get hold of any one, he swore he would shoot, where he heard the next sound come from, let him hit innocent or guilty, he cared not which.

He had no sooner broached the word shoot, than he found to his dismay that Sailors knew what that meant too and that more than one could play at that Game, for hardly were the words out of his mouth, than Bang, Bang, Bang went 3 muskets and the balls whistled merrily round his head.

Like all other tyrants he was a coward and no sooner did he hear the first report than he fell on his hands and knees and crawled out

5. Warner was with the U.S. Topographical Engineers, and had come to California with Kearny. He was wounded at San Pascual. Bancroft, *History of California*, v, p. 768.

of the Barracks leaving his Pistols on the floor and a Midshipman, whom he had brought with him, to fight his way out in the best manner he could. The Reefer had no great cause for quarrel but determined not to leave like a dog, he fired both his pistols in some direction or other and then walked man fashion out of the house.

A great row was kicked up about the discharge of the guns but as it was to the interest of R – – w to say nothing about it, he did not report the circumstance and it was put down as a false alarm.

Matters were now getting so bad that by far the great majority began to wish for a remove and long to join their Ships again, and but few were displeased when the order came to pack and prepare to march to San Pedro, a distance of 30 miles, where we were to embark on board the Whale Ship *Stonington* and go down to San Diego. The reading of this order was hailed with joy and all hands were on the "qui vive" for the march, which was to commence on the morning of the 20th, having remained in Barracks in Los Angeles 10 days.

As we had celebrated our entry, of course we were in duty bound to celebrate our departure, and the night of the 19th joy was kept up in fine style, all hands were not exactly to say drunk, but pretty royally corned, and but few of the command slept any that night.

The Dragoons resumed the line of march, back the way we had come on the 19th and the many stirrup cups that were to be emptied at the parting of friends, the toasts that were to be drunk and bottles that were to be deprived of their contents to moisten the wishes for good luck, on both sides, to say nothing of the number of Gallons that were finished in drinking "Long Life and a Merry One" to the Old Soldier himself, contributed not a little to start our last spree.

The Commodore too, with a Body Guard started back on the Old Route, and as we were now left to the tender mercies of the lesser Gents, we were determined to have a good one for the last. And a Glorious night it was too, and so well was it kept up that next morning, when the Revilee was sounded, there were lots of sore headed chaps, to be seen crawling out, from all sorts of holes and digging off for their Quarters.

"A hair from the same Dog" cured the bite and most of them took so many hairs that when the assembly sounded, though they were all there, it would have taken a tolerable stout board fence in the rear, and another in front of the Line to have kept them straight and upright, long enough to be mustered. It made no odds however, we were bound off and when the advance sounded we started, but such a start. The Bare recollection of that days march causes a roar of Laughter whenever I think of it.

They undertook to march by platoon, with the carts in the rear, but such marching, such reeling to and fro of whole platoons, such rolling and reeling about, such slipping up to go up the hills which seemed to rise at every step, such awful efforts was made to appear sober, such hitching up of muskets and stubbing of toes, such dancing and hoeing down all over the road, such a knocking off of caps, hats, and tin pots, and such shouting and bellowing of Patriotic, Sentimental and Comic Songs, was never heard before and will require an abler pen than mine to describe.

Every now and then some poor fellow, would stumble and fall headlong on the ground where he would lay, clinging on to his musket, like death, until the rear guard picked him up and stuck him in a waggon or cart to sleep off his debauch. Some of these cart passengers who were not drunk enough to sleep beguiled the time away by sundry Gymnastic Performances, song, and various other exertions which taken as a whole were immensely edifying to the spectators.

One of our Whistlers, not Sergeant Jo, but private John, a New York Gentleman, took one of our Marines who was gifted with such an awful ugly face that it always seemed to me as if it must have hurt him, and started off in hot chase of water. His scuppers and those of his companion were hot and Aquadiente could not assuage their thirst, and nothing short of water could satisfy them. Off they trudged, and soon came to a fine running stream, some 5 or 6 yards in width and 2 or 3 feet deep, down they dropped their muskets and off knapsacks, and down on their marrow bones they went and began to lap up the delicious fluid. By some means, unknown to himself, or perhaps to any one else, the Marine got over on the opposite side of the stream and when they rose their heads, after taking a good drink, there they sat, gazing at each other.

"Hello," says the Whistler, "how did you get on that side?"

"But how did you get on that side?" said the Marine.

"I didn't get on this side at all," says the Whistle, "I was here first, you have crossed over the stream."

"No I have not" replied the Marine, "It is you that have crossed over the stream."

"No," says Whistle, "'tis you."

"I say most emphatically," said Musket, "I have not, do you dare call me a Liar?"

"No," says Whistle, "I dont mean to say you are a liar, but you do travel a long way round the truth."

"That's an insinuation," says Musket, "and if you repeat it I will knock you down!"

"You'll either have to come across that brook again, or make a long arm before you do that!"

"Will I?" said Musket, who was too drunk to notice distances, "take that!" So saying, he struck out and finding nothing to resist the blow he made, the impetus pitched him headlong into the water. Whistle laid down and rolled in his excessive delight and made the air ring with his shouts of Laughter, while poor Musket crawled out, and sat himself down on the bank to dry.

At length the mirth of Whistle having subsided, he arose and an idea seemed to have struck him that he would go over to Musket. He acted upon it, and entered the water to wade across. At the same moment the Soldier arose and waded across too, and when each arrived at the opposite bank they found that the water yet rolled between them. This was a mystery; they looked at one another for some moments and then mutually tried the same move over again.

Three or four times the same movement was executed with the same success, and at last despairing of being able to join one another they gave it up and each one took his way to join the army; Musket happened to be on the right side and was soon on the Road. Poor Whistle however had a weary time of it; he was on the wrong side of the start and as he took a last look at the stream to take his departure his hat fell off, and away it floated and to save his life he could not catch it. He dared not leave his musket but off he trudged in hot chase of his Hat. Now it would get into some eddy, and float near the shore, but on the opposite side from where he was. He would plunge in and just as he was about to grab it off it would be whirled, and all his work was to do over again. For at least a dozen of times it fooled him in this way, until at last he pinned it, and happening this time to be on the right side of the River, he pulled foot after the Command but did not arrive until long after we were encamped.

We of course did not travel far that day, and camped soon, but early next morning we resumed the march but not before we had one more taste of Lt H – – s [Higgins]. This man had never got over the rebuff he met at the hands of the Genl at St. Louis, about the "Cats" and burned to get a chance to spit his spite out on the head of some poor devil, and this night he had a chance. Some of the men who had not got perfectly sober were growling and grumbling in one of the Tents and making considerable noise, one had got outside and was daring all hands out for a fight, but had just been persuaded to go away, when up comes this valorous spark (who for the sake of humanity we will suppose was well corned too, for no man in his sober senses would have done the act) and sung out, "If there's any body in there that wants any satisfaction let him come on, and I'll give it to him!"

The poor half drunken Tar, supposing it was his comrade who wished to see him a check, crawled out, and said, "Here I am." No sooner were the words out of his mouth than H – – s sprang upon him and struck him over the head with a cutlass. The second blow brought the man to the ground, stunned and motionless, and yet this fiend continued to strike until he had laid his head open in two places, and then was only stopped by two officers who were *men,* who jumped in and dragged him off.

Oh Valorous Man! Oh ornament to the U.S. Naval Service! If ever these pages meet your eye, and you do not blush with shame at the recital of this damning tale, we blush for you at the bare recollection of it. You are yet a young man, and may become a good Officer, but if you do not leave the Cup, and mend your ways, disgrace in life, and a drunkard's grave is your certain doom.

On the morning of the 21st we resumed our march for San Pedro and our Ships Company, together with the Cyane's arrived at Pedro that night, and prepared to embark in the *Stonington.* Previous to our leaving however we squared yards with our two mules who had served us for pack Animals the whole tramp and patient enduring and useful they were too, though one of them did lay down in the river and lose his pack, thereby causing a woeful deficit in the Pea Jacket and Blanket Line.

They had stuck to us the whole way and upon parting Sam—the

Devil, wrote a written discharge for them from the service of the U. States, and gave them a check for their pay in the shape of an order on the first Rancho where they might fetch up for a peck of corn or wheat. These documents were sewed in a Bag and fastened around the neck of the elder and of course the steadiest one and they were about being turned adrift, when an order came to detain them as our Commander wished to send an Express back to the Main Body.

Old Fore Jack, one of our Corporals, accordingly having received the letter, made an attempt to ride the Old Mule but he had been a long time with Sailors, and had got up to the movers [?]. He knew his time was out, he got no quarter more Pay. He had his discharge and check, consequently like a true Tar he refused duty, and in furtherance of his plan, first kicked old Fore Jack off, then kicked him down for falling off and wound up by kicking him when down for falling.

He did not hurt him much, but Fore Jack swore he would mount him no more. Bye the Bye then made the attempt, but he had no better luck and at last an order was sent to belay the Express and we let the Mules go, and marched down to the boats, and were soon snug on board the *Stonington*. There was lots of room for all of us on her lower deck and for one night we were comfortable enough, but the next—oh Lord.

The next day the balance of the Battalion came on board and then commenced a scene of misery, which I despair of attempting to portray in colors sufficiently high to give the reader a good idea of it. There were near 600 souls on board and the whole of them, except the officers were domiciled on the two decks, and as she was a small ship there was not space enough to accomodate, with any degree of comfort any more than 100 men. Yet into this hog hole we were crammed and bade make ourselves comfortable. Comfort, oh what a cheering word to look at on paper and what glorious recollections are called up at the bare mention of that word. But the sort of comfort we enjoyed on board this barky causes nothing but a thrill of horror.

There had been lots of Grub put on board for our use but by a sad mistake there were no means of cooking it, and we were obliged to make out the best we could, by scoffing our bread and Pork raw. Now raw Pork was bad enough but to mend the matter, our most sapient and valorous Marine Officer, one day sent forward an order to have the Ration changed and serve out Salt Beef instead of Pork. Now this same Mahogany Beef of Uncle Sam's is bad enough even when boiled but hungry indeed must the poor devil have been who could have made a meal of it raw. And this order was issued by one who had taken good care to deprive even the regular Ship's Company of the *Stonington* of the use of the Gally in order to have the Grub for the Officers well cooked. My God! are we not all men? and "What is sauce for a Goose, should be sauce for a Gander" also; are we because we are by rank removed a little below these Gentry to be ranked as wild cannibals, and doomed to eat Raw Meat, and worse than all the rest, Raw Salt Meat, while they revel in the best and all because they are Officers and we are Men?

But this Grub Matter was easily got over and totally lost sight of in the greater evil of want of room to sleep or even roost. If we had been packed in bulk, spoon fashion and laid away in two layers, we might perhaps have been crowded down on to her lower deck and hold, but as we had no fancy for that mode of stowage, it was not tried on. Well we got underway on the morning of the 22nd of January, and stood out of the Bay bound to the Southward; the first day and night, the weather was cool but fair, and we got along some how or other but on the morning of the 23rd it came on to blow from the S.E. and accompanied with a heavy rain. Now indeed our situation was deplorable, stay on the lower deck you could not, for fear of suffocation, and if you came on to the spar deck you were soon wet through and numbed with the cold, for there was no shelter for you there. All day long we suffered with some sort of patience, but when night came on, our horrors were filled up to over flowing, there was no place to stand, sit or lie, and as for sleeping, that was out of the question, there was no place even to roost, where you could be dry. Some 200 or so packed themselves on the lower deck and ran the risk of drowning and 100 stowed themselves in the blubber room and forecastle while the rest were doomed to take the upper deck for it. Around the Hatches they were piled in heaps, and under the Boats, they stowed in Bulk, keeping the water from falling on them, although it ran in streams underneath them.

For two days and one night this Storm continued and it blew a perfect gale a part of the time, and at last, in the evening or rather early part of the night of the 24th [January], we got into San Diego and were soon put on board our own Ships and truly did we thank God, when we put our foot over her side.

Our ration of Grog had been kept from us the last three days, although twas sent up for us, and had been drank by the Officers and for once our Autocrat opened his heart and ordered the Grog Tub to be got up. This was the first and only time we had ever spliced the Main Brace, what wonder then that the Jacks doubled the Tub, and the Pursers Steward, winking at the misdemeanor said nothing about it—here we are at last and God grant we may never have to go ashore soldiering again.

COMMODORE JOHN DRAKE SLOAT, *Commanding*

FRIGATES

U.S.S. *Savannah* (44 guns), Commodore John D. Sloat
U.S.S. *Constitution* (44 guns), Captain John Percival
U.S.S. *Congress* (44 guns), Captain Robert F. Stockton

SLOOPS

U.S.S. *Portsmouth* (20 guns), Commander John B. Montgomery
U.S.S. *Levant* (20 guns), Commander Hugh N. Page
U.S.S. *Warren* (20 guns), Captain Joseph B. Hull
U.S.S. *Cyane* (20 guns), Captain William Mervine

STORESHIPS

U.S.S. *Erie* (8 guns), Lt. Commander Charles C. Turner
U.S.S. *Relief* (6 guns), Lt. Commander Robert G. Robb

MUSTER ROLL OF THE PORTSMOUTH
June, 1846

JOHN BERRIEN MONTGOMERY, *Commander*

Lieutenants:

WASHINGTON A. BARTLETT
JOHN L. MISSROON
JOSEPH W. REVERE

Passed Midshipmen:

NAPOLEON B. HARRISON (*Acting Sailing Master*)
BEN F. B. HUNTER

Midshipmen:

CHARLES S. BELL
STANWIX GANSEVOORT
EDWARD C. GRAFTON
DANIEL C. HUGUNIN
ELLIOTT JOHNSTON
JOSEPH PARRISH

Assistant Surgeons:

MARIUS DUVALL
ANDREW A. HENDERSON

Purser:

JAMES H. WATMOUGH

PERSONNEL

RICHARD AIMES, *Ordinary Seaman*
FRANCIS ALIAS, *Cook*
GEORGE BAKER, *Gunner's Mate*
JAMES M. BALL, *Steward*
CHARLES S. BELLOWS, *Ordinary Seaman*
CHARLES BERRY, *Captain of the After Guard*
ALEX BLAIR, *Quartermaster*
ALVIN BOODY, *Landsman*

BATTISTE BRAY, *Seaman*
ALEXANDER BRINKFIELD, *Landsman*
CHARLES BROWN, *Ordinary Seaman*
CHARLES A. BROWN, *Seaman*
JOHN BROWN, II, *Ordinary Seaman*
JOHN BROWN, III, *Ordinary Seaman*
WILLIAM BROWN, I, *Seaman*
WILLIAM BROWN, II, *Seaman*
WILLIAM M. BROWN, *Ordinary Seaman*

STEPHEN BROWNELL, *Seaman*
DAVID BRUCE, *Sailmaker*
THOMAS BUCKLEY, *Apprentice*
JOSEPH BUCKMAN, *Landsman*
JAMES H. BUTTER, *Landsman*
JOHN A. BUTTERFIELD, *Landsman*
HANS CARL, *Seaman*
JAMES R. CARSON, *Ordinary Seaman*
JOHN C. CARTER, *Seaman*
EZRA CHAMBERLAIN, *Bosun's Mate*
SAMUEL D. CHICHESTER, *Landsman*
THOMAS CLAREY, *Seaman*
JOHN CLARK, *Seaman*
WILLIAM COBB, *Landsman*
JOHN L. B. CONNOLLY, *Surgeon's Steward*
CHARLES CONSUL, *Seaman*
EDWARD CORYGAN, *Ordinary Seaman*
JOSEPH COX, *Seaman*
SEWALL CRAM, *Seaman*
THOMAS CURRY, *Cabin Boy*
THEODORE DALE, *Landsman*
JOHN DALEY, *Ordinary Seaman*
JOHN DANCER, *Seaman*
HENRY DENNIS, *Carpenter's Mate*
ROBERT DENNISON, *Seaman*
WILLIAM DENSIFORD, *Ordinary Seaman*
WILLIAM DHU, *Quarter Gunner*
SAMUEL DIBBLE, *Ordinary Seaman*
JOHN DILLABEY, *Ordinary Seaman*
JAMES DIXON, *Seaman*
WILLIAM H. DORSEY, *Landsman*
JOSEPH T. DOWNEY, *Ordinary Seaman*
WILLIAM DUNLEY, *Captain of the Top*
JOHN ERWIN, *Ordinary Seaman*
WILLIAM O. FRIEL, *Seaman*
JOHN FROST, *Yeoman*
CHARLES GARDNER, *Landsman*
IRA GILE, *Quarter Gunner*
PETER A. GRAHAM, *Cabin Boy*
GEORGE GRIFFITH, *Seaman*
WILLIAM GRIFFITHS, *Captain of the Forecastle*
LEWIS GREEN, *Ordinary Seaman*
JOHN HADLEY, *Seaman*
JOSEPH HAM, *Quarter Gunner*
JOSEPH HANNAH, *Landsman*
THOMAS HANSON, *Seaman*

WILLIAM H. HARRINGTON, *Ordinary Seaman*
HENRY HARRIS, *Captain of the Top*
CARLOS C. HARVEY, *Landsman*
ALMORAN HOLMES, *Landsman*
GILMAN T. HOOK, *Landsman*
GEORGE HORTON, *Seaman*
JOHN HUDSON, *Captain of the Top*
GEORGE HURST, *Sailmaker's Mate*
DAVID HUTCHINS, *Captain of the After Guard*
WILLIAM HUTCHINSON, *Seaman*
JOHN JENKINS, *Landsman*
CHARLES JOHNSON, *Seaman*
WILLIAM JOHNSON, *Seaman*
WILLIAM H. JOHNSON, *Ordinary Seaman*
CHARLES JONES, *Armorer*
WILLIAM JONES, *Seaman*
WILLIAM H. KENNEDY, *Landsman*
WILLIAM KNOWLTON, *Ordinary Seaman*
JOHN MCNELLY, *Seaman*
NATHANIEL MARTINDALE, *Ordinary Seaman*
JAMES MASON, *Landsman*
DANIEL C. MELLUS, *Ordinary Seaman*
THOMAS MESSER, *Seaman*
JOHN E. MONTGOMERY, *Clerk*
S. W. L. MONTGOMERY, *Passenger*
JOHN MORGAN, *Master at Arms*
WILLIAM J. MORRIS, *Quartermaster*
HENRY MYERS, *Seaman*
GEORGE W. NEAL, *Steward*
JACOB NEWMAN, *Cabin Boy*
SOUTH NEWMAN, *Cabin Boy*
FRANCIS NICHOLS, *Seaman*
ANDREW NUTTER, *Cook*
HENRY OSBORNE, *Ship's Corporal*
JOSEPH OSBORNE, *Ordinary Seaman*
HIRAM PAINE, *Seaman*
ANDREW I. PALFREY, *Ordinary Seaman*
SAMUEL PARKER, *Seaman*
ROBERT PARMENTIER, *Landsman*
JOHN PATTISON, *Seaman*
WILLIAM I. PAYER, *Cabin Boy*
WILLIAM PENDEGRAST, *Ordinary Seaman*
CHARLES PETERS, *Seaman*

JAMES PETERS, *Quartermaster*
CHARLES H. PHILLIPS, *Ordinary
Seaman*
GEORGE PIERCE, *Landsman*
GEORGE PIERCE, *Seaman*
RICHARD PRICE, *Ordinary Seaman*
ANDREW A. RANDELL, *Gunner*
JOHN REESE, *Ordinary Seaman*
JONAS RHOADES, *Cabin Boy*
FRANCIS RICE, *Quartermaster*
THOMAS RICHE, *Seaman*
HENRY RITINGBURG, *Ordinary
Seaman*
ANDREW ROBINSON, *Cook*
JAMES ROBINSON, *Steward*
JOHN ROBINSON, *Seaman*
CHARLES SANGSTER, *Ordinary Seaman*
JOHN SEAMAN, *Captain of the Top*
JOHN SELKY, *Bosun's Mate*
JOSEPH SENGGIE, *Captain of the
Forecastle*
WILLIAM SHELDON, *Ordinary Seaman*
ANDREW SMITH, I, *Quarter Gunner*
ANDREW SMITH, II, *Landsman*
DANIEL SMITH, *Ordinary Seaman*
HENRY SMITH, *Bosun's Mate*

THOMAS SMITH, *Captain of the Top*
THOMAS L. SMITH, *Ordinary Seaman*
WARREN SPENCER, *Seaman*
CALVIN SPOONER, *Landsman*
CHARLES M. SPOONER, *Captain of
the Top*
JAMES H. STEWARD, *Ordinary
Seaman*
JOHN STINCHFIELD, *Captain of
the Hold*
FREDERICK STRAUS, *Ordinary Seaman*
ROBERT THOMPSON, *Seaman*
WILLIAM A. THOMPSON, *Landsman*
THOMAS TOBIN, *Ordinary Seaman*
JOHN B. TURKINGTON, *Purser's
Steward*
JAMES VANDYNE, *Landsman*
WILLIAM WALKER, *Ordinary Seaman*
TIMOTHY WHELAN, *Ordinary
Seaman*
ROBERT WHITTAKER, *Bosun*
JOHN R. WILKINS, *Ordinary Seaman*
GEORGE WILLIAMS, *Seaman*
WILLIAM WILSON, *Landsman*
GEORGE WISNER, *Carpenter*
CHARLES WRENCH, *Seaman*

ELDRIDGE C. YORK, *Cooper*

MARINES

JOHN D. AREY, *Private*
SAMUEL S. BARTLETT, *Private*
JOHN W. BELFORD, *Private*
RUFUS BRIGGS, *Private*
ERASTUS A. BURNHAM, *Private*
PETER BURNS, *Private*
SAMUEL G. CARLTON, *Private*
HENRY COOLIDGE, *Private*
JAMES H. CROCKER, *Fifer*
MICHAEL CUNNINGHAM, *Private*
PETER HUYLER, *Corporal*
JAMES O. KEARNY, *Private*
PHILIP McGOWAN, *Private*

GEORGE M. MILLER, *Sergeant*
JOHN H. MILLER, *Private*
THOMAS MOULTON, *Private*
JOHN RICHARDSON, *Private*
SAMUEL SAMPLE, *Private*
HENRY SCOTT, *Private*
WILLIAM SCOTT, *Private*
WILLIAM SMITH, *Corporal*
WILLIAM F. STEELE, *Drummer*
EZEKIEL D. WALKER, *Private*
HENRY B. WATSON, *Second
Lieutenant*
JAMES M. WIATT, *Orderly Sergeant*

JAMES M. WILDER, *Private*

240

Index